The Dewsweepers

THE
DEWSWEEPERS

*Seasons of
Golf and Friendship*

James Dodson

Century · London

Published by Century in 2001

1 3 5 7 9 10 8 6 4 2

Copyright © James Dodson 2001

James Dodson has asserted his right under the Copyright, Designs and Patents Act, 1988
to be identified as the author of this work

First published in the United Kingdom in 2001 by Century
The Random House Group Ltd
20 Vauxhall Bridge Road, London SW1V 2SA

Random House Australia (Pty) Limited
20 Alfred Street, Milsons Point, Sydney,
New South Wales 2061, Australia

Random House New Zealand Limited
18 Poland Road, Glenfield
Auckland 10, New Zealand

Random House (Pty) Limited
Endulini, 5a Jubilee Road, Parktown 2193, South Africa

The Random House Group Limited Reg. No 954009

www.randomhouse.co.uk

A CIP catalogue record for this book is available from the British Library

Papers used by Random House are natural, recyclable products
made from wood grown in sustainable forests. The manufacturing processes
conform to the environmental regulations of the country of origin

ISBN 0 7126 8469 7

Typeset by SX composing DTP, Rayleigh, Essex
Printed and bound in Great Britain by
Clays Ltd, Bungay, Suffolk

To Mrs. Congeniality

CONTENTS

ACKNOWLEDGMENTS

A BOOK of this nature is rarely the creation of one person, and so it is in this instance. Many hands gathered and shaped this golfing yeoman's tale. They include, to begin, the eight men who lent their fraternal name, unflinching honesty, and abiding good humor to this unlikely enterprise, the Dewsweepers themselves: Dr. Lester Austin, Russ King, Tom Cahill, Bill "Friar" Tuck, Peter Marshall, John Zawadzki, Jim Hathaway, and last but not least, Jonathan Sager, Esq., the funniest guy I ever met and, I hope, a golf pal for life. While I'm at it, I'd be greatly remiss not to thank several Dewsweeper wives for their gentle forbearance of our adventures—Sheila Austin, Jiggy King, Nancy "Who?" Cahill, Cynthia Marshall, and the irrepressible Karen Sager.

I must say, once again, thank you to my oldest buddy on the planet, Patrick McDaid, whose wisdom and wit are only exceeded by his spectacular inability since childhood to beat me at the game we love most—though, alas, I hear his footsteps and know that day of reckoning approaches. I must thank Terry, his saintly wife, again, too.

Speaking of wives who are saints, much of the impetus for this book came from the late Winnie Palmer, who knew I hoped to someday write a book about the unique place golf friendship holds in the lives of men, and enthusiastically urged me to write it.

And, as if she whispered the same thing in Arnold's *good* ear, thank you, Arnold, for urging me to play more golf "just for fun." You really are the King. Long may you reign.

I don't know whether Rees Jones is the Donald Steel of America or Donald Steel is the Rees Jones of Britain. But in either case, they are two exceptionally graceful, wise, and gifted course architects who make playing golf a Darwinist pleasure for millions of men and women around the world. Ditto Ed Seay, the bellowing leather-necked Gator who has forgotten more about designing a good golf course than most architects even know. I value the insights and fun I've had palely loitering at the elbows of these three talented men.

David Chapman, former North Carolina junior amateur champ turned course developer *extraordinaire*; thank you for having me as a partner in the King's Crown. Even if you payed a rather dear price for that folly—twice. Thanks, as well, to several of your members and staff at The Tradition, for making a bloke from snow country feel right at home in the desert.

Golf pals don't come better than Sid Watson, Tom Dugan, and Terry Meagher, three good reasons I'll skip work and be at the club in fifteen minutes any old summer day. Ditto Rollin Ives. Your friendship, your stories, mean more than you can possibly know.

A salutatory pint, if you will, to the lads of the Massachusetts Golf Association: Tom Landy, Cary Jubenville, Bill Van Faazen, and the lucky members of Kittansett Club. And, while we're toasting: Larry Smuckler, Lee Tomlinson, and the "friends" of the Friends Classic. Thank you, Laird and Honor Small, for your generous wisdom and friendship over the years.

There are several debts to pay to those "across the pond" as well: to Martin Ebert for his pungent wit and great hosting skills, and the gracious members at Woking Golf Club; to Charles Churchill and historian David Stirk of Westward Ho! for one of the most memorable days ever; to the delightfully engaging Peter

Gardiner-Hill at fabulous Rye Golf Club; to Peter and Lady Mason of Wormil Hall for golf in their dreamy estate garden; to David Kirkwood and the lairds of Gullane for the thrashing and fellowship administered; to the generous staff at Kingsbarns Golf Club at the finest new track in golf's Holy Land; to my admired friend and colleague John Hopkins of *The Times*; to Andy McKillop, fine editor and even better friend; Gordon and Colin Dalgleish of PerryGolf, and not least of all the unsinkable Dove Jones, a dewsweepering Dame if there ever was one.

Once again, I regard as great fortune to have Brian Tart as my editor and Ginger Barber of William Morris Agency for her wisdom and support. They don't come better on either count. Thanks, in addition, to George Peper, Jim Frank, and Mike Purkey of *Golf Magazine*. I'm honored to work for you guys.

A few more will do, and then on with it.

Thanks to Daphne Williams, Merle Corry, Midge Hudson, and Ginny Franks—four classy ladies who made my mom's life happy to the end. Thanks to Bobby and Claire Tracy for being the closest thing I have to blood kin.

Thank you, Mom, for infusing my life with your huge spirit and vast generosity, and for granting my children and me the gift of your final days.

Thank you, Wendy, for walking through that door.

Thank you, Jack, for coming to golf when I needed you, and it, most.

THE
DEWSWEEPERS

"Golf, thou art a gentle Sprite. I owe thee much."
—*The Golfing Manual,* 1857

PROLOGUE

I SPRINT *across the club parking lot yanking furiously at my necktie, late for a round on the greatest golf course on earth. The locker room steward lifts his drowsy head with surprise as I hurtle by his post, shedding clothing as I go. Moments later, I stagger onto the first tee, hastily buttoning up my polo shirt, offering deep apologies and hopelessly inadequate oaths about delayed flights, missed interviews, and lost baggage.*

"Not to worry," assures the old club secretary, a rosy-faced Alec Guinness sort in a blue crested blazer, consulting his expensive gold watch. His expression hardens. "But we do have very firm rules about tee times. As a consequence, I'm afraid, your friends have been allowed to play ahead as a three-ball."

I stare down the fairway and, sure enough, see my three best golf pals ambling toward one of the most famous opening holes in golf. They glance back and wave like giddy passengers from the rail of a departing cruise ship—or maybe more like thieves safely across the border, for without my professional connections these scoundrels never would have set foot on these hallowed hectares of turf, this elite ancient Elysium of the game.

"Maybe I'll just run and join them," I propose.

The secretary shakes his head. "Oh, no. Not possible, I'm afraid. We have very firm rules about that sort of thing." He solemnly clears his throat and then, startlingly, bursts out giggling. "Besides," he says as his dignified face turns alarmingly red, "you seem to be missing a few . . . essentials."

I am stunned to discover that the golf bag on my shoulder is empty; incredibly, in my haste, I've somehow neglected to bring my golf clubs. But that's minor compared to a larger problem. I hear polite snickering and turn around to see a small gallery of people looking on with amusement—a rogue's gallery that includes, of all people, my eighth-grade civics teacher, the angry lady from the dry cleaners, a convicted murderer I interviewed many years ago, the idiot snowplow guy, a Delta Airlines clerk, my mother, and my girlfriend, Wendy.

"Honey," says my mother, unable to stop herself from laughing, "you really ought to run back inside and put on some nice trousers."

Glancing down, I discover to my acute horror that in my mad dash to the tee I've arrived without benefit of pants. There I stand, flapping in the breeze, so to speak, a red-faced buffoon in new white boxers, a polo shirt, shoes, and socks.

"Our rules are very clear on such matters," chortles the old secretary as he slips his arm around my mother. "Proper attire must be worn at all times! We explicitly mention trousers!"

The gallery howls and the secretary says something to my mom about coming along for a "nice pink gin," and everybody starts to wander away shaking their heads and wiping their eyes except for Wendy who is helping the murderer figure out how to work a disposable camera. I hear him ask her for a date and open my mouth to warn her that this creep is supposed to be doing fifty-to-life for chopping up his girlfriend and burying her remains across three southern states.

But I can't speak. I turn to see where my buddies have gone but they've rounded the dogleg on the greatest golf day of their lives.

Then, mercifully, I wake up.

ONE

KING OF SOMETHING

G OLF, and sometimes life, is full of new beginnings.
That's what I told myself, at any rate, as I rubbed my
sore elbow and waited to tee up an unblemished Titleist on the
twelfth morning of a brand new century at the Kings Crown
member-guest golf tournament in the California desert, hoping
this might be the year I found a new beginning to my old and ailing game.

For almost two decades, golf writing had been my home and
the life I liked best, and I would even say I loved it because golf
had taken me to places I never would have gone, introduced me
to the most amazing sorts of people, and forged my deepest
friendships. *A man who stumbles upon the work he was meant to do,* the
poet Thomas Carlyle was supposed to have said, *is destined to become a king of something.* If I wasn't quite a king, I was at least a
king of something.

But like many men who reach the so-called prime of life and
find themselves pleasantly surprised at how well most things have
turned out despite their youthful ambitions, I felt a vague dissat-
isfaction with one particular aspect of life. Fortunately, I didn't

require the services of an expensive shrink or urologist to diagnose what was quietly ailing me. The nature of the problem was as black-and-white as the scribbled ciphers on my scorecard, as near as my seldom used golf clubs.

I was no longer a good golfer. I'd lost, or seemed to be losing, my golf game.

I realize how completely ridiculous that sounds. After all, in a world where, as I write, polar continents are vanishing at alarming rates and two million children will sleep on the streets of America tonight and no less than eleven civil wars are raging and the Middle East is once again aflame with inscrutable ancient hostilities, moping about the sorry state of one's golf game, I'll grant you, seems a tad, well, *shallow* at best—like whining about having too many dessert choices at the Ritz Sunday brunch or complaining that you didn't get the window seat you requested in your unexpected upgrade to first class.

In other words, when you think about how hard some people on this troubled planet have it just to make ends meet or even just make it to the end of the day, an ailing golf game doesn't seem such a big deal after all.

On the other hand, if you accept the premise that golf writing had been my happily chosen profession for almost two decades, it follows that golf *playing* was an abiding passion long before I made this lucky matriculation, and from there it's only a short leap to appreciating that playing the game reasonably well had always been a modest little badge of personal distinction. For me at least, over the years and even decades of life, nothing I could think of had given me so much consistent pleasure and reliable companionship, such exquisite pain and private satisfaction on any number of levels, for so well and for so long, serving both man and boy, entertaining through lean years and lush, providing succor and safe harbor from any storm or turmoil, offering a polite means of ready escape and an endless stream of off-color jokes punctuated by occasional moments of high-minded inspiration . . . than the simple act of playing golf.

Of course, having said all of that, there really is nothing re-motely *simple* about playing golf. Any fool with a five-iron knows that much.

Part of golf's eternal attraction, it seems to me, stems exclusively from the fact that no game is harder to play and play *well*. Golf is a beguiling *belle dame sans merci* of a sport that will shamelessly consume your finances and eviscerate your emotions if you permit it to, provoking otherwise sane and socially responsible grown men to shamelessly abandon their families for extended periods of time, and women who are similarly afflicted to blithely ignore the obligations of career, home, and hearth, a curiously complicated Presbyterian pastime that can loft your soul to dizzying heights of spiritual nobility one minute—and wring you out like filthy floor mop the next.

Not to put *too* fine a point on it, for these reasons *alone* the woeful deterioration of one's real or imagined golfing skills that comes with the passage of time or a sudden shift of circumstance is a violently unpleasant thing to have to witness, particularly from the viewing bleachers inside one's own head.

The older I get, Lee Buck Trevino once quipped, *the better I used to be.* That was certainly true in my case. Ten years ago, according to the yellowing state golf association card I still carried nostalgically in my wallet (and slipped out to gaze upon with the private fondness of a long married man peeking at a dim provocative snapshot of his old college sweetheart) I was once a highly respectable two handicap, a good if not great stick, a friendly lug whose game was theoretically within lob wedge distance of attaining every hacker's dream of being scratch.

I became a shaky, nine-handicap fortysomething who was slipping rapidly down the sodden grassy bank toward confirmed mediocrity. On a good day, I broke 82. On a *very* good day I achieved my so-called official USGA handicap and felt giddy with gratitude.

A golfing psychologist friend of mine says we inhabit the

"Age of Reasons" and I suppose it's only natural that even I—a guy who regularly complains about people who complain—had my own little laundry list of perfectly good reasons why my golf game wasn't what it used to be. Assuming you're willing to sit and listen to a grown man whine, they included, in no particular order of significance: the necessity of making a living, watching too much cable news, keeping up with the relentless obligations of my twelve-year-old daughter's growing social life, dealing with increasingly cranky house pets, coming to grips with a mysteriously expanding waistline, too many unmatched socks in the laundry, a general worry about a killer asteroid flattening my house, youth hockey practice, pesky telemarketers who disturb domestic tranquility at meal time, a far-too-short gardening season, the Victoria's Secret catalog, a chronic biological need for eight hours of sleep, talking to my girlfriend Wendy on the phone, perpetually lost car keys, and heretofore uncomplaining body parts that recently announced they were fast approaching AARP eligibility—these are just some of the obvious suspects to finger for blame. I could probably think of plenty more but who wants to hear that sort of thing?

The point I'm trying to make, in any case, is that to whatever "reason" I could assign this woeful golf attrition, the inescapable truth was that I'd taken to regularly jilting my standing Wednesday foursome at my club back home in Maine. Sid, Terry, and Tom had taken to making unflattering side bets about what particular day, month, or year I might actually show my face again at Brunswick Golf Club. And Chris Doyle, the club's otherwise taciturn head professional, once cruelly joked that my average golf rounds there were costing more than a day at Pebble Beach. Including caddie, lunch, and lost Nassau.

Like an overworked man of the cloth who gradually realizes he's somehow lost his Vardon grip on the point of faith, it slowly began to penetrate my cranium that I wasn't just losing my ability to play my favorite game the way I once had. Something far more elusive and valuable than a once respectable golf swing was slipping away faster than the hairs on Gary McCord's head.

I can't think how to say it so I'll just say it. The most unthinkable thought of all.

Golf was ceasing to be *fun*.

And if that weren't excruciatingly painful enough to have to admit to oneself, there was finally the cautionary tale of my own "silent" mentor and literary god, Henry Longhurst, to consider.

As my travels, writings, and broadcasting increased, to say nothing of my age, Longhurst wrote the same year I graduated from high school and wandered out to the Greater Greensboro Open aiming, absurdly as it turned out, to snag a job as a professional caddie for a "few months" before my first college term commenced and was delighted to encounter one of my literary heroes anchoring the corner of the bar at the old Sedgefield Inn, entertaining a small crowd of friends with rich anecdotes from his journey across the game's decades . . . *my golf fell away and it became less and less fun to do progressively more badly something that one had once done reasonably well. I had every reason to believe that I should turn out in middle age, and even later, to be an accurate and crafty player, always liable to beat an undergraduate, but it was not to be. My swing disintegrated and I became quite pathetically bad. I kept meaning to take myself in hand and go in for a fortnight's serious practice, which I knew was all that was needed, but somehow, with all the traveling about, I never got down to it.*

I think that sums it up pretty nicely.

· · ·

WHICH, in a nutshell, explains what I was doing that morning at the beautiful Tradition Golf Club in La Quinta, California, bathed in the romantic desert light of the New Millennium, infused with the foolish optimism that always comes to hackers like me on the threshold of a brave new golf season.

True, my right elbow still throbbed mysteriously and United Airlines had apparently seen fit to send my clubs on an extended tour of Fiji. But I told myself these were mere *distractions* on the path to recovery and regained golf fulfillment because the cagey golf gods, as either Homer or maybe Homero Blancas was alleged to have said, refuse to do for a man what he will not do for himself.

Not to dwell on an unpleasant subject, I simply realized it was either time for me to quietly toss in the game towel and go with the ceremonial dignity Father Longhurst had exhibited or else take my faltering game by the scruff of the neck and rededicate myself to the proposition that old golfers never die—they just piss and moan until they can't stand the sound of their own whining anymore and actually *do* something about their pathetic games before not even their golf partners will agree to play with them.

The good news in this instance was that my partner in the Kings Crown was a *very* fine stick named David Chapman, a slow-talking, sweet swinging scratch golfer and former North Carolina junior state champion who grew up to build the spectacular Tradition Golf Club. Lucky for me, he knew every inch of the challenging Palmer-Seay golf course there like the back of his own golf glove.

The bad news was, for our opening nine-hole four-ball match of the tournament, David and I had been unlucky enough to draw my recent employer, the tournament's namesake and the King of Golf himself, one Arnold Daniel Palmer, and his close friend, Cessna Aviation CEO Russ Meyers.

As a cluster of early-rising spectators (a few still in pajamas but curiously clad in bright ski parkas) huddled over their steaming coffee mugs on the adjacent terrace, attempting to ward off the desert's penetrating morning chill, Arnold teed up and drilled one of his patented "Big Mamoos" over the corner of the dangerous lake that borders the opening par-five hole, surgically reducing the difficult three-shotter to a long par-four he could easily reach in two. The pajamaed gallery *oohed* and *aahed* admiringly over their gourmet grinds.

Russ teed up next and smacked a crisp, intelligent drive off the right corner of the lake, the safe approach to the hole. There was another approving murmur of support from the terrace crowd.

My talented partner teed up his ball and winked at me, made a majestic swing and pushed his drive far into the desert rocks. The chorus fell respectfully silent, ducking heads safely back into their coffee mugs. "Sorry, boss," David apologized to me, looking sheepish but also clearly annoyed with himself.

"Oh, no *problem*. That's why you've got a partner," I heard myself breezily reply, the oldest chestnut in golf, confidently waggling my borrowed driver, massaging my aching elbow and suddenly, inexplicably, recalling the unsettling little dream that had been dogging me for months in which I show up at a world-famous club to play with my best friends only to discover I have brought neither clubs nor pants. Suddenly, as I realized David was now hitting his *third* shot and we were playing *Arnold Palmer* in a real-life golf tournament I felt about as lonely and exposed and ridiculous and terrified as I've ever felt on a golf course. Maybe the dream was some kind of premonitory warning that I had no business trying to play the game with such *serious* golfers.

· · ·

DURING the three years I helped Arnold Palmer write his memoirs, we'd played perhaps ten or fifteen full rounds of golf together at Bay Hill and Latrobe Country Club, and even though I thoroughly enjoyed those rounds and played passingly well in spots, I confess that I never quite got over the incomparable thrill—and silent terror—of knowing I was playing golf with the king of the game. My nervous unease, if that's the right word for it, had nothing to do with Arnold. He was the soul of hospitality and down-to-earth charm, quick to offer an encouraging word after a poor shot and a needling grin and affectionate barb for a good one—especially those rare moments where I had the temerity to out-drive him from the tee. Whenever some adoring foot soldier from Arnie's vast army asked me what their hero Arnold Palmer was *really* like, I replied that he was exactly what he appeared to be—only better. After three years of close proximity to the man and the legend, the best thing I could say about Palmer was that I liked him even *more* than when, like twenty million kids, I knew and adored him only from afar. In public and private settings he was commendably the same man, a superstar so obviously comfortable in his own skin he had a genuine ability to make anyone—doorman or CEO, President of the United States or even a pesky fan—feel remarkably at ease. He made solid eye contact. He gripped your hand the way a blacksmith holds his hammer. He made you feel damn good about being in his army.

And so, I took a deep cleansing breath and attempted to focus my mind on the positive aspects of the situation, telling myself this was only a meaningless golf club member-guest golf tournament, for Pete's sake, and not the bloody United States Open and, even though I was suddenly playing against Arnold Palmer instead of with him, with a little luck and a lot of positive concentration I might not miserably top the ball and thoroughly embarrass myself and anyone who happened to know me. I only wished I could get my hands to stop visibly shaking.

For an instant, poised over that all-important opening swing, I think I may have even believed some of this mental drivel—for golfers are nothing if not a race of incurably cockeyed optimists who desperately cling to the ridiculous delusion that if only we remember to integrate a few of the basic swing principles we've known almost from infancy, keep our heads perfectly still and our grips pleasantly loose, make a smooth slow shoulder turn with our new forged Tour irons glinting in the sun at the precise moment the Dow achieves a new upward benchmark and the moon and planets mysteriously align themselves in the heavens, why wondrous things can and will surely happen—world peace, for example, or a lasting cure for the common cold, or at the very least the greatest golf year of our lives.

Not this time, I'm afraid. Maybe it was the borrowed clubs or the annoying ache in my elbow. Anyway, I made a decent swing and watched my ball hook straight into the heart of the lake. It grew so quiet, David told me later over a beer, or something to that effect, you could hear a mouse pass gas in his pajamas.

"Too much work, not enough play, eh Shakespeare?" The King of Golf said quietly to the horrified King of Something, chuckling in that engaging way where his chin slips down into his leathery bull neck and his massive blacksmith shoulders merrily hop.

Everyone on the tee smiled sympathetically and I smiled, too, wishing the desert ground would just yawn open so I could jump in and hide. No sport exposes your flaws of mind and body quite as ruthlessly as golf does, which is why the shot that *follows* a terrible one is often even more memorable.

I teed up a second ball, determined to hit my own "Big Mamoo" out there where the king had placed his, and if I say so myself, I managed to lay an even finer golf swing upon that innocent thermoplastic sphere.

This one went even farther into the lake.

• • •

WE were two down after three, three down after four, basically getting beaten like a Navajo war drum when David strolled over to have a word with one of his maintenance men who was planting rows of a beautiful heatherlike shrub on the border of the fifth tee. Arnold pulled out a cell phone and began chatting with Ely Callaway and Russ walked up to the tee to hit his next perfect drive whilst I slunk to the plastic cooler and drew a cup of ice water, wondering if it would appear unseemly for the guest of such a classy establishment to pry off the lid and politely soak his elbow and maybe his head for a while. My new century of rededicated golf had yielded a triple bogey followed by a pair of double bogeys followed by a bogey, my worst start since about the seventh grade, the year I first broke 100—proof that I maybe should give all due consideration to following Longhurst into the sunset. Not only had I managed to disgrace myself in front of my childhood hero and his friends, but also a bunch of nice people in their designer pajamas.

That's when my golf bag rang.

As a rule, I'm offended by people carrying cell phones on golf courses (unless your name happens to be Arnold Palmer) and have long been on record as advocating the Iranian remedy of a severed dialing digit for such unholy trespasses into the realm of the sacred. In this case, I suddenly remembered that I'd stuck my own cell phone in one of the zippered side pockets of my borrowed clubs on the wildly improbable chance United Airlines might phone up to say they'd found the rest of my luggage and a set of golf clubs with my name on them as well, so I wouldn't have to go purchase an expensive sports jacket to wear to the tournament dinner where I fully expected to hide out behind the ice sculpture in order to avoid meeting anyone who might have watched me tee off that morning.

"Hey, pal," droned a familiar flat nasal voice, "where do they get virgin wool?"

"I dunno," I admitted.

"V-e-r-y ugly sheep."

I laughed. Sort of. My mood at that moment, truthfully, was not wildly upbeat.

It was my friend Jonathan Sager, who sounds a lot like the actor Charles Grodin, and come to think of it, resembles him a bit, as well, including his smarty-pants smirk and naturally thinning topknot.

"So, where are you and what are you doing?" Sager demanded

cheerfully. "I live vicariously through your work life, you know. And just in case you really care, it's twenty-two degrees and snowing again here in Syracuse."

"I'm on a golf course in Palm Desert, three down in a golf match to Arnold Palmer," I said without a trace of irony or, I'm afraid, enthusiasm.

"*C'mon,*" he said. "Remember I'm a lawyer. You can't con a conner."

I assured him I wasn't lying. I explained, in so many words, that I was indeed playing in a golf tournament against Arnold Palmer and, for what it was worth, field-testing a positive new mental approach for reviving my ailing golf skills, hoping to rediscover my old zest for the game in the new millennium.

"Really?" he said warily. "How's it going?"

"Great," I replied. "Except for the fact that I seem to have the same sorry golf swing and couldn't play worse if I had one arm and was blindfolded and am making a complete imbecile of myself, everything's fabulous. Just *peachy.*"

Counselor Sager chuckled, which usually means a smart remark or blue joke is on the way. He's like Charles Grodin that way, too.

"Well, just remember the immortal words of Miles Murphy."

"Who's he?"

"Lost but not forgotten Dewsweeper. He's the guy who used to screw up a hole, hurl his club, and say, 'I really hate this *damn* game. But it's the only fun I ever have.' Just remind yourself of that. Golf is supposed to be fun, Lumpy."

I hated when Jon called me Lumpy. But then again, *everybody* he really liked turned into a nickname, a true indication that he considered you his kind of guy—not unlike the way Arnold barked at and needled friends who were closest to him. *You're only young once,* went the Sager golf mantra, *but among golf buddies you can be immature forever.*

"Hey," he said. "Is Arnold Palmer *really* there?"

For as long as I'd known him, which was approaching four years, Jon Sager had wanted to meet Arnold Palmer. But then, I suppose, so does roughly every other golfing male between the ages of thirty and ninety walking the planet. Even so, I'd promised Jon the day would come when I took him to meet his childhood hero. Perhaps a brief phone chat would suffice.

"*Yes,*" I said with exasperation. "Do you want to speak to him?"

"Are you *serious*? Listen, pal, I just had to approve of the company's termination of a contract with our cleaning service whose apparent motto is 'We never break a sweat' and whose idea of cleaning a bathroom is to leave out last Sunday's *Times* for toilet paper. By this time tomorrow we'll be lucky if pickets aren't up around the building and Hillary Clinton isn't out there standing on the roof of my car leading the protest with a bullhorn. You have no idea how speaking to Arnold Palmer would make my day! Put <u>him</u> on. Tell him I've got a great Dewsweeper joke for him . . . "

It was touching to hear a forty-six-year-old senior legal counsel for a large financial institution sound like a giddy six-year-old about to meet the real Santa Claus.

Arnold happened to be five feet away, finished with Ely Callaway. So I presented him my cell phone.

"Who is it, your *girlfriend*?" he demanded with a gruff bark that meant he approved of Wendy.

"No. It's a Dewsweeper. One of your loyal subjects and he dearly wishes to say hello."

The king put the phone to his good ear.

"Hello?" he said good-naturedly, squinting into the desert sun like golf's Gary Cooper. "What the hell is a *Dewsweeper* anyway?"

Arnold's tanned face went blank. After a few seconds he handed me back the phone with a disapproving smirk that could have come straight from his unsympathetic Pap.

"It went dead," he said to me, then shook his head. "You obviously forgot to charge it up."

· · ·

SOMETHING truly inexplicable happened after that. I still can't fully explain it. David and I won the fifth hole with a birdie putt. Oddly enough, mine.

Then we won the seventh with another birdie. Even more unexpectedly, also mine.

We halved eight with four pars.

Then, at nine, I rapped a long birdie attempt across the green and couldn't believe what I witnessed. It fell into the hole, too. David let out a little rebel yell and Arnold looked over at Russ as if we all must be hallucinating. Both our opponents missed their birdie putts and the match ended, officially halved.

"*Three* birdies in four holes!" the king snarled, thrusting out one of his huge paws for the customary shake. "You've obviously been playing *way* too much golf and ignoring your work, Shakespeare!"

Then he slapped me vigorously on the back and gave me that lopsided hero's grin of his. My heart did a little flutter step of joy, I must say, and my knees went a little weak.

I was still puzzling on this breathtaking reversal of fortune several hours later when, showered and dressed for a night out with Arnold and his friends, I sat alone on the Palmer patio having a whiskey and watching the sun slip behind the desert mountains.

Arnold, cocktail in hand, suddenly appeared. He drew up a chair and sat down. His eyes were moist with emotion. He'd just been in the bedroom, I realized, reading my latest column in *Golf Magazine*, due to hit the newsstands in a few days. It was my personal tribute to his late wife, Winnie.

Winnie had been gone only eight or nine weeks. The last time I'd seen him, in fact, was at her funeral in Latrobe. As I wrote in the column, getting to know Arnold Palmer and his family on an intimate basis was a golf writer's dream come true. But the unexpected bonus of the project was forming a deep friendship with Winnie Walzer Palmer.

I greatly missed Winnie and couldn't even begin to fathom the emptiness he must be feeling. So I sat there saying nothing, unable to speak, waiting for the Boss, as Ed Seay always called him, to speak, allowing the ice in my bourbon to melt in the dusk.

Finally, he cleared his throat.

"What the hell is a Dewsweeper?" he asked.

I smiled with relief. We were back on safe turf now, the give and take of golf. I took a sip of my drink.

"A kid who goes out at dawn to sweep the dew from the greens with a long cane pole. They still do it in Britain and a few places in America."

"I *know* that," he said with gentle annoyance. "What I meant was, who was that guy you wanted me to speak to?"

I explained that Jon Sager was just one of my best golf buddies, the de facto leader of a group of seven or eight close friends who played every Saturday and Sunday morning, rain or shine, from May to November, at a hundred-year-old golf club in upstate New York, just outside Syracuse. It was called the Onondaga Golf and Country Club. Every golf club in America had a group of golf nuts like the Dewsweepers, I said. But these guys were sort of special. They ranged in age from forty-six to seventy-one and their friendship was based on a shared passion for golf—or maybe it was the other way around. In any case, they were Arnold Palmer's kind of guys and they'd more or less adopted me.

"Adopted you?"

I explained that Sager introduced me to the rest of the Dewsweepers when I went to Syracuse a few years ago to make a speech for the Lung Association. Since then, we'd played a lot of golf together and Jon had even introduced me to the woman I'd been dating now for almost two years—a woman, though I didn't dare say it, who reminded me of Winnie Palmer in a lot of wonderful ways.

Arnold smiled slyly. "Wendy."

"Correct."

"So I guess you make it to Syracuse pretty often. For love if not golf."

"For both, as a matter of fact."

"Good for you," he said and fell silent. For a moment, we sat and stared out at a desert mountain's blue profile in the dusk. He sipped his scotch.

"Well, Shakespeare," he said with a sigh. "Where do you suppose I'm going to find another Winnie?"

I liked it when Arnold called me Shakespeare. But I couldn't begin to answer his heartbreaking question. Fortunately, it didn't require an answer from me or anybody else. To Arnold Palmer, golf was life and life was golf. But both of us knew he would never find another Winnie Walzer.

There was stirring inside the house. David Chapman had arrived and Ed Seay was bellowing to the Boss that it was time to go.

Arnold slapped my knee vigorously and went inside to fetch his jacket and I sat there finishing my drink, thinking about how difficult the year ahead was probably going to be for him. Fortunately he had a circle of close and trusted friends, his devoted daughters Amy and Peg, his grandchildren and the abiding pleasure he still took in teeing it up and chasing the game to fill his days and perhaps buffer his grief.

What was my excuse for being unhappy? I suddenly wondered—hearing a distant familiar voice of one I'd loved and lost, too, and realizing, as I did, that I may have had the proposition about fixing my game and rekindling my pleasure in golf entirely *backward*.

· · ·

MY father, an ad man with a poet's heart, whom I grew up calling Opti the Mystic due to his abundant goodwill and goofy optimism, used to say that he never had a bad day on the golf course. *Whatever life throws at you,* he would say regardless of the round's outcome, *you can always rely on golf and your friends for a laugh.*

Essentially I shared this level-headed perspective on life's hardest game, but lately it seemed that I'd forgotten this fact. Opti played with the same three guys every Saturday morning, season upon season, for nearly two decades—a group of Carolina dewsweepers who were always the first group off the tee and just as swift to congratulate as they were to needle, faithful golf templars quick to convey the latest blue joke meant just for the guys or share a thoughtful confidence knowing that in the right setting they really *could* be boys again.

If it's true that sons dream their fathers' dreams, as Carl Jung insists, perhaps that explained my attachment to Jon Sager and Onondaga's Dewsweepers, an even larger bag-carrying brotherhood of golfing oddfellows who faithfully showed up in any weather and played mostly for the competitive pleasure of each other's company and seldom even wagered on the outcome of their matches—or, for that matter, even bothered to keep a formal scorecard. They gathered, they played, they counted on the pleasure of each other's company. Friendship and rowdy camaraderie seemed to be at least as important as their golf and yet golf was somewhere near the epicenter of their lives.

That was *precisely* what was missing from my own busy golf life, I realized—playing for kicks, for laughs, for nothing more than the cold drinks afterward, for the simply unalloyed joy of beating your buddies at their own game.

I'm not sure if this sudden insight qualified as a personal epiphany or a psychological breakthrough of any kind, but it certainly struck me as a possible cure for what was really ailing me out there on the magestic Tradition course today.

Instead of turning myself into a raving desert lunatic unbuttoned by the fact that he could no longer summon his "old" game, perhaps I'd be much much better off to forget adding up scores and play the game for whatever pleasures golf would give me—honest laughs, new friends, good shots if they happened, whatever came along the fairway.

Simply put, corny as it sounds, regardless of whatever life in the New Millennium threw at me, perhaps it was time for me to try and get back in touch with the faith of my father and the fundamental quality that made me fall in love with the golf in the first place—the joy of playing with my friends.

I rattled the ice in my tumbler and tried to pick out the shape of the desert mountain, now completely covered in darkness, thinking how the simplest truths are almost always the most difficult to accept. Sometimes, like that beautiful mountain, you just can't see what's been standing right in front of you all along.

The truth was, for whatever reason I cared to name, I'd fallen out of love with playing golf—and I needed to be in love again. Perhaps by working less and playing more, I decided, going in search of Dewsweeper *joy* instead of a better game, I could somehow rekindle that love affair and neatly avoid Father Longhurst's fate entirely.

Just then, the King of Golf reappeared at the patio door. He was wearing his zippered windbreaker, collar turned up, ready to go. For an instant, he looked like his old self again, the world-famous public man who is so comfortable in his own skin. He gave me another withering Pap look.

"You going with us or *what?*" he barked in a way that meant he was glad I was tagging along—this time for fun and not work.

I apologized for dawdling and hopped straight up. Arnold, however, stopped me at the door with a massive hand on my shoulder.

"That was pretty *interesting* what you did out there today on the golf course," he said, adding with a softer note, his eyes watering just a bit, "and thank you for what you wrote about Winnie. You got it *right*."

I told him I was happy that he thought so. Then I shrugged and admitted I certainly would never forget halving *Arnold Palmer* in a golf match.

"You should play more often," he said, clearing his throat, still clutching my shoulder, giving me a bit of the famous hero grin.

"Life's way too hard and way too short, Shakespeare, *not* to play golf."

I admitted I'd been thinking a little bit along those same lines lately, now that I was living my life again instead of his, as autobiographers must do.

"Just don't *ever* do what you did this morning again!" he barked at me, and then smiled in a way that meant he was pleased I'd done just that.

TWO

ZEROCUSE

I sometimes think I'm going to be the last one out of this place, the guy who shuts off the light and locks the door for good," Jon Sager observed with a wry smile.

He was standing at a window on the fourteenth floor of the corporate headquarters in downtown Syracuse, staring out over a Midwestern-looking urban landscape of ornate Victorian rooftops and gray municipal buildings and squared off city blocks and leaking smokestacks, a city being swallowed whole by a fresh foot of Lake Ontario snow.

"See that building down there?" he said, nodding below to the roof of the city's war memorial auditorium where the bas-relief words *Marne* and *Normandy* were raised in stone and just visble through the swirling maelstrom. "That's where the Nats used to play ball. Man, were *they* great. I remember one summer after college when I was out west visiting my grandmother in Laguna Beach and my Uncle Jack introduced me to George 'The Bird' Yardley who held the Detroit Pistons' scoring record until Syracuse University graduate Dave Bing broke it. Yardley had been my favorite, as a kid. You can't imagine the thrill it was for me to finally meet the guy. I lived for basketball in those days. It was even more important to me than golf, if you can believe it."

"You miss them?" I asked.

"The Nats? You betcha."

"I meant those days."

Jon glanced at me as if surprised I could ask such a lame-brained question.

"Sure. Don't you? Is there anything better than being a kid?" He laughed like Charles Grodin and fixed me with a skeptical little smile. "And, who know, someday I might even get to finally meet my *other* childhood hero, Arnold Palmer."

"Patience, counselor. It'll happen."

An hour or so before, I'd found my way to his office out of the winter tumult, unannounced and on my way to California, and discovered Jon burrowed into a legal brief the size of a Guttenberg Bible on his desk.

Because of the storm, most of the company's employees had been sent home for the afternoon, a Friday in early February—Groundhog Day, as it just so happened, my forty-sixth birthday.

"Hey, look what the storm blew in," he declared the instant he saw me, waving me to a large leather chair by the window and wondering aloud what brought me through "Zerocuse" in the dead of winter, aside from the obvious physical attractions of his neighbor, Wendy Buynak.

"The usual," I said, dropping into the chair and picking up a copy of *Golf World* magazine that had a photograph of Tiger Woods on the cover and editorially wondered if this might be his "best season ever." I was mildly curious about the same thing—only, selfishly I guess, for me rather than him.

"Work," I replied. "And a birthday cake."

"Wendy really doesn't look a day over thirty," he said.

"It's *my* birthday."

"Oh," he said, then smiled the Charles Grodin smile. "Well, in that case, happy birthday and look on the bright side. You may not

be getting any younger, Lump, but you can still have your birthday cake and eat it, too. Probably the whole cake, in your case.
Someone should warn Wendy."

"How's your monk's patch growing? I read that they've made
some promising breakthroughs against male pattern baldness."

Whenever Jon needled me about my stubborn waistline, I reminded him of the ever-expanding bald spot on the crown of his
head that had him well on the path to looking like a medieval
monk by fifty.

"It only hurts when I bend over and look at myself in the mir-
ror," he admitted, slamming shut a huge law book. "Hey, this calls
for an emergency meeting of the Dewsweepers. They'll kick me
off the bowling team if they discover you were in town and we
didn't hoist a brew with you. Especially on your birthday."

"Don't make them come out in this mess," I protested. "Besides, one of the gifts I'm giving myself this year is less beer and
more exercise—preferably in the form of golf. Pretty soon there
won't be as much of me for you to abuse."

"Are you *kidding*? This is America's snowiest city, pal. Average
snowfall thirteen *feet*. At least we still lead the nation in *that* cate-
gory. A blizzard is nothing to the Dewsweepers. Hell, Russell and
Lester will probably ski over. Besides, we've got serious business
to discuss. When the guys heard you and I were sneaking off to
Pebble Beach they felt left out and started making noises about a
spring golf trip."

And with that, he picked up his telephone and began dialing
the boys.

• • •

THERE's an old saying that golf pals are God's compensation for
being unable to pick your family members.

I sometimes think that's true—especially when you glance
around to discover that you've grown inexplicably fond of a
bunch of characters you never expected to know and powerfully

attached to the inhabitants of an out-of-the-way place that's the butt of a lot of bad weather jokes.

So it was with me and the Dewsweepers and America's self-described "Snowiest City," a place I'd frankly never given even a passing thought to visiting until a very official-looking legal letter arrived in my mailbox in Maine, as if delivered by the unseen hand of Fate itself, one reluctant spring day almost four years before.

The letter was from Jonathan Sager, Esq., politely inviting me to come in my capacity as a golf writer to Syracuse and make a speech at a charity fund-raiser for the American Lung Association of Central New York. Counselor Sager, who was joint chairman of the event, had read a book I wrote about taking my father back to England and Scotland to visit places where he'd learned to play golf during World War Two and thought the author might have something interesting to say about golf's role in forging lasting friendships.

I wrote this guy Sager straight back, thanking him for the invitation but politely declining, noting that I was about to take off on a publicity tour for my latest book—which was about fly-fishing with my young daughter—and part of that commitment fell over the same weekend as his fund-raiser. I thanked him for considering me as a speaker, though, and wished him the best of British luck raising money for his cause.

A few days later, another official letter arrived.

Dear Jim:

Here are the TOP TEN REASONS TO COME TO SYRACUSE, NEW YORK:

10. You can see Richard Gere's boyhood home in North Syracuse and meet his father, Homer.

 9. You can get the room (and bed!) at the Brewster Inn where Alec Baldwin and Kim Basinger stay when they visit Alec's mother and sister here.

 8. You can see the world's first drive-in teller at a bank—at the former Merchant's Bank on Erie Boulevard. Also, visit

the village of Chittenango where Frank Baum, author of *The Wizard of Oz*, grew up.

7. You can go to the Irish side of town to see the only traffic signal in the U.S. (manufactured locally by Crouse-Hinds) where the green is on the top.

6. See the private school where Walter Hagen's son attended classes and the little golf course called Lyndon where The Haig stopped and set the course record on a drive over from Rochester.

5. Visit the alma mater (Cornell University) of Robert Trent Jones, see and play three of his finest early designs (Cornell University Golf Course, Seven Oaks at Colgate, and Green Lakes State Park) and also play his worst one (Hill-N-Dale in Tully, NY, which he designed at the request of our then local New York congressman, reportedly on a cocktail napkin).

4. Meet Jim Boeheim, coach of the Syracuse Orangemen, Sandy Burton (one of Arnold's teammates at Wake Forest) or maybe even find Al Devendorf (who once worked with Karsten Solheim at the General Electric plant in Liverpool and some say co-invented the first Ping putter—which still hangs behind the bar at one of his favorite haunts).

3. See the Boxing Hall of Fame in Canastota, Robert De Niro's mother's house, or stroll all fifty yards of the Syracuse Walk of Fame where such "native" luminaries as Bob Costas, Bobcat Goldthwaite, Grace Jones, Gordon MacRae, Joanna Cassidy, Frank Langella, and Jackie Coogan—that's right, Uncle Fester from *The Addams Family*—are all represented in cement!

2. See famous Onondaga Lake where Native American legend holds that the warrior Hiawatha stuck his magic paddle into the water and created the Great Peace that led the way to the formation of the Iroquois Confederacy—America's first functioning democracy. The lake later became home of America's second largest salt industry and many years later achieved the top spot on the EPA's hit list of New York's most polluted waterways, thanks to Allied Chemical.

1. Visit and play Oak Hill Country Club in nearby Rochester (Site of 1995 Ryder Cup) or Country Club of Rochester (the course where Walter Hagen grew up playing as a kid) or play Onondaga Golf and Country Club, my home club, designed by Walter Travis in 1920, host of numerous state championships and U.S. Open qualifying site, not to mention the home of the Dewsweepers.

I figured this guy was either *really* desperate for a speaker or *really* cheap. He'd probably heard that I'd only recently begun making club and charity speeches and my going rate was reasonable—translation: free—or else was some aging Arnold Palmer groupie who really just wanted a signed photograph for his office wall.

Whatever else was true, you had to admire this guy's wit and determination. For reasons that still somewhat elude me, a little voice inside my head said I really ought to go to visit Syracuse. In retrospect, I think the possibility of playing Trent Jones's *worst* golf course and tracking down this Al Devendorf cat, whoever the heck he was, must have piqued my journalistic interests.

In any case, I promptly wrote him back that I would see if I could arrange to conclude my book tour in Syracuse. By any chance, I wondered, attempting to give him back a bit of cheek, did they have book stores *and* golf courses there?

Two days later, Counselor Sager phoned me. He sounded like we were fraternity brothers who hadn't seen each other since we accidentally burned down the frat house after too much Purple Jesus that crazy night thirty years ago.

"Hey, *pal,* not only do we play golf and read books over here," he said, with an air of mock woundedness, "but we even have female authors who are as drop-dead gorgeous as our golf courses. I read in your fly fishing book that you're divorced . . ."

He mentioned a local bestselling author named Mona Crump

whose racy novel about a girl growing up in the South with too much booze and not enough proper adult supervision was riding high on bestseller lists and delightfully shocking book club matrons across the Republic. As books go, hers was the spiritual antithesis of the modest family memoir I'd written about my dad and our golfing exploits.

"Maybe I can set you up with Mona Crump for dinner at the club. She's literary *and* beautiful. Ever catch her author photo? Not bad on the eyeballs, if you know what I mean."

I told him I knew what he meant, but I was sort of seeing a woman in Maine, neglecting to mention that the pretty young woman I'd been seeing in Maine really lived in a Boston loft, hated golf and fly-fishing, wasn't particularly wild about children, thought snow was "icky," was half my age, and had recently burst out sobbing inconsolably in a crowded restaurant when I couldn't explain to her satisfaction—I swear this is true—the "meaning of life." It had come as a profound relief to us both when we finally agreed that either I was too old for her or she was too young for me and we probably ought to call it quits. She went back to her former boyfriend, the moody but brilliant computer games designer, and I drove back to Maine to pick up my kids for soccer practice and a piano lesson.

"Is it true Maine men go to family reunions to pick up chicks?" Jon wondered.

"I wouldn't mind playing Robert Trent Jones's worst golf course and meeting the Ping Putter guy," I said, ignoring this wiseguy—who was starting to grow on me, I must admit, I dunno, like an amusing skin rash, if there is such a thing.

"Done. I'll introduce you to the Dewsweepers, too. Hey, by the way. I've got a buddy named Lloyd Martin who owns his own airplane. We'll even fly over and pick you up. What kind of beer do you like?"

Normally, these weren't two activities I closely associated with each other. On the other hand, it was free transportation and I was fairly sure my publisher, at least, would appreciate that frugal touch.

And so, at a designated time on the agreed-upon sunny morning in June, with only a few grave misgivings for my personal safety and my children's future livelihood, I watched a much-smaller-than-expected airplane taxi up to a hangar and three dudes hop out wearing Groucho glasses and rubber noses. They were either hitmen with a sense of humor, I decided, or the guys from Syracuse.

Jon and I shook hands.

"You're younger than you look in pictures," he said by way of greeting, "and bigger. You remind me of that Tim Heron guy on Tour they call Lumpy."

I thanked him—sort of—and replied that he reminded me of an old fraternity brother of mine who went on to a distinguished career in state politics and was now in charge of running the laundry service at the prison. Sager smiled back as if I was his kind of guy.

"Are you two planning to carry on like this *all* the way back to Syracuse?" wondered the pilot and cochair of the event, a nice chap named Bob Henderson.

"Not unless he says something really disgusting," Jon said, "like he wishes he could date Hillary 'Keg Legs' Clinton instead of Mona Crump or something."

"Absolutely," I assured him with a smile, putting on the thoughtful Groucho glasses they'd brought me, thinking that if the plane went down in the jungles of Vermont and our bodies weren't found for a year, at least my kids would know their old man went down laughing.

As we sat on the runway preparing to take off, the pilot gave a hand signal over the engine's roar—one finger raised followed by five fingers up.

"What's that mean?" I asked Jon and Bob in back.

Bob replied, "We've got only about a one in five chance of taking off."

• • •

WE flew to Hamilton, New York, home of Colgate University, first buzzing the frat house where Jon Sager partied like there was no tomorrow but still managed to earn a degree in religion and philosophy in three years ("I was on the Saint Augustine plan—Oh Lord give me strength and piety and eventually a college degree. But not just yet . . .") and then actually landed and played Trent Jones's Seven Oaks Golf Course, which turned out to be even better than advertised, a real sweetheart of a golf course. My host turned out to be better than advertised, too. He was a funny guy with a wild duck hook and a handicap almost identical to mine and kept breaking me up with his pungent one-liners. We played a close match that he won on the final hole, then he shook my hand and told me a great joke that Arnold Palmer would have loved but can't be printed here.

That evening, Jon and his lovely wife, Karen, took me to dinner at the Onondaga Club, which turned out to be a sophisticated fieldstone clubhouse set upon a high sweeping hill east of Syracuse near the pretty village of Fayetteville (childhood home of Grover Cleveland—a juicy morsel Jon somehow neglected to include on his list) and even somehow arranged for Mona Crump to join us for dinner. She sashayed into the old-line conservative club wearing a slinky cocktail dress and a worried expression, much better looking than advertised, also.

"So, Mona, gosh, what does your *mother* think of your book?" Karen cheerfully asked the famous author, as we setttled down for a pre-dinner libation.

Karen Sager was the kind of bouncy, upbeat person who could probably convince a death row inmate to sing a few heart-felt stanzas of the Barney song before his date with destiny—a former high school championship swimmer from Liverpool who attended Notre Dame on an academic scholarship but these days worked part time at a local travel agency, ferried her four handsome kids from swim practice to track meets, and was locally known for the unusual Christmas and Easter decorations she made by painting discarded stuff like light bulbs, used bowling pins, and so forth.

"You know," Mona snapped, visibly on guard, "I really don't want to talk about my book *or* my mother."

"Oops."

"Okay," Karen chirped and smiled pleasantly at me as if to say, *Well, it's your turn, Lumpy . . . Don't just sit there on your hands.*

Jon slapped his knee.

"I have an idea. Let's go in to dinner."

Dinner was on the east porch of the club, overlooking what I soon learned was the third tee of the golf course where a few happy stragglers were playing along in the summer twilight. I sat there sipping iced tea wishing I could be out there with them, only periodically tuning in as Karen and Jon labored to break the ice with Mona.

The club's dining room was crowded with patrons, most of them of the elderly variety that can be riled up fairly easily if you make unseemly silverware noise or say something particularly nice about Hillary Clinton.

I was sitting there minding my own business, more or less, following an imaginary white ball over the grass in my head when a pair of hands suddenly and violently seized my shoulders from behind and Jon and Karen both appeared startled. For an instant, I thought I might be about to be given the bum's rush to the door for making too much ruckus with my linen napkin, but then I heard a familiar Southern voice drawl inches from my ear, "Well *hey*, Precious. You mean to say they even let educated white trash like you in a *purty* place this nice?"

Heads turned, soup spoons paused in flight, brows knitted.

It was, of *all* people, Patrick McDaid—my oldest friend, my closest pal, my greatest nemesis on Planet Golf. To say we're like brothers doesn't quite cover it. We're Hope and Crosby without the personal baggage, Lea and Perrins without the sauce, Funk and Wagnalls without the funk. Not to belabor the point, McDaid and I are spiritual blood brothers and happily sworn childhood adversaries who walk this terrestrial orb in the eternal hope of beating each other at a game—any game—and I can't imagine life being any dang fun without him. I just deeply pity his lovely wife, Terry.

"It's the Irish Antichrist," Jon declared, anointing Patrick with a perfect nickname that would stick like flypaper. Jon, it turns out, had convinced Pat—who resembles an aging oversized leprechaun—to fly up from North Carolina and be a surprise guest at the fund-raiser where I still hadn't figured out yet what I was supposed to talk about.

His effect on Mona Crump was fascinating to behold. Her worried frown vanished, her pretty brow relaxed, her lovely dark eyes lit up and before you could say *New York Times Book Review* they were sitting there chatting pleasantly about everything from crop-dusting to new Bordeaux wine. McDaid, I'll concede, is a pretty worldly cuss. He marks his golf ball with a special Irish harp coin, has a personal swing guru who was an LPGA player, and once sold the industrial cowlings that house the fans that cool the putting greens at Augusta National. Politically speaking, he used to be slightly left of Jane Fonda but now, one of the South's top industrial reps, was slightly right of Ted Turner. When he wasn't rebuilding his golf swing from start to finish or closing some mega-deal involving chain stores the size of ocean liners, he doted lavishly on his daughter Emily, taught Sunday school at the Methodist church, and actually read the kinds of books most of us wouldn't dare pick up unless we needed to, say, graduate from college or find a sure-fire cure for insomnia—stuff about "shifting global paradigms" or "coming class war over ideas" or the perkier writings of famous dead white guys like Baruch Spinoza, Bede the Younger, and Immanuel "Iggy" Kant.

Anyway, as he and Mona fell into avid conversation about the woeful state of American letters or worrying declines in Third World honeybee populations or some other such elevated topic, Karen Sager slipped me a sympathetic look and wondered how

I'd liked Jon's funny little "fan letter" promoting the surprising charms of Syracuse.

I admitted that I liked it a lot. As fan letters went, I replied, it was so funny and endearing I simply had to come here just to see if anything he said was true.

"Jon Boy is nothing if not *endearing*, all right," she agreed sarcastically. "Do you get much fan mail?"

I admitted that I got more than I ever thought I would just for writing a *golf* book or two. I thought of it as "friend" mail, though, because the people who wrote me tended to feel such easy familiarity with the subject they often provided vivid descriptions of their own favorite golf courses and memorable rounds. I loved these accounts from the field, I admitted, particularly the ones that included photographs of golf spouses, kids, and regular golf foursomes. It was reassuring to know there were other people out there just like us.

"That's *nothing*," Mona Crump declared, suddenly dropping Pat like a hot brick and jumping into our conversation. "I get fan mail from prisoners."

The table fell silent. The entire dining room did too, come to think of it. I saw the Irish Antichrist smile.

"You *do*? Prisoners?" he said wonderingly.

"Yeah," she declared loud enough to wake anyone slumbering over their vichyssoise. "They send me pictures of their *dicks!*"

Utensils clattered on fine Syracuse china, abrupt gasps for air were heard and chairs began to scrape across the polished marble floor as dessert courses were hastily abandoned and the elders of Onondaga fled into the night for their own moral safety.

"What a fascinating woman," Karen Sager remarked a little while later when Mona finally got bored with us and trotted away, perhaps headed for a late-night reading at a rave club or an assignation with a wanted felon, her reputation for shocking Republicans safely intact.

"You know, Jon." I pointed to my host. "You really don't have to try to procure me dates. I'm old enough to ask them on my own."

"Hey, who said it was a *date?*" Jon chortled. "I just wanted to see if she looked as good in real life as on the cover of her books."

Karen laughed. "Nonsense," she declared. "Jon Boy *loves* to matchmake his single friends. He could have been born a girl—except for his bald spot."

. . .

THE morning after the speech, I finally got to meet the Dewsweepers.

There were seven of them assembled on the first tee that morning at Onondaga—Lester, Tom, Tuck, Russ, Jon, Peter, and some guy they called Zawadzki, or " Z-Man" for short. At first, like the Seven Dwarfs, I could scarcely tell them all apart. But then, all white, rich, Republican golfers seem depressingly the same to me. If I had any money I might say it takes one to know one.

We shook hands and then, without much ado, the Dewsweepers began teeing up golf balls and drilling them down the first fairway, a short par four that ran steeply down the hill to a small round green silvered with morning dew—hence, I gathered, without even having to be told, their golf group's name.

The first four Dewsweepers were dangerously still in range when the rest began teeing up and hitting.

"Aren't you afraid you'll hit them?" I ventured to inquire.

Jon smiled, waggling his big and scarred Terminator driver.

"Nah. We like to keep things moving. Balls in the air by seven rain or shine, and no dawdling—that's our motto."

After nine holes, the groups switched places and even swapped personnel. No one appeared to be keeping score, so far as I could tell, but the conversations and barbs were nonstop and I slowly began to differentiate between the players—put faces, as it were, with names, and even attain lively snatches of the group's personalities.

Bill Tuck was the wiry little guy with big bushy white eye-brows and a neatly trimmed Mitch Miller beard who'd just re-tired as president of some well-known company in Syracuse called Crouse-Hinds and taken to exercising like a madman and playing golf like crazy. His wife, Toni, trained champion bearded collies and Jon engagingly referred to him as "Friar Tuck, the man with a swing like a full-body dry heave."

Lester Austin was also short, also retired, a trim and youthful former anesthesiologist with a beautifully compact golf swing that sent his tee shots drawing to the center of the fairway almost every time. Lester, who once had been a star athlete of some kind at Syracuse University—a champion wrestler, I later learned—now tended a vast vegetable garden with the devotion of a Bene-dictine monk, had a crazy Weimaraner dog named Woody Austin, and was married to an accomplished pianist and crack lady golfer named Sheila. Lester took a constant ribbing from Jon about his "munchkin" size, general forgetfulness, and his frequent visits to the woods to urinate. "The world is Lester's urinal but I think he likes to mark his progress around the golf course the way Woody Austin would. By the way," Jon added helpfully, "Woody's not named for the Tour player. A word of caution: he's named Woody because he always *has* one when he jumps on visitors and knocks them down. You've been warned."

Zawadzki, I learned, was the spiritual leader of the Dew-sweeper bowling team. The others weren't particularly keen on bowling, I discovered, they mostly did it to break the monotony of Syracuse's fierce and interminable winters until their beloved Onondaga course re-opened. Z-Man hailed from North Syracuse and was Polish by birth, sweet by disposition, the regional presi-dent of Fleet Bank and, as Jon pointed out, not only did he have the most amazing golf swing of the Dewsweepers but also a coif of hair that defied the laws of nature. Z-Man's precisely cali-brated swing actually paused eerily for a couple seconds at the top—"Long enough to fit him for a full wardrobe," as Jon sum-marized it—then clipped shots neatly into the short grass with depressing accuracy. Somewhere in his past, Zawadzki had beaten out Richard Gere for the lead in the senior play at North Syracuse High which, also according to Jon, sent Gere packing to Hollywood to look for a decent job. Z-Man was married to a beautiful woman named Saskia and, true enough, his hair never moved a bit.

Peter Marshall, on the other hand, had actually *been* in a movie—a bit part in the seventies film *A Separate Peace*, filmed at Exeter Academy shortly before Peter claims he was almost kicked out of the famous prep school. Chatty, personable, married to a passionate Greek blonde named Cynthia and father of a couple athletic teenagers, Peter functioned as chief financial officer for an international holding company whose job it was, I gathered, to travel the world buying up promising small companies and collecting company logo golf shirts. Peter, a self-declared fifteen handicap, sometimes rode his beloved Harley-Davidson motorcycle to the golf course with his golf clubs strapped dramatically to his back, and swore by a ridiculous "swing trainer" device that brought him steady ridicule from the others. The same age as Jon and me, Peter was coming off a back injury that had recently kept him out of action and purportedly in the therapeutic grip of a Swedish therapeutic masseuse called Inga. "We won't even go there," Jon explained, shaking his head sorrowfully.

Russ King, on the other hand, was nicely wrinkled and slow of foot, relatively speaking, a former president of Onondaga who helped write the club's recent centennial history book and, I quickly learned, the genial, dignified patriarch of the city's oldest architectural firm. Russ had recently finished building his post-and-beam "dream house" high on a hilltop east of the city. "You can see Onondaga from my porch but not my porch from Onondaga," he related to me as we trudged together up the long uphill eighteenth hole, pointing toward a set of pretty green hills in the distance. "And my wife, Jiggy, and I sort of like it that way, if you know what I mean."

The last Dewsweeper I met that morning was Tom Cahill. He

didn't say a whole lot during the round where nobody miraculously got beaned, but I learned from the others that Tom, too, was a recent president of the club and once upon a time he'd been a Syracuse city counselor and soon planned to retire from the defense contracting firm where he managed the contracts department. Tom was rangy, tall, and exceedingly courteous in an engagingly old-fashioned sort of way—a fine player and classy guy whose youngest son Patrick belonged to Country Club of Rochester, the club where Walter Hagen had grown up. As we finished up that first round at Onondaga during which everybody seemed to play against everybody else and with nobody in particular, Tom turned to me and said, the soul of Dewsweeper hospitality, "If you ever come back to Syracuse, we'll hop in the car and go over to Rochester and play."

As we shook hands, I heard myself replying that I would like that very much and would certainly make a point to come back to Syracuse as soon as possible.

Jon, I think, thought I was just attempting to be polite. But the truth was, even then, something about the easy camaraderie of the Dewsweepers greatly appealed to me.

"Well," my host said at the airport, extending a handshake as I prepared to climb aboard the tiny little plane for the ride back to Maine, "thanks for coming. I really appreciate you doing this. I think the guys really liked you."

I told him that was good because I liked the guys. The weekend, in fact, had been great—seeing my old pal McDaid, boring Mona Crump to tears, playing golf with those zany Dewsweepers.

"There was only one problem," I said solemnly, greatly enjoying the sudden look of proprietary panic he gave me, as if his spectacular hospitality were all for naught.

"You never introduced me to Al Devendorf or showed me Trent Jones's worst golf course. Some host *you* turned out to be."

Jon smiled slyly. It's funny how a great friendship begins.

"In that case, Lumpy, you'll *definitely* have to come back."

• • •

Now, almost three years later, four Dewsweepers were already assembled and waiting for us at Mulligans, a small tavern off the main drag in Fayetteville, just down the hill from the pretty white house where Grover Cleveland grew up wishing he could hit a lob wedge the way Phil Mickelson does and settled, instead, for being president.

The overwhelming consensus among the guys, according to Peter Marshall, who presented me with a pint of beer seconds after we entered the place, was that the Dewsweepers needed a spring golf road trip. I was happy to hear he wanted me to tag along with them.

"It's not spring yet," I reminded him, indicating the blizzard outside.

"More the reason to go someplace warm and green as quickly as possible. Forget the road. We'll fly. I'm thinking someplace classy—maybe Pinehurst."

Peter looked thinner than I remembered. I asked if he'd recently been in prison.

"No. The Beverly Hills Diet. There's fifteen pounds less of me for Cynthia to love."

"Cynthia doesn't love your old body," Bill Tuck spoke up, wielding a huge unlit Dominican cigar, "nearly as much as she loves her new Navigator."

"That's probably true. Did I mention that a guy flashed her last week while she was driving in it downtown," Peter said. "She was at a stoplight, looked over, and there was this pervert with his pants pulled down—looking up at her with all three eyes."

"What happened?" asked Dr. Lester Austin, who was straining to hear.

"His cucumber had left the salad, Les. You know. He was paddling the putter in public."

"So what'd did she do?" wondered Tuck—who also seemed to be little more than a shadow of himself due to the relentless daily workout routine he'd been on since I'd first met him. During that time, impressively, Tuck had dropped forty pounds and ten strokes off his golf handicap. Jon joked that he was eating only about as much of one of Toni's champion canines. He'd also shaved off the Mitch Miller goatee, which made the cigar in his mouth look bigger than he looked.

"Picked up her cell phone and started dialing."

"Was she dialing the pervert?" wondered Jon.

"I was stationed in the army near there during the war," remembered Lester fondly, perhaps missing the drift of the conversation due to his slight hearing impediment, or maybe was simply choosing to ignore the others as he sipped his nonalcoholic beverage. Lester, who looked as fit as Jack Lalanne, also had a small heart condition that sometimes flared up from too much alcohol or bad Sager humor.

"Would that be the Civil War or the Spanish-American War, Lester?" Jon asked sweetly.

"Very funny. Careful, sonny, or I'll hop up on this stool and punch you in the throat."

I asked anyone who cared to answer where Russ King and Tom Cahill were. On the drive to the pub, Jon had explained that good old John Zawadzki had just been relocated to Rochester where he was now the head honcho of all of Fleet Bank's northern New York operations. He still returned faithfully on weekends, though, to bowl with the Dewsweepers because, as Jon put it, "he's ethnically predisposed to bowling."

"Russ is competing in the downhill slalom up at Stowe," Jon now further explained. "I understand that he's the man to beat in the Super Senior metal-walker division. You should see how the great-grandmothers flutter when Russell skis by them. Beneath that dignified mien and all those layers of expensive clothing, the man is a real lady killer."

"Tom's down on the Cape with Nancy," Tuck provided, firing up the log in his chompers. A cloud of dense blue smoke momentarily enveloped his tiny head, making him look like a guy with his head in the clouds. "I think they're trying to forget that they live in Syracuse in the winter."

"Nancy *Who?*" the Dewsweepers all chimed on cue, more or less in unison.

This was a running Dewsweeper gag. Once upon a time the Dewsweepers were having a post-round drink at the club when an attendant approached and informed Tom that he had an urgent telephone call. Nancy was on the phone, the attendant said, needing a word with him.

"Nancy *who?*" Tom wondered innocently, momentarily forgetting the lovely woman he'd been married to for almost forty years.

The Dewsweeepers never let *him* forget it.

I asked Lester how Woody Austin was doing. The last time I'd gone over to see how Lester's lettuce patch was growing, I remembered with a faint wince, Woody bounded joyfully toward me and rammed his long cold snout directly into my groin, doubling me over with pain. As personal injuries went, though, that was nothing compared to what he did to Tom Cahill. He was once so delighted to see Tom arrive, he flattened him and tore cartilage in his knee, sidelining him for six months from rounds with the Dewsweepers.

Lester, Sheila, and Woody shared an attractive though remarkably modest bungalow set on a pretty forested ridge surrounded by the Onondaga Indian Reservation, a few miles south of Syracuse. The rumor around Onondaga was that Lester was so frugal he'd saved half of his physician's six-figure income for many years before retiring. The scuttlebutt was that he could "buy or sell just about anybody," as one admiring and obviously jealous Onondagan said to me.

"Woody's doing okay," Les allowed. "The winter gets him down. I can't let him out or one of the crazy teenagers who roars up and down our road all hours of the night might run over him. They don't even have to have licenses."

"Does Woody?" asked Peter, chuckling into his light beer.

Lester ignored that barb and explained his big news. He'd just given his Subaru to his daughter Wendy in Boston and had recently ordered himself a brand new Chrysler PT Cruiser, which was supposed to be delivered sometime in the spring. He planned to get vanity plates that said *Dewsweeper 2*.

Jon said, "Lester's the guy to ask for a car loan. He'll never admit he's a little short."

"Who's Dewsweeper number one?" This seemed like a reasonable question for me to ask.

"I'm thinking of getting *Dewsweeeper 3* for my Harley," explained Peter, who also missed most of a recent golf season due to a pulled muscle in his neck but turned up on several occasions bearing hot sticky buns from Wegman's to greet his mates at the turn, a measure of how much he missed the guys.

"Whose got the biggest mouth?" Lester replied, glancing over at Jon Boy and back at me again. "Who are you taking to play golf at Pebble Beach?"

"I wish somebody would invite *me* to play in a golf tournament at Pebble Beach," Peter said with a wounded little sniff.

"C'mon guys," I said, explaining that it was just a silly private tournament called the Friends Classic that I'd attended only once or twice at most—a small confab of old chums who convened at Spanish Bay every winter to drink, play golf, and temporarily forestall the terrors and obligations of middle age. It was no big deal, I said, hoping my nose wasn't growing, not even all *that* much fun.

"In that case," Lester said, "why are you going?"

"This year," I explained, "my objective is to play more and work less, hang out more with you guys and McDaid and my neglected golf pals back in Maine. That way, maybe playing golf will *become* fun again."

Somewhat sappily, I heard myself say to them what Arnold Palmer had said to me in the desert. "Besides, life's way too short not to play golf."

"We're your friends, too," Bill Tuck pointed out. "In that case you should take us *all* to Pebble Beach."

"I can only take *one* friend to the Friends Classic," I said. "I'm not even telling McDaid about it, quite frankly. "

"Besides," Jon injected with a smirk, "Wendy is coming out there a few days ahead of me. He probably won't have any strength left for the golf tournament." He sipped his beer and wiggled his eyebrows provocatively. "If you catch my snowdrift."

"It's your very own fault," I pointed out. "You introduced me to her."

"Then we *have* to do a spring road trip," Peter said with feeling. "How about Myrtle Beach? Guys say it's great, wall to wall golf. Decent motels and seafood."

Jon observed seriously, "Lots of exotic dancers for *après* golf, they say. As an old friend of mine down South used to say, you can whet your appetite wherever you want, as long as you always eat at home."

"Are you talking about food?" Lester inquired.

"Never mind. Take a ginkgo biloba."

Just then, someone's cell phone rang. It was good old John Zawadzki calling, trapped by the snow in his new office in Rochester, phoning to say he wouldn't be bowling that weekend due to the weather.

"Forget bowling," Jon told him, "we're talking something even more important—a spring golf trip to the Oasis of Sanity, Myrtle Beach. Sunny skies and all the steak, fried food, beer, golf, gluttony, and grease your body can tolerate."

"Count both me and my hair in," Z-Man enthusiastically told him from snowbound Rochester, or words to that effect.

"That settles it," declared Jon. "The Angry Yoots will play the Hostile Elders in the Battle of Myrtle Beach! Now all we have to do is get decent airline tickets and permission slips from our wives."

"You mean for the golf or the topless bars?" wondered the

ever diminishing Tuck, lurking somewhere beneath his dictator-sized cigar.

"Both," Jon told him. "When it comes to golf trips my wife's policy is the same as Mister Clinton's on gays in the military. Don't ask, don't tell. Karen just has a third rule—don't touch, either, or you soon won't have any feeling in that arm."

And with that, we drank a toast to springtime in Myrtle Beach, my birthday, and the reluctant northern golf season that was still buried somewhere outside underneath four feet of Great Lake snow.

•   •   •

It was dark when we left Mulligans, but the snowfall had stopped. Instead of driving me to Wendy's house so I could dutifully eat my birthday cake, Jon wondered if I might wish to see how nice Onondaga looked under all that snow.

We drove up the hill and turned up the long winding driveway to the club. The great stone building was completely dark but resembled a Currier and Ives print, reminding me that the building and Walter Travis course had been put there at the peak of golf's so-called golden days in the early 1920s, when mighty Syracuse was one of the most lively industrial boom towns in America. Thanks to Jon's famous introduction letter and all the time I'd spent loitering with Dewsweepers and nosing around town lately, I'd become something of a visiting scholar on the city's illustrious history and personality.

The Erie Canal, which split downtown, once made Syracuse the biggest transportation hub between New York City and Chicago and influxes of hungry immigrants made it a self-made man's promised land of opportunity. Agricultural implements that plowed open the great American prairie, newfangled bicycles that carried a nation on the move, wondrous typewriting machines that created the nation's first secretarial boom, and various gears and switching devices that made the first municipal electric street lamps possible were just the start of the flood of civilizing innovations. Washing machines, deluxe motor cars, and air conditioning came next, followed by color television, electronic innovations of all sorts, and the kind of over-the-horizon radar that won a world war—even the little metal device used for taking an accurate measure of the human foot was invented there, something called the Brannock Device. It wouldn't have surprised me one bit to learn the Ping putter was invented there. Just about everything else in America, it seemed, had roots beneath the frozen tundra of America's snowiest city.

As we were parking in Onondaga's empty lot, though, that knowledge only made the afternoon's news summary sound as bleak as the winter wind itself—and perhaps explained Jon's odd comment by the window at his office about feeling like the last guy to leave the place and shut off the lights.

Carrier Corporation, it was being reported, the world leader in air conditioning and a vital cog in the city's life since the worst days of the Great Depression, was announcing its intention to leave town and relocate its TR-1 division to Charlotte, North Carolina—taking the better part of five hundred jobs with it. It was the *fourth* major manufacturing firm to shut its doors and decamp from Syracuse in the past two years.

On the plus side of the municipal ledger, it was reported in the same news broadcast that a sprawling, glitzy shopping mall called Carousel Center and presently located on the northern fringe of downtown planned to double and maybe even *triple* its size sometime in the next few years—with aims of making it larger than the leviathan Mall of America in suburban Minneapolis. The owners of Carousel contended the mall would be a financial windfall to the flagging Syracusan economy—attracting hordes of out-of-town shoppers to the famous old industrial city.

"Great," Jon said, snapping off the radio and sitting there beside me in the darkness for a moment. "They want to create twice as many places to shop so people who've lost their jobs because the good companies have gone elsewhere will have someplace nice to spend money they no longer have. Now *that's* the definition of progress."

He got out and started walking across the empty lot toward the member's entrance of the club. I got out and tagged after him, recalling the poet George Herbert's view that "every step in winter feels like two" as we mushed through the deep clingy snow and into the lighted vestibule of the members' locker room.

Jon paused and glanced around. The lights were on, the air warm and redolent of Clubman talc and Bay Rum aftershave. But nobody seemed to be around, though the club remained open for dinner on weekends during the winter months.

I followed Jon through the locker room and out into the handsome dark-paneled grillroom, where large windows overlooked the first tee where I'd first met the other Dewsweepers that first entertaining summer morning several years ago. Jon walked to the window and stared out. I joined him there, noting how our reflections superimposed over the darkened golf course made us look more like winter-starved accountants than fun-loving golf amigos. Funny how reflections seldom lie.

"You know what's really interesting about those guys?" he asked quietly. *Uncharacteristically* quietly, I thought.

It took me a moment to realize he meant Lester, Tuck, and Russ and the rest of the Dewsweepers near and far and not the greedy empire builders who thought the answer to Syracuse's economic woes lay in a hundred more boring chain stores and an expanded food court.

"They could live anywhere they want. But they want to live here. They choose to live in Zerocuse."

I nodded, intrigued that he'd chosen to use the derogatory nickname of his hometown and vaguely wondering if *I* could ever choose to live there, too. I'd come to fancy the place, to be quite honest—even if it did feel a little like golf season yielded to nuclear winter eight long months of the average year. Maine, I supposed, was only slightly better than that. At least we had the ocean to look at.

That's when it hit me what Jon was doing. He was taking inventory of who he was and where he'd come from. I know that sounds kind of dopey but middle-aged men do far stranger things than that when the cold winds of change begin to blow.

Jon's family burrowed back over 150 years into Syracuse's history, coinciding with the opening of the Erie Canal, when old Jacob Sager and his progeny stumped over the mountains from the Dutch settlements of the New Albany Valley to open dry goods stores and start churches aimed at cultivating the wilds of Onondaga County and a burgeoning, rowdy town, named for a famous Italian lake town called *Syracusa*, that would soon be full of immigrant dreamers, fiery abolishionists, and Free Soil Republicans.

Jon's great grandfather Rev. Theron Cooper, a circuit riding Methodist minister, was one of the first men to graduate from the fledgling institution that eventually became Syracuse University, and ended his days on the board of trustees of the school and preaching every weekend from the same pulpit where Norman Vincent Peale would later preach his gospel of positive thinking.

Another of Jon's forebears was a renowned journalist who worked at the New York City paper that sponsored Admiral Peary's famous expedition to the North Pole—a yellowing framed telegram still hung in Jon's father house, reading simply: *Stars and stripes nailed to the North Pole—A. Peary*—and until recently the large fading logo of the famous Sager Brothers could be seen on the side of an historic brick building on Clinton Street in downtown Syracuse. That firm, operated by Jon's great grandfather and great uncle respectively, employed thousands of local women to knit luxury wool garments in their homes that were then shipped in massive steamer trunks to the finest shops as far away as San Francisco.

Jon's great-grandfather had been one of the earliest members of Onondaga Golf Club, the place where America's golf craze took root on the banks of the Erie Canal just before the end of the nineteenth century; his father, Roderick, was a longtime member, too.

If Willis Carrier's corporation and those other former titans of industry were willing to bail out of a place that worked so hard and meant so much and made them wealthy beyond their wildest dreams, it was easy enough to understand why that deeply bothered a native son like Jonathan Sager, Esq. He was, for better or worse, the ultimate progeny of the New World's Syracusa, listed in half a dozen volumes of *Who's Who in America* and the product of generations of the city's boldest dreams and finer ambitions.

"I've been offered a job," Jon said—suddenly and thoughtfully, basically shooting this grand theory of social evolution straight in the temple.

"No kidding." I was surprised. "What and where?"

"Virginia. A good company."

"You don't sound overjoyed about it."

He shrugged.

"It's an attractive offer. But I don't know. I've got a lot of years in here."

"Is that the only hitch?"

"No. There's the kids. Karen. They're happy here. This is home. My parents are getting on, too. I'd have to uproot everybody. Plus . . ." He paused and smiled at himself in the glass. "I've supposedly got a promotion to vice president in the works. That amounts to the keys to the kingdom around here."

I congratulated him and admitted I could see how that complicated whatever decision he had to make. One veep in the old hometown was worth two great jobs in Virginny, or something along those lines.

I didn't dare say it, given his sudden wintery introspection, but I frankly couldn't picture Jon leaving Syracuse in his dust—or, as it were, snow. I knew he had far more than years invested in his company, and for what it was worth I couldn't picture him getting along without the Dewsweepers, either. He really was the Number One Dewsweeper.

"Whatever life throws at you," I heard myself telling him what my father used to say, "you've still got golf and friends."

"Yeah. They're special guys."

"Is there really a decision to make?"

He thought about it a moment, then turned and smiled the wily Chuck Grodin smile.

"You bet there is. What are you going to hit on the first tee at Pebble Beach? That place scares the hell out of me."

THREE

MRS. CONGENIALITY

I telephoned my mom clear across America to say good morning.

"Hi, babe," she chirped. "You've got good timing. I just came back from the continental breakfast. Hey, are you and the kids still coming for supper tonight? I need to make a reservation."

I reminded her that I was in California, driving up the coast toward Pebble Beach at that moment, purportedly working.

"Oh, that's *right*," she said. "I forgot. In that case, maybe I'll have to have dinner with Stan after all."

"Who's Stan?" I asked.

"I don't know. Some tall good-looking old man who came up to me as I left the dining room last night and said, 'Excuse me, ma'am. I need to tell you something. You're the best-looking babe in the entire place.' Then he asked me to have dinner with him tonight and come to his apartment to have a cocktail and see his fly-rod collection before that. These northern men certainly move fast."

My mother, widowed almost exactly five years, laughed like a girl who'd just been named Miss Congeniality in a beauty pageant, which in fact she been once upon a time, winning a trip to the 1939 World's Fair as Miss Western Maryland.

"I think he used to be a fishing guide or something," she elaborated coyly.

"Tell him you're not old enough to date yet," I said. "Tell him your son needs to speak to his parents first."

She laughed merrily again and said, "Okay, babe. Whatever you say."

It was nice to hear her laughing. My mom was almost eighty and gamely adjusting to a brand-new kind of life my older brother and I had gently but firmly forced upon her. There was no other way to say it than that. For almost forty years, she'd lived happily on a dogwood- and azalea-strewn residential street in Greensboro, North Carolina, the town where I grew up and my older brother still lived. But one Indian Summer evening the previous October, her two best buddies Daphne and Midge pulled me aside and said, in no uncertain terms, as we strolled together down the block during a family gathering, that it was "time" to do something about Mrs. Congeniality's living situation. I got the distinct feeling they'd been waiting politely to gang up on me for weeks.

Midge Hudson, who lived a few doors down and drove my mother anywhere she needed to go in town, expressed her grave concern that Mom had taken several "nasty" falls but either refused to tell her sons about it or, worse, failed to remember.

"Her memory is really slipping away fast," Midge said, shaking her snowy head. "I worry that she'll leave on the stove or an iron and burn down the house with both she and Molly in it." Molly was my father's aging yellow Lab.

Daphne Williams, Mom's oldest living friend and my father's longtime secretary—a woman who knew the inside workings of my family maybe even better than I did—had worries that went even deeper.

"I think you need to check out your mother's finances," she

said, taking my arm as we strolled together in the aromatic fall darkness. "She asked me to balance her checkbook against her statement the other day and I was shocked to discover . . ." she paused as if she dared not say it ". . . a lot of money has vanished from her accounts. And she recently took out a home equity loan. A very *large* one."

I paused and asked her how much we were talking about—wondering, as I did, why on earth my mother would take out a loan of *any* kind. My father had left her debt-free, a healthy monthly income, plus a pretty house that was fully owned and appraised into six figures, on a popular street where similar older houses were being gutted, renovated, and resold for upward of three times as much. This fact had always comforted me because, on his death bed, my father had reminded my brother and me that under the terms of our parents' wills, the property would eventually pass jointly to us both—but *only* if we didn't need it as an asset to take care of our mother and any of her medical or living needs after his death. My brother and I both promised to do whatever it took to make her comfortable and happy till the end of her days.

"About what the house is worth," Daphne said, grimacing.

I was startled, to say the least. My mother had no debts that I knew of and even fewer material wants, which was good because, as all Mom's closest chums knew, she had no capacity whatsoever for managing her own financial affairs. She was generous to a fault and would happily give anyone anything they asked for, as she painfully illustrated once by "loaning" a complete stranger with a sob story ten grand from her life's savings while standing in the checkout line at the Big Star grocery store. The woman, according to the police, turned out to be a flimflam artist and was never seen again. Neither was my mother's money.

"What on *earth* did she use that money for?" I asked Daphne and Midge, still a little dazed by this unexpected development on the home front. I couldn't imagine what she would have spent that kind of money on—or why she would have needed it in the first place.

"I don't know," Daphne admitted. "But her savings are way down, too, and I think you'd better do something *fast*. Your father wouldn't be happy about this at all."

I promised her I would investigate this troubling news but urged her not to worry because I had joint power-of-attorney over Mom's estate and nothing all that serious could happen without me knowing about it.

"I hope you're right."

With that, we strolled back to the house where, ironically, a lively wedding rehearsal party was going on in the backyard. My older brother was getting remarried. The wedding had been set for the previous spring then postponed, according to my brother, because of the groom's shaky financial situation. Since our father's death, my brother had worked several different jobs, never quite finding his proper niche, though it seemed to me just a matter of time until he settled down and found whatever he was meant to do in life.

He was a good guy, jovial and funny, the life of any party, and we'd always been unusually close. If I had concerns about what I'd just learned from Daphne regarding Mom's finances, I also had a great deal of faith in my brother—the son who'd stayed behind in the old hometown and was supposedly keeping close tabs on the day-to-day life of the family matriarch. I had every reason to believe he would do a good job at this because we were both Eagle Scouts who grew up sharing the same philosophical diet of Aesop's fables and Greek myths, tales of medieval valor and transcendental poetry fed to us by Opti the Mystic. We'd traveled abroad in each other's company and sailed ships across darkened oceans together, and to say I trusted him with my life would not be overstating the fact.

Our mother, not surprisingly, hadn't been overjoyed at the reason for his wedding's delay, nor the fact that the bride had been married several times before, but Mom was a Southern lady through and through and it was *his* life and a new beginning and all of us were choosing to look upon the bright side of the situation.

Change was in the winds, as the blind poet of the Aegean might have said, and for two years my brother and I had been discussing how, when the moment was right, we would convince Mom to move to a lovely assisted-care facility in Maine called the Highlands where I and her Yankee grandchildren could take over keeping a close eye on her doings and my brother and his new wife could get along with a new life of their own. In accordance with our father's will, we'd agreed that either my brother and I would purchase the house outright from Mom and reinvest the money for her to live off, or my brother and his bride would pay her a nominal rent for the house and she would retain ownership until the asset was needed and could be cashed out. Either way, Mom's financial situation would theoretically be protected, ready for whatever rainy day came along.

And so, despite friendly warnings, I chose to think Daphne had probably simply *misread* my mom's bank statements and happily stood up as best man for my brother, believing everything would be just fine in the end. Six weeks later, following the game plan we'd all agreed upon, I flew to the Old North State and loaded up Mrs. Congeniality's most treasured belongings in a truck, placed old Molly onto the big bench seat, and drove straight up the interstate to the Highlands in Maine. Within twenty-four hours, I had Mom's brand-new apartment at the award-winning senior community waiting for her arrival—she was flying up, of course—her favorite paintings hung, her beloved Persian rug down, her familiar furnishings placed, and various family photos and her beloved porcelain birds ready to greet her.

She cried when she saw the place—although, in retrospect, maybe that was because she already missed Greensboro more than either of us thought she might. In any case, she kissed me and said it felt "almost like home" and wondered if we might go out to eat seafood at Cook's that night with my children.

· · ·

"Oh, sweetie. One more thing . . ." she said almost casually as we prepared to say good-bye across the vast American Republic. "I got the oddest phone call from Merle Corry this morning. She said she'd heard I'd given my house to *you know who.* I told her, 'Dumbhead. Why would I do *that?*'"

Merle lived two doors down from Mom. They were still swapping neighborhood gossip almost daily on the phone. I asked my mother who she meant and what she was talking about.

"I don't know, babe. Merle seems to think I gave my house to Miss Clairol."

Miss Clairol was what my mom sometimes called my brother's new wife. She found the woman's ever-shifting hairdos, I suppose, kind of amusing.

"You didn't do that, did you?" I asked her gently, thinking as I said this how that scenario was basically impossible due to the power-of-attorney clause and my father's will.

"Didn't do what, sugar?" My mom's memory was going faster than any of us realized.

It was pretty obvious that Daphne and Midge had been right and I hadn't gotten her safely to Maine a minute too soon.

"Given your house to . . ." I hesitated. I knew the woman only vaguely. "Miss Clairol."

Mom laughed as if that was the craziest thing she'd ever heard.

"Of course *not,*" she declared. "Besides, I may want to move back there in a few months."

This remark reassured me because, in fact, that was part of the deal I made her in negotiating her relocation to Maine. If she came north and hated the Highlands and couldn't stand the weather or whatever, I agreed to move her home and either *hire* someone to live with her on Dogwood Drive or else find a nice assisted-care place in Greensboro.

"Okay," I said. "Just checking."

"Relax, babe," she said. "So where are you going?"

I explained that I was on my way to San Francisco airport to pick up Wendy, who was flying in for a couple days of golf at Pebble Beach before my friend Jon Sager met me there for a golf tournament.

"You're not playing in the *Crosby?*" she said with excitement. My mom was a big-time golf fan and loved to watch the PGA Tour on television. She had an almost indecent crush on Ernie Els, for some peculiar reason.

"No, ma'am. That's *next* week. This is just a thing called the Friends Classic. Bunch of guys who get together every year to talk about their wives and tell dirty jokes. My buddy Jon always has lots of good jokes."

"*Wonderful!*" declared Mrs. Congeniality. "That place is magical. Did I ever tell you about the time your father took me to Pebble Beach to play golf? We actually saw Bob Hope at the Lodge, and Doug Sanders, too—wearing normal clothes! It was very romantic—but also kind of painful . . ."

"I'm not sure I need to hear that part," I informed her, merging into the City by the Bay's main airport exit. "I hope it didn't involve small animals or leather constraints in the Bing Crosby suite . . ."

"Of course *not*, silly," she said chastely. "Don't be vulgar. I'm talking about on the golf course! I missed the ball four times and topped it probably six times—and that was just on the first hole! Your father kept telling me, 'Pick up, Jan, pick up, *for heavens sake!*' But I wouldn't do it. I said I intended to play every shot and, by golly, I did, too! I think I drove him crazy but he later bought me flowers and we went down to look at all of those lovely galleries in Carmel and then went to some really nice place to eat and even went dancing. Your father could be so . . . romantic."

"I remember," I said, "but he never could reach a par five in two."

"Maybe not," she said, somewhat wistfully, "but I really miss him."

I said I knew she did. I admitted I did, too.

"Please say hi to Wendy for me," she said brightly. "She's such a lovely girl. I really wish you two. . . ."

The cell phone began to break up, muted by the sizzle of three thousand miles of electronic snow.

"Mom," I said. "Are you *there?*"

A second or two later, Mrs. Congeniality was gone.

I knew exactly what my mom was trying to say. She was attempting to say that she thought Wendy and I ought to get married, which is what she more or less slipped into any conversation in which anyone mentioned Wendy Buynak.

Mom really liked Wendy, but then so did everybody who knew her. Wendy was smart, funny, honest as a Syracuse summer day is long, a devoted divorced mother of two energetic small boys, an actress turned cake baker who never seemed to stop smiling even when life threw the cake in her pretty face.

Meeting Wendy, I sometimes thought, was the best thing to happen to me since I rode my tricycle around the block and discovered there was a whole other street on Planet Earth and, delighted beyond words, kept peddling. Recently Mom had told my kids Maggie and Jack how their dad once ran away on his new tricycle and came home six hours later with an ice cream and a police escort—my very own version of Baby's Day Out, which might explain why I was still on the road peddling like mad forty years later.

Among other things, I now had Wendy in my life and Jon Sager to thank for making the introduction—though it nearly hadn't come off at all. Perhaps I should explain.

A week or so before my second official (non-speechmaking) sortie to Dewsweeperland, Jon faxed me a piece of paper listing six eligible single women in the greater Syracuse metropolitan area he thought I might like to meet—a sort of Michelin Guide to the Onondagan divorced mother set, a sorority of handpicked

Sager-approved potential dinner companions that included neat categorical summaries such as "General Appearance," "Interest in Golf Quotient," "Taste in Books," and "Ready-to-Date Index," plus starred ratings and Jon's own amusing personal side commentaries. ("Ta-tas till Tuesday. Junoesque physique. My personal fantasy pick.")

I don't know why I played along with such middle-aged nonsense. I phoned Counselor Sager and told him blind dates weren't my thing and reminded him that Mona Crump had found me about as appealing as Kenneth Starr in a thong.

"I know," he said. "But that was just a first effort—like the first time I played golf with the Dewsweepers ten or twelve years ago. Russ King was a venerated captain of industry and scared the hell out of me. I was afraid he'd tell my parents if he heard any profanity or jokes of any kind. Frankly, it took a couple of rounds for me to even to begin to feel at ease."

The moral of this little golf parable, apparently, was *So shut up, Lumpy, and send in the sheet.*

Maybe I was in the mood to meet somebody new or at least see what kind of real women Syracuse had to offer besides best-selling authors.

For whatever reason, I checked a couple of the candidates and faxed him back the sheet, particularly intrigued by the description of one *Wendy Buynak, divorced, 35ish, "E" for appearance but all other factors "UNK." Very cute and sweet neighbor who may not yet be back in the saddle, socially speaking. Couple of young kids. Mom and Dad moved into former marital residence with her. 5'5", petite, brunette.*

I frankly hadn't expected him to line up *two* blind dates in a row, though.

The first one was with a pretty woman named Melody. That's not her real name, of course, because the innocent must always be protected—in this instance, me. The date went beautifully, at least for the first three or four minutes.

Melody settled down next to me in the plush backseat of the

Sager Acura, turned to me, and said, "I understand you're a big fan of golf."

"My favorite four-letter word," I assured her.

"I hate golf," she declared. "Everybody in my family plays that moronic game. It's the invention of elitist, Eurocentric, angry white males who are bent on repressing women and minorities. It's something only fascist Republicans and redneck Democrats do. So which are *you*?"

Jonathan Sager chortled. Melody glared at his monk's patch and Karen Sager slipped me the faintest smile of sympathy from the front seat. A moment later, a distinct muted thump was discerned where, I believe, Mrs. Sager gave the Professor of Love a swift boot in the shin.

That next morning at Onondaga, playing along the front nine with Les, Tuck, and Jon, I demanded that Jon give me that evening's designated victim's telephone number so I could phone her at the halfway point and relieve her anxiety about having to come to the Sager house for dinner with some fascist golf-loving chump she'd never met.

"Are you kidding?" Jon said with alarm. "Karen worked on Wendy for two solid weeks to come to dinner. She only said yes last night. Don't take it personally, pal, but we may have to begin *paying* women to go out with you."

"There's a name for that sort of thing," Tuck said, most unhelpfully.

And Lester said, "Wendy sounds great. My daughter is named Wendy, you know. Hey, if you don't want to go out with her, maybe I will."

"You're *far* too short," Jon told him sharply. "Besides, you've already had your wonder years. Sheila probably wouldn't like it a bit if you started dating again."

Six hours later, I was sitting in a comfortable leather wing chair chatting mindlessly with one of the other Sager dinner party guests when Billy Sager, age ten, the precocious swimmer, appeared and grinned slyly at me over his braces.

"Your *date* is here Mis-ter Dod-son. Maybe you'll like *this* one," he singsonged and then wiggled his ruthless preteen eyebrows provocatively in a manner that seemed to suggest a stark naked lady had just arrived on the front porch bearing a nice tuna casserole dish. With that, he smiled and made an infamous curvy gesture known to teenage boys across the ages, proving the apple really doesn't fall far from the tree.

There are moments in life you never forget—the first time, for example, you reach your first par five in two and watch everyone on the green scatter wildly with their hands shielding their heads and moments later raise their collective fists in a way that could, one supposes, be considered a kind of salute to your golfing prowess.

Well, this was even better than that.

To begin with, Wendy Buynak was sensational looking—either Northern Italian or Southern Irish, I couldn't decide which. She smelled deliciously of Chanel and the fabulous hazelnut shortbread cookies dipped in bittersweet chocolate she'd thoughtfully contributed to the evening meal.

Women always say men don't notice things. Well, I'm here to tell you, fair citizens of Venus, I even remember exactly what Dame Wendy was wearing that first enchanted evening: a pair of veddy British-looking hound's-tooth tweed slacks and a sleek beautiful black velvet blouse that proved Billy Sager's rough estimations had been remarkably on target.

We shook hands—beautiful skin, creamy as Shropshire butter— and sat down at the end of the table and looked up again a couple of hours later. I'm told there had been a rather lively dinner table discussion about a host of important and timely subjects, ranging from the new Middle East peace talks to how to hit a proper full-explosion sand shot, but frankly, I was far too busy and interested in Wendy Anne Buynak to pay much attention to anything else.

It's amazing what you can learn in an hour of perfect Rotella-like concentration. Wendy was a spirited baker of work-of-art wedding cakes, a mother of small rambunctious boys, with a fondness for Tootsie Rolls and Italian Renaissance art, a former stage actress who knew Manhattan like the back of her hand and adored the Met, the New York Giants, Miles Davis, and white lilacs.

Far too soon, I walked her home. It was only a block. Standing close together on her front porch, with all the Dawley Farm neighborhood watch committee and probably her father, Bill, observing from the bathroom window upstairs, she permitted me to kiss her. That's when I told her there was something critically important I needed to ask her.

Wendy smiled and looked at me, the very picture of Soccer Mom innocence.

"Do you, by any chance, play . . . golf?"

"You know," she confided with a little laugh, "my old boss at the bank where I worked a few years ago was a total golf nut. He got me to join an after-work league that played at this little par three course on the west side of town. I thought it would be a hoot, you know—just something to do with the girls." She blushed adorably. "Holy *crow!* I had no idea golf was so much fun! I think I could really get hooked."

Did I hear angels singing?

A week later, I must confess, I beat a path straight back to Syracuse and we struck out on our first formal date, not to a golf course as you might expect but upon a leisurely afternoon drive down through the Finger Lakes wine region to Ithaca, where she was thoughtful enough to point out various historical interests along the way and I was careful to note that Ithaca was where Robert Trent Jones had learned his craft and had built a swell golf course at Cornell, his alma mater.

That night, unforgettably, we skipped our dinner reservations at the fancy restaurant in Ithaca and ate instead at a lakeside roadhouse called the Glenwood Pines, played shuffleboard pool and drank longneck beers, talked of parenthood and perennial flowers, politics and religion—all the stuff dating experts, in other words, warn you to avoid on a true first date, which may explain why they are still dating and everyone else is getting married. We wound up parked by the lake in Ithaca, necking in the moonlight like teenagers.

Anyway, at some point during the greatest date of my life, somewhere between the formal wine tasting and the informal making out, I innocently wondered if Wendy might be interested in going to hit golf balls sometime. "I don't mean *tonight* or anything," I was careful to add, in case she got the wrong impression of my intentions.

"Okay. How about tomorrow?" she replied simply and smiled.

The next afternoon, we drove to a domed golf center in the northern suburbs of *Syracusa* and I watched her take two warm-up swings that were far more technically accomplished than anything I expected to see. She topped a ball and asked if I saw anything wrong with her swing.

Not much, I had to admit, then fiddled with her grip a bit, rendering it more neutral and the V's on top of the shaft. I suggested she turn more with her shoulders, less with her hips. Maybe plant her feet a bit wider for better stability.

With no more than that, she swung and drilled a ball to the rear of the indoor golf dome. The hairy ape ripping low duck hooks off the rubber mats in the stall beside us paused and glanced over at Wendy with naked envy and manly contempt.

For a rank beginner, she had an incredible golf swing and, or so it seemed to me, *unlimited* potential. Not to put too fine a point on it, I was not only deeply impressed but maybe even deeply in *love* with this suburban cake-making Wonder Woman.

It would be ridiculous, I suppose, to posit that I fell madly in love with Wendy Anne Buynak then and there—at some stupid indoor golf center, where hairy apes in Syracuse University sweats were ripping chunks out of the driving mats, based on only two days together and one fluent swing of her golf driver.

Why, even she would probably tell you it took at least an *entire* bucket of range balls in order for that to occur.

·   ·   ·

You can therefore understand, perhaps, why I felt a tiny spasm of guilt for throwing sweet Wendy Buynak to the wolves of Fate otherwise known as Pebble Beach Golf Links.

Signing in for our noon tee time that sunny but brisk February morning a couple days before Jon and I were supposed to tee off in the Friends Classic, I neglected to inform the management that Wendy had never played an *entire* eighteen holes in her life.

I didn't think that was such a big deal, frankly. She'd had a personal golf lesson from Jackie Pung, the first lady of Hawaiian golf, and she'd enthusiastically played parts of several golf courses with me around Syracuse and on business trips out west, always operating on the rule that if golf became *too* frustrating to bear, she would just pick up her ball.

Even for a highly skilled player, the first tee at Pebble Beach can be a deeply unsettling experience. Regardless of the time of day, there's always a crowd of people milling about and standing to watch you tee off, a gallery of onlookers that may include famous guests of the Lodge, Japanese tourists armed with video cameras, baffled auto travelers, celebrity stalkers, blood relatives you haven't seen in many years, fragile women hoping to catch a glimpse of Kevin Costner, and other golfers waiting to play and secretly hoping you'll top up your opening shot so they won't look quite so ridiculous when it's their turn to play.

We were paired with a nice couple named Donnie and Marie ("That's us—just like the TV show!") Kluttzenhooper from Fort Pierce, Florida, and a man named Roger from Bayonne, New Jersey, whose wife, Irma, gave him a trip to Pebble Beach for his fortieth birthday. Irma was dutifully snapping photographs of Roger with her new digital camera. The Kluttzenhoopers were wealthy retirees, dressed as if they planned to go straight from the links to a cocktail party on the poop deck of a Carnival Cruise ship with Kathie Lee. Only Marie was playing golf, though; Donnie was driving their cart and handling the videotaping chores. He casually mentioned that he'd had a couple coronaries and "didn't want to push my luck."

"Is this place always this crowded?" Wendy wondered quietly as we waited for Roger to tee off.

I looked at her and smiled, fearing she might have gotten a case of the Pebble Beach jitters. Who could possibly blame her? I'd played the course maybe ten times and I had them, too.

"Relax, babe," I said, sounding just like my mom. "You'll do fine. Nice and slow, let it go."

Several Japanese tourists and Irma had their lenses fixed firmly on Roger, who'd been hovering over his ball for a preternaturally long amount of time. Finally, he slowly drew back his club and swung wildly, sending a crazy slice veering toward the hotel balconies on the immediate right, reminding me of actor Jack Lemmon's famous toe-shot that penetrated one of the Lodge's finer bedrooms—his own, as it turned out. Roger, blushing, reteed and pelted a provisional tee shot into the right-side rough.

With one quick unthinking poke, I placed my Titleist safely in the short grass, 230 yards from the tee. The sense of personal relief that flooded me was immense.

Up at the ladies tee, Marie Kluttzenhooper had an endearing preshot routine. Jingling musically from numerous gold wrist bracelets, she pegged up her ball, crouched directly behind it, and squared the face of her driver with the target. Then, ever so slowly, still holding the shaft in her right hand, she rose stealthily and sort of *crept* around the east side of her ball and carefully placed her feet in position. At that point, weirdly, she appeared to go into some kind of yogic trance that lasted close to a full minute, breathing deeply, opening and closing her eyes, squeezing her club.

Turning her head, she scrutinized the distant target as if she were zeroing in on the "fine jewelry segment" on QVC, wound up, and swung. For all of this dramatic build-up, her actual golf shot was a disappointing little punch that sent her ball looping ninety yards out into the fairway. Not bad. It just took forever to happen.

Wendy, clearly a Dewsweeper at heart, teed up her ball with minimal fanfare, took a nice smooth warm-up swing, then swung and . . . topped her ball—trickling it only a few yards off the tee.

"Why don't you try another one," I said.

Wendy's caddie, Bob something, who appeared to have come straight from an all-night bachelor party judging by the roadmaps in his eyes, moved to fetch her ball but she waved him off and marched after the ball as if to say she meant business this time. She took a more careful bead before swinging again, producing another miserable top, and advanced her ball only four more feet.

In the normal golfer, shock and a plunging feeling of disbelief usually sets in about this point in time, quickly followed by a wave of personal mortification and a giddy desire to sprint into the crowd never to be seen again.

With all those eyes and cameras trained on her, the last thing I wanted Wendy to think was that a bunch of people she didn't even know would soon be sitting around their video monitors in Kobe and Sioux City laughing their backsides off at a rank beginner's first encounter with mighty Pebble Beach.

In short, the last thing I really wanted her to do was try and hit that ball again.

"Hey, Wen, here's an idea," I said cheerfully, remembering my mom's big adventure at Pebble. "Just pick up and start at the edge of the green."

"No *way*," she muttered. Meaning, *Stuff it, Lumpy.*

What a fierce and wondrous thing it is to watch a golf nut be born to the game, perhaps the closest any of us will ever come to hearing the yawp of the expanding universe or witnessing the birth explosion of a celestial star. Just think of it! Here stands an ever-upbeat middle-aged mother of two, wily veteran of school bake sales and weekend memory book seminars, church volunteer, and registered Democrat, Martha Stewart subscriber and dedicated dawn neighborhood walker, bearing down upon a dimpled polyurethane-covered ball with the focused intensity of a Balanchine dancer on opening night, utterly oblivious to the opinion of the world, determined to shake the cosmos to its very roots!

Wendy swung again and *pulverized* the ball, sending it soaring through the air. Her caddie's bloodshot eyes widened as if he'd just been awakened by an air horn. Someone in the gallery actually applauded. Wendy wheeled and blushed triumphantly at me. The game was on and we were off!

On the seventh tee, the famous par three hole, standing on the windy headland above a magnificently churning sea, Wendy came up to me as I prepared to hit a 9-iron directly into the stiffening breeze. She waved the scorecard and smiled.

"Are you aware that you are three under par?"

"Really? I guess I hadn't noticed. I've been watching you."

"Liar," she replied and poked me in the ribs.

I really *had* been watching her, I protested, thinking how marvelous her uncomplicated approach to the game was and worthy of emulation but, okay, I was aware that I had a respectable score going.

"You call three under par just *respectable?*"

"Okay. Very respectable. I'm trying not to notice. It's probably because I'm simply enjoying you so much and not worrying too much about my own game. I call it being in the blessed state of *stupid happy*."

I told her that was very close to being in what Laird Small called "NATO"—as in *Not Attached To Outcome*. Laird was director of Pebble Beach's renowned teaching academy, tutor to PGA Tour star Kirk Triplet and a host of fine players, and a close friend of many years. If I recalled correctly, Laird had proposed to his wife, Honor, on the magestic third tee at neighboring Spyglass Hill, and later sealed their deal by actually getting hitched there as well. Now Honor and Laird had a pair of small wiggling sons and probably rarely if ever managed to get out to the golf course together. But they seemed almost *stupid happy* in their busy married lives and that's exactly how Wendy made me feel. With her as a companion, I wasn't particularly attached to any outcome or challenge life could throw us and watching her hit the ball, march after it, and hit it again, I admitted, gave me a peaceful and *very* stupid happy feeling.

She laughed. "Stupid happy, huh? I like that. I really love this game, too," she said simply, pushing a strand of auburn hair out of her eyes, sounding as if she really meant it.

"I love you," I heard myself say, dopey as that sounds, really meaning it, too.

A crazily appealing thought suddenly came to me—to take Wendy's hand then and there, drop to a suitor's earnestly bended knee à la Laird Small, and gently beseech this fabulous golfing woman to marry me. Mrs. Congeniality would certainly have approved of an impromptu marriage proposal on a bluff at Pebble Beach and the breathtaking seventh hole was the perfect place to do it. Who cared if I hadn't had the foresight to even bring along a diamond engagement ring to seal the deal in the unlikely event she agreed to honor and cherish and tee it up together whenever life and our own children's busy lives permitted us to.

For a moment, I stared at Wendy's pretty face and she stared pleasantly and a bit expectantly at me, no doubt wondering what accounted for my idiotic grin. That's when I happened to glance over to find Donnie Kluttzenhooper filming us for his personal video travelogue of the Monterey coast.

"Hey, love birds!" he barked out. "Let's see somebody hit."

The moment to make my move, alas, abruptly passed. With a shrug of annoyance that was perhaps visible on camera, I dropped a ball and hit it into the front left bunker.

"Too bad," Donnie called out. "Not your best shot."

On the positive side of the ledger, though, Wendy put her

shot nimbly on the green and nearly made her first birdie ever. Somehow I scraped a shot close out of the bunker and made the putt, despite a sudden sense of *something* besides Donnie Kluttzen-hooper rudely intruding on my rarified state of happiness. For what it's worth, I even managed to par the great headland hole Jack Nicklaus claims is the greatest four-par on earth, Pebble's vaunted eighth hole.

Just as I prepared to tee off at nine, though, Marie Kluttzen-hooper waddled across my line of sight, headed from her cart to the ladies tee, oblivious to the fact that it was my turn to play. Even worse, Donnie stopped their cart directly in front of the men's tee, his video camera plugged to his eye. Wendy looked horrified. Even Roger looked at me and shrugged sheepishly.

We waited for Marie to do her peculiar pre-shot routine, which now seemed about as endearing as a William Shatner TV commercial. I motioned for Wendy to hit next, which she re-luctantly did, and then suggested to Roger that he play while I gathered my wits back. Something I couldn't quite name was suddenly chewing at me and for some reason Marie's small breech of etiquette completely unbuttoned me—or so I thought at that particular moment. The ease and comfort I felt swinging my golf club up till then abruptly vanished, too, replaced by a palpable tension that must have been visible to others.

Something told me I was going to hit my teeshot over the cliff on the right into the ocean. And, of course, I did just that.

I teed up a second ball and, shades of my disgrace at Kings Crown, did the identical thing.

I teed up a *third* ball and hit it as hard as I humanly could. This ball missed going over the edge by about ten inches. I finished the hole with a nice fat *nine*. That's a quintuple bogey if you care to count that high. I sure as hell didn't. Whatever *stupid happiness* I'd achieved was now gone. I was just plain *stupid*.

I triple-bogied ten, double-bogied eleven and, walking off in a silent sulk, realized that Wendy was studying me the same way she looks at her four-year-old son, Liam, after he's thrown up cookies on himself.

"You okay?" she finally asked.

I nodded and grunted yes, grumbling something about murdering a perfectly decent score and wondering why I suddenly felt so . . . worried and angry. In the space of three holes, I'd gone from three *under* to seven *over* par—from a man at peace with the world and joyfully swept up by the romantic possibilities of love on the links to just another stalking, pissed-off, facist Republican or redneck Democrat who couldn't find a par with one brain and both hands. I might have attempted to explain all of this to Wendy, but she clearly saw it for herself.

"Hey, tell me something," she said almost jauntily, falling in stride beside me and looking at me with sympathy and a certain amusement. "I thought you were the guy who was going to play the game for fun this year? Not attached to outcome or anything else."

"Yeah, well, I *was*," I sulked. "That was the big theory, at any rate," I admitted as we trekked up the twelfth fairway. "Guess I've got some work to do yet, huh?"

She shrugged, glanced at the sea, and smiled. "This sure is gorgeous, don't you think?" She walked a little farther, still looking at the water, and added, "I have an idea. Let's quit keeping score and play like the Dewsweepers."

"Let me think about it," I said idiotically, remembering as I did that Laird Small had once suggested the exact same thing after a few disappointing holes at Spyglass; we'd ditched the scorecard and played for the pleasure of each other's company and had one of the most enjoyable afternoons of my life. This seemed to be a lesson I was destined to have to repeat over and over until the message finally sunk in, though clearly something else was percolating up through my consciousness and ruining an otherwise perfect day.

So I thought about it for the next five holes and slowly, torturously, all but oblivious to the charms of the most spectacular

120 acres of public golf on earth, began to figure out that what was really bothering and unbuttoning me had nothing to do whatsoever with the Kluttzenhoopers or even my poor swings at nine.

Finally, at seventeen, the famous par three where you fire your ball directly at Japan, I emerged out of my personal Monterey fog long enough to realize Wendy was still happily attacking the game for all she was worth, having fun the way I way I damn well *ought* to be in such a magical spot, oblivious to her score or the way she appeared to others as she continued topping balls and occasionally making solid contact with that fine evolving swing of hers.

As I watched, she hit a tee shot with her five wood that floated up through the sea air and landed softly on the putting surface. She joyfully pumped the air with her gloved fist, Tiger-style, excited as a kid, and wheeled around to find me unable to stop myself from smiling at her antics again.

"You're right," I said. "I'm sorry about my mood. I guess I'm kind of worried about something." I kissed her on the cheek and added, "Lovely shot. You're something else."

She didn't ask what I was worrying about and I didn't volunteer the information until we were halfway down the eighteenth fairway, walking side by side and holding hands in the frisky February seawind. The Kluttzenhoopers and Roger had gone on ahead in their riding carts, hurrying to finish before darkness.

That's when I told her about the odd conversation with my mother and explained that I had an unsettling feeling that something funny might be going on back in Greensboro. That worry had killed *stupid happy* and replaced it with *foreboding concern* and I admitted being embarrassed that I'd allowed something that may or may not even be a problem to spoil a good walk with her.

"Whatever it is, we'll handle it," she said calmly, squeezing my hand and slipping closer for a little human warmth, pushing another strand of hair adorably beneath her golf cap. Her cute button nose had turned very pink with cold. "The walk can't be spoiled if we don't let it."

She was right, of course. Wendy was Mrs. Congeniality's kind of gal and Laird Small's kind of golfer and it was only fitting that we were headed directly from golf to Laird and Honor's place in Pacific Grove for a visit.

Whatever else was true, as I look back on it, I think that moment, walking quietly together up the eighteenth hole in the cold seawind and gathering darkness, was when I really knew for sure that someday and somewhere down the fairway, I would absolutely find the perfect moment to ask this amazing upbeat woman to marry me and become my golf partner for life. With a little luck and a nice diamond ring in hand, she might even say yes. So, in the end, the walk hadn't been spoiled.

Maybe I was learning to play this game the right way, after all.

FOUR

THE GOOD FIGHT

"You have to wonder sometimes why we play this silly game," Bill Kimpton said with a philosophical smile, settling behind his bowl of navy bean soup.

We were having a quick late lunch after a round of golf in the nearly empty members' dining room at San Francisco Golf Club, beneath a photograph of Ben Hogan, several hours after I put Wendy on an early morning flight to see her sister Karen in Seattle and a couple hours before Jon Sager arrived on a flight from Orlando for the Friends Classic.

"I think I played today just for the soup and your company," I said, tasting mine, thinking how neither one of us had exactly brought the fine old Tillinghast course outside to heel. "Who knows? Maybe I'll become a good golfing Buddhist like you."

Kimp smiled. He and I had been friends only three years but it felt like we'd known each other for at least a couple previous lifetimes. Destiny and a clever chap named Tom Rohr had brought us together as teammates at Rohr's annual golf tournament and autumn shindig called the King's Cup on Hawaii's Big Island. The tournament's pairings were determined by a "blind draw," but I knew for a fact that Rohr had personally teamed his old pal Kimp with me because he knew we would have a grand time together regardless of the quality of our games—a strategy that proved as accurate as it was enlightening. We'd played our way straight out of contention by the end of the first day—but become fast friends in the process.

Kimp, as I affectionately called him, was sixty-four and father of several grown-up and accomplished children and, in my experience, that rarest of critters—a hugely successful businessman who'd found the deeper meaning of life in the realm of the spirit and—as a result of this growth, according to Bill—the love of his life almost simultaneously. Kimp was chairman and CEO of a group of small luxury "boutique" hotels that bore his imprimatur but lived a life of increasing simplicity with his Swedish girlfriend Isabel on a small houseboat in Sausalito. While Kimp and I had foozled our way around the Waikaloa Kings Course talking about Eastern philosophy and Western business, Wendy and Isabel had wandered around a tropical rain forest and forged a natural alliance on their own.

"I've been trying to teach the game to Isabel a little bit," Kimp confided with obvious pleasure. "She gets *so* excited when she hits a good shot, and so dramatically angry when she misses. I must confess I really love that quality in her. She wants to take life in her hands and eat it raw. She's teaching me to swear in Swedish."

"Funny you'd say that," I said, and then told him about Wendy's big adventure at Pebble Beach and her similar dogged newborn passion for the game. No wonder she and Isabel were such natural saddle pals. They both wanted to take golf and eat it with their hands.

"You and Wendy will have to come to our place in the desert," Kimp said. "It's not far from Arnold's house at the Tradition." He paused and smiled in that way that made him look like a skinny Buddha. "Keep it under your golf cap but Isabel and I are talking about getting married."

I smiled and congratulated him, then observed that golf pals must think alike because I was seriously considering asking Wendy to marry me, as well. If she said no, I might have to ask Isabel to teach me to swear in Swedish, too.

"She'll say yes," Kimp assured me, sounding remarkably like my own father. "She loves golf because she loves you. She knows what it means to you and probably loves sharing it with you."

"You're kind to say so. We have some complications to work through first—a former husband who appears determined to keep her in Syracuse."

"Time and patience, lad," he said. "People reveal themselves for what they are. Just give it time and be patient."

Fresh glasses of iced tea arrived, along with slices of apple pie. I thanked Kimp for his sagely insights and excused myself to answer the call of nature. As I was returning through the men's locker room to my pie, I paused and stepped into the phone booth thinking now was an opportune moment to try and *uncomplicate* my life a bit.

I dialed my brother's phone number in North Carolina and heard it ring. A few yards away, an elderly man still dripping from the shower was laboring to put on his underpants and simultaneously watch TV where reporters were talking excitedly about Miami Cubans protesting the Clinton administration's efforts to send little Elian Gonzalez to his grandmothers and father back in Cuba.

My brother answered. He sounded like his old self and we chatted pleasantly for several minutes and then I casually asked him if anything unusual was going on with Mom's house.

"No," he said, and then paused. "Well, I guess I should tell you if Mom hasn't." Another longer pause. "She sold us the house."

I said I wasn't sure I heard him correctly. He cleared his throat.

"I said, Mom sold us the house."

I was, to say the least, dumbfounded. I sat down on the edge of a wooden chair in the booth, opened the door, and leaned out a bit for some useful oxygen.

"How much did she sell it to you for?"

It was the same number Daphne had told me.

"Really?" Now I paused, wondering what the hell to ask my brother next. I felt winded, blindsided, astonished.

"When was this?" I managed.

"I don't know," he said uneasily. "Back in November or December."

"Let me see if I've got this straight. We've been talking for months about how we were going to handle Mom's estate and take care of her living and medical needs and now you say she up and *sold* you the house out of the blue. And you didn't think I had a right to be told this?"

Complete silence in North Carolina.

"If nothing else," I pointed out with a firm but even voice, "under the terms of her own will that couldn't have taken place without me learning about it."

"She changed her will, Jim. Mother did it herself. She wanted us to have the house." Another uneasy pause on his end. "She was supposed to tell you about it."

"Wow." I rubbed my face. Maybe thirty seconds of silence trickled past before either of us said a thing.

"Okay. We'll forget the fact that you or she or both of you cut me out of the will. We'll concentrate instead on Mother's assets— the money she will undoubtedly need down the road. Where, if I may ask, is the money?" I reminded him of the vow he and I had both made while seated by our dying father—that the house or its proceeds were supposed to take care of our mother and whatever she needed.

This question was followed by another lengthy uncomfortable silence on his end of the line. Finally, as if exasperated by my nosy inquiry, he sighed and replied, "Look, Jim. It was all on . . . paper."

"On paper?" I was even more confused now. "What does *that* mean?" I said, speaking loudly enough to cause the old fella to glance over at me in the open booth. He now had his underpants safely on and was slowly wiggling up his stockings. The Cuban protesters were now visibly agitated, too, promising to make Janet Reno's life a living nightmare.

"Are you saying," I said carefully, "that she *gave* you her house?"

"Look," he said again, "it's all legal. It was all on paper. Mom wanted us to have the house."

"But where is the money?"

"It was . . . part of the transfer. We took on Mom's debt in exchange for the house . . ."

"What *debt?*" I said angrily. "Mom didn't *have* any debts! And what transfer of what to *whom?*"

Of course, I knew exactly what debt he meant. He meant the home equity loan Daphne and Midge had mentioned to me which I hadn't fully investigated yet but knew my mother had never spent—either gave to my brother or another hard-luck soul in a grocery store line.

"So who actually owns the home now?" I demanded. The old guy had given up on getting dressed and was sitting on his bench, placidly eavesdropping with open fascination on my little family crisis. For all I knew or cared, the angry Cubans on Liberty Boulevard were listening, too.

"Well . . ." He paused again. Then my brother told me the most astonishing thing of all. Merle Corry had been correct. Crazy as it sounded, his new *wife* owned my mother's house.

"You *have* to be joking," I said.

"No," he said. "I'm not."

I called my brother a son of a bitch. Regrettably, I heard myself saying things to him I couldn't believe were coming from my mouth. I told him he was at best a coward, at worst a thief—and clearly no brother of mine.

"You're just mad because you won't get any money," he said.

"Forget the damn *money*," I flared at him. "This is about betraying family trust."

Suddenly his new wife joined the conversation. Apparently she'd been listening on the telephone extension the whole time.

"Let me tell *you* something," she said angrily. "There are things here you don't know anything about. And, besides, your mother *wanted* me to have that house. We were very close. It was all legal and we even had witnesses."

I actually laughed at this point, though a bit hysterically, I confess.

I told her witnesses were meaningless. She could have assembled a Vatican Council to serve as witnesses to whatever unholy transaction they cooked up and it wouldn't amount to beans in my book. Technically speaking, what they'd done might be "legal" but it certainly wasn't right. In fact, it was ethically indefensible. In my opinion they'd taken advantage of a generous but mentally frail woman who couldn't remember what she had for breakfast that morning and given away the very asset that was supposed to take care of her—the very reason I'd moved her to Maine in the first place. Even if she wanted them to have the house, I volleyed back, how on earth could they justify accepting it, given Mom's limited circumstances?

"You'll have to ask your brother that," she replied.

She was right. My beef wasn't with her. Whatever else was true—whatever else I wasn't seeing—none of it could have transpired without my brother condoning or even orchestrating it.

Flush with a biblical rage I'd never experienced, I quietly asked him how he planned to take care of our mother in the event she fell ill and required a greater level of assisted care. Her current budget, I pointed out, was tighter than my balled fist which was about to come down the telephone line directly onto his snoot.

"Hey, Bro . . ." My brother switched to his old jaunty approach, apparently trying to make me appreciate the humor in this situation and lighten up a bit. "You need to calm down. We'll do our part to care of her. Trust me. You need to calm down."

"Yeah, you're right. Good-bye."

And with that, I hung up the phone and discovered the old fella staring at me solemnly.

"Sounds like you need a good lawyer, son," he said gently from his bench across the frayed carpet, fully dressed now and trying to wiggle on a wingtip shoe. The Cubans were gone and a Wall Street update was now on the TV. The Nasdaq was up eighty-two points.

"Yes sir," I said, looking at him, still shaking from the encounter. "I think I do."

I walked slowly back into the dining room. Kimpton glanced up from his pie.

"You don't look so good," he said. "Is something wrong?"

I sat down and told him my breathtaking news. He listened until I was finished; then, wiping his mouth with his napkin, he shook his head.

"It's amazing what money can do to a good family. It brings out the worst in people. Were you and your brother close?"

I replied that we had always been, exceptionallly so, or so I thought. That's what made this turn of events so difficult to believe, so impossible to stomach. But now I wasn't sure about anything—except that I'd love the opportunity to flatten my brother. I was half tempted to bail out of the Friends Classic, fly to North Carolina, and do just that.

"Maybe you ought to feel sorry for him," Kimp said. "One way or another, you'll fight the good fight and get through this crisis and so will your mother. But I'm not so sure about your brother."

I looked at him and nodded. It was a point worth considering, something my father himself might have said, though it still didn't stop me from wanting to hurl a punch.

• • •

A DAY later, I sat alone beneath my own private rain cloud in the noisy and crowded bar just off the hotel lobby at Spanish Bay, waiting for Jon Sager to come down from our room where he'd gone to check in via phone with Karen and the kids at Universal Studios, on winter break from the snows of Syracuse. My anger had now morphed into something akin to general disillusionment and a growing sense of indecision and panic.

I'd spent most of the afternoon on the telephone, using my reporter skills to chase down legal documents and assemble a paper trail, speaking to a pair of top estate lawyers, and putting together a fairly extensive picture of what had transpired in Greensboro. Mere hours before I arrived in North Carolina the previous December to move my mother and her belongings to Maine, my brother had taken my mom to see his old high school chum, the lawyer-turned-city-councilman, who produced a codicil to her existing will which indeed granted the deed to her house on Dogwood Drive *exclusively* to my brother's new wife. They'd blithely ignored the power-of-attorney agreement because my mother was clearly, at least for their purposes, of "sound" mind.

As if that weren't wildly improbable and deeply disturbing enough, I'd also discovered that my brother had mystifyingly signed a prenuptial agreement with his new wife that granted her complete legal ownership of anything she acquired *after* their marriage, meaning the new owner of my mother's home could simply, if she chose, toss my brother out on his ear and he wouldn't have a legal leg to stand on.

• • •

"We can have an injuction from a judge in hand by tomorrow," a top attorney in Greensboro assured me, "to protect whatever is left of your mother's property and make sure they don't sink it all into a brand new Mercedes. But there are a couple things you need to think about—and I mean long and hard."

I had to realize, he said matter-of-factly, that we would probably need to have my mother declared mentally incompetent to handle her own affairs—was I willing or able to take that step? I assured him this wasn't a problem because that was *precisely* why

I'd moved her to Maine in the first place. Besides, my mother's closest friends and neighbors would all corroborate that she was incapable of handling her financial affairs and probably had no clue what she was signing away in that lawyer's office. The best evidence of this fact was that, whenever asked, Mom still doggedly maintained that the house was still *hers.*

The second thing the lawyer said I needed to ponder was the fact that there were federal Medicare laws in place designed to protect the assets of people just like my mother.

"What I'm saying to you is, and I want to be very clear on this if we are to proceed, regardless of whether we manage to get back your mother's estate or any part of it or not, if you pursue this case in your mother's behalf, there is a chance someone could wind up being prosecuted."

At which point, he paused meaningfully.

"And the chances are pretty good it *won't* be the woman who now owns your mother's house."

So there is was—the ultimate *risk-reward* par five hole. It took me a moment for the reality of what he was saying to sink in. If I pursued a remedy through the courts, I might get back my mother's house all right—but possibly get my brother into trouble with the law, maybe even send him to jail. It was, to say the least, completely boggling to even contemplate such a denouement. All I could picture was my angry father somewhere wanting to punch *both* of us in the snoots.

In any case, that more or less explains why I was sitting desolately alone beneath the blaring TV in the Spanish Bay bar sipping on a double Maker's Mark and waiting for Jon to come down from talking to Karen and the kids about their day at Islands of Adventure. I was pondering these inscrutable matters, trying to figure out what the heck to do *next.*

I'd already phoned McDaid and explained the whole thing to him. It was he who placed me in touch with the lawyer and true pal that he was, he even cheerfully volunteered to go find my brother and punch him in the nose on my behalf, if it would make me feel better. I'd phoned six or seven of our family's closest friends, revealed my biblical tale of woe and solicited their frankest opinions. Every one of them said essentially the same thing and nothing I really wanted to hear—that I had a "moral obligation" to protect my mom's assets and do whatever it took to get them back. One asserted that it was "high time" my brother finally grew up and learned there were consequences in life. Another said my father wouldn't hesitate to seek a legal remedy— all of which, I confess, only deepened my confusion and gloom.

Only Wendy, when I explained the full extent of the situation to her, seemed to grasp the bleak implications of my options, and the fact that the last thing I really wanted to do was take my brother to court.

Oddly enough, despite all of this, Jon and I had acquitted ourselves pretty decently in the opening round of the Friends Classic, ham-and-egging our way nicely over the beautiful, links-style golf course created by Sandy Tatum and Tom Watson to finish with a team best-ball total of 68, good enough for third place in the field.

"She's some filly, huh? I'd marry her."

I realized that the young guy in the expensive golf duds seated next to me was staring up at the TV screen but speaking to me. He looked about fourteen except he wore a neatly trimmed goatee. I glanced up at the screen, too. The evening news was on, if you wished to call it news.

A pretty blonde in a ball gown was standing on a glitzy stage chastely kissing a guy who turned out to be a tinhorn millionare. It was a clip from a controversial "reality" TV show during which the woman, whoever she was, claimed to have been duped into marrying the guy on national TV. He turned out *not* to have a million bucks, as advertised, but *did* have a police record and now the woman, according to the report, was holed up in a $400-a-day hotel suite in Manhattan, consoling herself with fistfuls of Godiva chocolate, fielding marriage proposals from lonely aces across the planet, trying to decide whether posing nude for *Playboy* would compromise her dignity.

"Everyone's got troubles," I heard myself philosophize, Sri Kimplike, vaguely wondering if I'd rather have her immediate problems or mine—then realized nobody in their right mind would pay good money to see a photograph of me naked.

"Yeah, I guess so. Not me," he added, hoisting his beer. He took a huge swallow and exhaled with enormous satisfaction. I half expected him to belch.

"I broke eighty today."

I congratulated him, hoping he didn't hurt himself or any innocent bystanders.

"I don't mean to brag or anything," he said. "But my buddy and I have only been playing golf since last November. Man, are we ever *hooked*. Golf is, like, running our freaking lives now."

"Golf is like that," I agreed. "Easy to start, hard to stop."

I asked what he did before the golf bug bit him because he looked like the kind of guy who had other recreational interests before an Old Fart pastime like golf came along—skateboarding through crowded shopping malls, perhaps, or taking his father's Beemer on late-night joyrides.

"We were wind surfers up at the Russian River," he explained and then his face brightened with a vast smile. "Hey, man," he nodded up at the TV, "that's *us!*"

The evening newscast had moved on to a story about the explosion of "dotcom" millionaires in California. According to one report, thirty new millionares a week were being created in California's booming Silicon Valley and there was so much New Economy money floating around among twentysomething internet entrepreneurs, quoth the reporter, some young lions of e-commerce were actually suffering from a newly diagnosed mental fatigue called "Sudden Wealth Syndrome."

I had to smile at this, and almost repeated my lame comment about everybody having troubles these days, but then realized the

kid really *was* in the news story—there in the background, swinging a golf club while some other young guy was holding forth to
the reporter. The bar had grown so crowded and noisy I had to
strain to hear what his friend was saying.

"Hey," I said, "that is you."

"Told you, man."

I recognized the comely first tee at Spanish Bay, as well. The
guy being interviewed was talking about a new information web
site for "overstressed dotcomers" who needed advice about stuff
like where to safely invest their sudden windfalls, what to do to
avoid paying major capital gains taxes, where to take unique adventure vacations specifically aimed at "chilling out" overworked
internet executives, even tips on how to recognize signs of, and
seek counseling for, Sudden Wealth Syndrome.

"That was done this morning," the guy on TV's goateed friend
explained, grinning up at the sight of himself on television.

I had a disturbing thought.

"Are you here for the Friends Classic?"

"Nope. Montana is doing a couple talks down here this weekend. I'm just here for the awesome golf and any nice looking
ladies I can find who are under *fifty*."

I looked at this *dude* and wondered if he might be a dot-com
millionaire, too. He looked like my ten-year-old son Jack wearing a fake beard.

"Is your friend really named Montana?"

He laughed. "Nah. It's Chuck. I just call him that 'cause he
loves Montana, wants to buy a big farm there, like, *major* soon.
He got me into golf and now we can't stop playing. We just came
back from Butch Harmon's school."

"Great," I said, thinking how youth *and* fortune really are
wasted on the young and wealthy.

"He's Tiger's teacher, you know."

I sipped my whiskey and said I knew that.

"You play Pebble yet?" he asked.

I said I'd played it a couple days ago with my girlfriend, and I was scheduled to play it again tomorrow with a friend.

"Two times in four days," I said, making a little joke. "I'm living like some depressed dot-com millionaire."

"Cool," he said, sounding as if my remark was anything *but*. He added that he and his buddy had played Spyglass twice, Poppy Hills once, and Pebble Beach Links already four times that week, neatly trumping my pair of anemic loops.

"Where you headed next?" he wanted to know.

"Home to Maine. I understand that my front sidewalk needs shoveling. You?"

He explained that he and his buddy and a group of golf nuts like them were taking their girlfriends to Australia to play that country's famed Gold Coast—then down to South Africa, followed by Spain and finally Scotland. They planned to be gone almost two months.

"Say, you know any dudes over at Cypress? We're trying to get on there before we go."

He meant, of course, *Cypress Point,* the number-two course in America and one of the most exclusive golf enclaves in California. As a matter of fact, I did know a few Cypress members who would probably hunt me down and put out my eyes with blunt wooden golf tees if I sent this dude and his friends up their driveway seeking a game.

"Sorry, man," I told him sympathetically, trying to do the math in my head for his green fees alone and wondering if this was possibly the new face of American golf. If so, it was kind of spooky to contemplate—or maybe I was just suffering from a case of Jealous Hacker Syndrome.

Mercifully, a hand slapped me sharply on the back, loosening a crown and giving me a reason to evacuate my bar stool.

"Hey, Lumpster. Sorry I took so long. Karen and the kids are fine, save for a bit of stomach flu. What's cookin'?"

"That guy back there just came from Butch Harmon's golf school," I explained to Jon, as we hoofed off toward the opening

Friends dinner. "If you can fathom it, he and his friends are playing their way around the world. Talk about a spring golf road
trip."

"Yeah, well," Jon said with perfect timing, "they better not
show up in Syracuse trying to buy a game with the Dewsweepers.
Personal wealth doesn't get you playing privileges with us, pal.
We'll play with anybody—assuming they're sufficiently irrever-
ent. Those guys sound like *pseudo* 'Sweepers."

The Friends Classic was beginning to show its wear—becoming
too much of a good thing, according to Larry Smuckler, one of its
founders.

A dozen years ago, Smuckler and his chum Lee Tomlinson
and a few other longtime golf pals decided it would be great to
assemble a handful of friends together at some garden spot of the
game "for a little talk and a lot of golf."

The event had commenced in Hawaii and finally moved to
Pebble Beach, and in the process, as friend invited friend, swelled
from ten or twelve original participants to sixty-eight competitors. "The problem nowadays," Larry confided to me that morning out on the golf course at Spanish Bay, "is that nobody really
talks the way we used to. The intimacy is gone. The thing has gotten too big and impersonal—guys bringing guys who just want
to take home one of the prizes and have no interest in the social
aspect of the event."

That was not the original intent of the Classic, Larry said,
and he and Lee hoped to return the event to its original atmosphere by severely limiting the field and getting rid of prizes in
future years.

Meanwhile, in an attempt to foster the kind of lively conversation that characterized the original intimacy of the Friends
Classic, Smuckler proposed that each dinner table have a formal
"discussion group," and he suggested that every "friend" share a
story he'd "never revealed to anyone" to see where the discussion
might lead.

Jon slipped me a doleful look, as if I'd gotten him into some sort of weird Left Coast encounter group where we would be doing "trust exercises" and having group hugs next.

The first "Friend" to spill his guts, so to speak, at our table managed a real estate company up in Sonoma County. His name was Tony. He told us that thirty years ago he gave up a "full ride" engineering scholarship to Cal Poly in order to marry the girl of his dreams—who only fooled around with his best friend and ditched him ten years later. He wished he'd gone to Cal Poly and built a great bridge instead of marrying her.

"I wonder if his best friend brought him to this golf tournament," Jon leaned over and chuckled in my ear before the next Friend could speak.

Larry, a dentist from the Midwest, talked about canceling his engagement to a girl back on Long Island the night before their wedding rehearsal dinner, and having to return all of the presents with his mom. He now had a happy marriage, several kids, a thriving dental practice, a twelve golf handicap, and apparently not too many regrets.

A professor from Berkeley, though, revealed how a college professor of his once invited him to sleep with his wife, which he obligingly did, wrecking his own marriage in the process—a stupid stunt that still haunted him forty years later, he admitted. He apparently still loved his first wife or the professor's wife, I wasn't quite clear which.

One by one, the stories emerged, more poignant than expected, creeping ever closer to Jon Sager and Friend.

A Japanese guy told a touching tale about a friend from Africa who phoned him in the night asking for a prayer or help or something and how he later discovered that the alarm on his bedside clock had gone off exactly at the moment his friend died, several hundred miles away.

After a respectful silence, a corporate psychologist named Brad revealed how he took the girl of his dreams away for a weekend the same weekend his mother passed away. Years later, he returned to her grave in Maine and wept. Brad was leading the

Friends Classic with his son Chip. They were rank beginners in the game, with handicaps listed as thirty plus on the pairing sheet. Chip was the star on his high school tennis team and hoped to attend Stanford University. He apologized for not having had much happen yet in his life yet—"That's bad, I mean," he allowed with a nervous laugh—though he did blush and freely admit recently setting off a stink bomb in a crowded classroom which made him feel sort of weird and later guilty.

Jon, I noticed, was poking vacantly at his salad, possibly preparing to divulge an old fraternity prank or tell about the time he and Karen were visiting the information center of a posh real estate development north of Syracuse when nature violently seized him, thereby causing him to flee into the nearest bathroom just off the reception lobby, which turned out to be for preschoolers. Karen described the ensuing racket from within the "mini-commode" as "the most embarrassing sound I've ever heard one human being make," and admitted she'd actually begun singing to try cover her husband's body racket—but I guess that story had already been told, so it didn't qualify.

In any case, a balding eye surgeon named Barry told movingly about why he became a surgeon who does volunteer work in developing countries. His father was a small town doctor in rural Minnesota. "People who were injured or dying came to our house fairly commonly," he said. "Once, a farmer brought in his little boy who'd ingested a balloon and was turning blue from lack of oxygen. I watched my father work like hell to save that kid, who was just a bit younger than me. The boy died anyway. I remember later sitting with my father in our living room. He was devastated, heartbroken that he couldn't save that boy. A couple weeks later, I came to him and said I planned to be a doctor. I think that changed both our lives."

It was suddenly my turn to speak. How on earth could I possibly follow *that,* I wondered.

Well, here's the deal, guys. Yesterday afternoon I learned my brother betrayed everything we were raised to believe. . . .

No. That wasn't something I could say—yet. I knew what he'd done. I just didn't know *why* he'd done it.

Instead, I heard myself saying that for a guy who grew up loving golf so intensely he even skipped his grandmother's funeral as a teenager to go play golf at the Dunes Club in Myrtle Beach, it really surprised me to reach midlife and discover that I'd "fallen out of love" with playing the game.

Several of my new intimate "friends" looked genuinely surprised at this admission.

"Why do you think that is?" Brad the psychologist perked right up.

"Too much work," I replied. "Not enough play. Who knows for sure?"

I explained about the strange golf dream and the unexpected insight at the Kings Crown back in January and joked that I planned to play more golf and hopefully "get back in touch with my inner golf child" with some swell guys from Syracuse called the Dewsweepers. I liked their approach to the game. I hoped it rubbed off on me.

"What's a Dewsweeeper?" the junior tennis whiz wondered.

"Him," I said, jerking a thumb at my silent tournament partner. All eyes shifted to Counselor Sager.

"Do you ever stop and think," he began, far more serious than I expected, "about where you are now in life, how far you've come, and whether or not you made the right choices as an adult? I mean, let's say you've got a good job, a great family that depends on you, a nice house, the whole nine yards. Do you ever wonder if you'd made a different choice you might have achieved more—or at least something else?"

This wasn't exactly the assigned topic but I was damned interested to hear where the Sage of Syracuse might be leading the witnesses.

"I do," volunteered the Berkeley professor who'd had biblical knowledge of his professor's wife. "I ask myself that all the time. I guess that possibility scares the hell out of me."

"*Golf* scares the hell out of me," added Larry the likable dentist.

"Interesting question. What you're really asking, I think, is what's enough?" Barry the thoughtful surgeon suggested.

"Yeah, I guess so, more or less," Jon replied, plunging his nose safely into his wineglass.

"It would be enough for me to realize there is *never* enough," said the guy who gave up his engineering scholarship to chase the girl who later fooled around on him. "That way, I could quit trying to outdo my father."

"Maybe," someone said, "for better or worse, we become our fathers."

"Now *that's* a scary thought," cracked Jon and glanced at me—knowing I knew his father Rod, a gentle, quiet, retired insurance company president to whom golf could be a sad affair, was really his personal hero and the man he would most likely resemble if he hadn't gotten his mother's sharp wit and handsome features instead. As far as I knew, though, his mom, Ruth Sager, didn't have a monk's patch.

Like an idiot who couldn't leave well enough alone, I spoke up again.

"I was just reading about a vain emperor named Qiri. He was the first emperor of China and Mao's personal hero, the guy who brought art and civilization to China by unifying the warlords. Among other things, he irrigated fields and built the nation's first roads, created the country's first written language, established a system of weights and standards, formed a legal system, and raised a standing army of two million men. On the down side, he buried four hundred Confucian scholars up to their necks and lopped their heads off with shovels. Like a David Leadbetter pitching drill."

"*Major* bummer," said Chip the teenage tennis star who was leading the tournament.

"Sounds like a mayor we once had in Syracuse," Jon observed dryly. "And your point would be . . . ?"

"Emperor Qiri did all of this before he turned forty-five. His stated aim was to swallow the world whole."

The table fell silent, and suddenly I forgot the point I was attempting to make.

"That would be enough for me," admitted the corporate psychologist, swallowing a bite of cheesecake.

"Yeah," quipped Jon, becoming his old self again. "But the bottom line remains—there's never been a Chinese guy who could chip and putt worth a damn in the Majors."

They all laughed at this. Jon was good for that sort of thing.

• • •

"**T**HAT was some neat lawyer trick you pulled last night at the dinner," I said to Jon the next morning as we walked up the first fairway at Pebble Beach. We'd both managed to get decent drives into the short grass—perhaps an omen of things to come.

"Yeah? How so?"

"You started to reveal something about yourself—but quickly turned it into a roundtable discussion on male life choices. Pretty nimble, Counselor."

"First rule of the law, pal. You can't take the stand as a witness if you're already trying the case for your client."

The Pacific sun was out but the winter wind was whipping again. Jon's game, though, was up to the challenge. He played the first five holes very well indeed, knocking off four pars and a birdie at the fourth hole. I, on the other hand, stumbled along like a rank beginner, scraping five bogeys and a lone par out of the first six holes.

"So," I said to him, thinking of the big career decision he had yet to make, somewhere about the long uphill sixth fairway, "any second thoughts about the road you *didn't* take?"

Jon gave me an annoyed Chuck Grodin look.

"Hey," he said, puffing a bit. "Can't we talk about something *really* interesting—like Markie Post's brilliant acting career or something?"

"I wasn't aware she had one," I said.

"Not funny. Now there is an actress *and* a woman. My dream date—if Karen would only agree to let me ask her out."

"My dream date would have to be either Natalie Allen or Marty Seidel," I volunteered.

"Who the heck are *they*?"

Natalie Allen, I explained, was the noontime anchor on CNN. Marty Seidel was a Dixie Chick, or as I put it—"the unnaturally blond fiddle player who was rumored to have recently undergone an unmistakable physical enhancement of her attractive person. I fondly think of her as the Tammy Wynette of the New Millennium."

"You're a sick puppy. I'm telling Wendy on you."

We paused and watched Larry Smuckler hit a nice approach shot to the sixth green, rolling his ball just past the hole.

"I almost came out here," Jon remarked simply and out of the blue, glancing at Stillwater Cove and we resumed our walk.

"Where. Pebble?"

"No. Los Angeles—Laguna Beach, actually. My grandmother, my father's mother, owned a small airline. My Uncle Jack ran it for her. It was called Air Catalina—small seaplanes that flew passengers between the mainland and Catalina Island. Really cool planes. The summer between Colgate and law school I worked for her as a baggage loader. By day I loaded planes and napped in the sun between flights, and by night I hung out with stewardesses and partied till it was time to go to work. I started seeing a girl named Gail. She was a cheerleader at UCLA. Really gorgeous." He smiled at the memory. "It was my own personal Summer of Love."

"You're a sick puppy," I told him. "I'm telling Karen on you if you don't tell me more."

He didn't tell me any more, though, until the eleventh hole. By then, my game was seriously foundering and Jon was barely keeping our team's hope of a respectable finish alive with bogeys and pars.

He talked about how he nearly went to seminary in Chicago but decided to follow his father's footsteps into law school instead, heading south to the hill of Washington and Lee, where he made law review and dated a pretty southern belle named Kathy, whose daddy ran the biggest bank in Danville and belonged to the country club where a former PGA Tour player named Bobby Mitchell was head pro; the family more or less adopted Jon and a powerful state senator offered him a clerking job in his law firm and later invited Jon to join his practice. It was more or less presumed by everybody that Jon and Kathy would get married as soon as he graduated—but Jon was still thinking about California, still wondering a bit.

"It might have been a perfect life, already assembled and ready to go," he explained, " a beautiful wife, her great family, a super job, membership in the country club, nice car, the whole nine yards."

"So . . . why didn't you say yes?"

"I don't know—well, yes I do. It wasn't me. It wasn't what I was used to, and I never learned to like grits. I kind of wanted to go back to California and I kind of wanted to just go home."

So, he just went home. I knew this part of the story from Karen Sager.

Not long after he earned his law degree and moved home to Syracuse to take a $300-per-week job at a prominent eight-partner law firm and found a miniscule apartment off Erie Boulevard, Jon wandered into a popular tavern off the S.U. campus and met Karen Wischerath, a striking strawberry blonde with an infectious laugh, the artistic daughter of a large Catholic family from Liverpool. Karen had just finished Notre Dame and was working as an insurance underwriter, about to relocate to a job nearer her boyfriend in Boston. Jon presented her with a business card and asked if he could call her sometime soon. She laughed, assuming it was just another lame pickup line and he would never really phone.

"I think I was the only girl who ever laughed in Jonny Boy's pretty face," Karen once explained to me. "The next night, though, he did call—and the night after that, too."

A few weeks after they met, Karen ditched her Boston boyfriend and began seeing Jon exclusively. One night in the spring of '79, Jon handed Karen a paper grocery sack with a bunch of tomatoes in it. They planned to make dinner at his place before going away on their first vacation together. Inside the bag, buried among the tomatoes, was a boxed diamond ring from Wilson's Jewelers. Jon, according to Karen, actually got down on one knee to propose. "Only so I could look her properly in the eye." She laughed and then she cried. The rest, as they say, was history.

"You know," I said to Jon as we stood waiting to hit on the sixteenth tee, both of our games now slipping into the land of Big Ugly Numbers, "we both could probably have played a whole lot better if you hadn't been talking so much about your midlife crisis."

"Hey, don't blame me," he protested. "I wanted to talk about Markie Post."

"Some fine team *we* make," I said. "Here you are trying to decide whether or not to leave Syracuse. Here I am trying to decide whether or not to take my brother to court. How did life get in the way of golf?"

Jon turned, surprised. I hadn't told him anything about my brother and the deeply disturbing things I'd learned in the previous seventy-two hours. With the tournament lost but the Pacific sun still shining, it seemed as good a place as any to run the highlights of *my* own evolving midlife crisis by *him*. Who else but a golf buddy who happened to be an expert in estate planning law would really understand?

So I did just that as we ambled along sixteen and moved on to seventeen—where, it was pleasant to recall, Wendy had struck that fine 5-wood shot that reached the green a couple days ago. Already, I missed that girl.

I talked, Jon listened. We finished the round with our bags on our backs, walking side by side through the warm low-angled California sunshine.

"You won't sue your brother," Jon predicted. "It's really awful what he did. But like my father used to say, family doesn't sue family."

I nodded, hoping I could really believe him. Somehow, though, I had to find a way to fight the good fight.

"You won't take that job in Virginia," I said.

He shrugged and smiled, perhaps thinking I had his number, too.

We completed the round with a couple bogeys and a better ball net team score of even par 78, miles back in the pack of the Friends Classic—which was won, as it turned out, perhaps as it should have been, by a couple of rank beginners, the corporate shrink and his cheeerful teenage son Chip, the tennis star.

FIVE

BUNNY DUGAN

I was struggling to jot down a few thoughts for a speech I was supposed to give in Boston when good old Bunny Dugan telephoned out of the blue.

"How's the weather?" he demanded cheerfully.

"Not exactly golf weather," I replied, staring moodily out my office window at my yard—or what might have been my yard if it had been actually visible. Being springtime in Maine, the calendar end of what a friend of mine likes to call "The Official Indoor Golf Season," it was snowing fitfully, piling up like America's *second* snowiest city. But just the sound of Tom "Bunny" Dugan's voice lifted my spirits because I hadn't seen him since he traitorously flew south for the winter almost five months before. Purely for a masochistic kick, I asked how the weather was where he was, knowing full well he would laugh and say it was sunny, seventies, perfect golf weather, the same old, same old, "Nothing too exciting, if you want to know the truth," and I should give thought to spending my winters in Florida, too.

"Isn't that strange," he said, "it's snowing here, too. Coming down pretty good. Almost like back home."

"In *Florida?*"

"Oh wait a minute. I am back home. Actually, I'm in town and thought I might buy you lunch—if you're not too busy."

"Not for you, partner." I explained that I was only wool-gathering over a golf speech I was supposed to deliver in less than 24 hours at the Harvard Club in Boston to the annual spring conference of the Massachusetts Golf Association.

"Another speech, huh? You must getting pretty good at that by now."

"Not really. I'm just cheaper than the Footjoy Sign Boy and slightly funnier than Frank Hannigan. At least they have to feed me dinner."

"Come downtown. I'll feed you lunch."

"I'll shovel out and see you in a few."

At seventy-nine, Tom was the elder statesman of my regular golf group at Brunswick Golf Club, but to look at him or watch him play golf you'd swear you were looking at a guy twenty years younger than that. A tall, fit, elegantly dressed gray-haired man with a dapper Irish face and mirthful blue eyes, he carries his own bag and purports to play off a handicap of twelve, a statistical anomaly you'd be well advised to accept as fact only at great peril to your wallet. With his brief but brisk caddie swing, Tom is sneaky long off the tee and seldom misses fairways. He chips surpassingly well and putts side-saddle the way Sam Snead did before the USGA told him to cut it out so some other geezer could win. Tom is fast with a compliment, smooth with the ladies, quick to buy drinks, and never fails to apologize charmingly when he takes every last *nickel* of your lunch money at golf.

He was waiting for me at the new upscale lunch place near the town common, dressed festively in a red wool sweater, a golf version of Father Christmas, looking tanned and far too fit to suit my tastes, a sight for winter-sore eyes nonetheless. We embraced and sat down and I immediately asked him how his Florida golf season was going. During the long winter months, Tom and his lovely wife, Jane, resided at St. Andrews South in balmy Punta

Gorda, Florida, where flamingo loll and exotic flowers bloom and dapper Dugan plays golf every Monday and Friday with men half his age who probably get sick and tired of going home without their lunch money.

"Oh well," he began with his usual courtly blush of modesty, watching a true sign of spring in Maine—a salt-stained snowplow with a broken headlight—rumble past the restaurant window, "it wasn't a bad season, I suppose . . ." and proceeded to admit he'd just shot his age and taken home enough winnings to take Jane on holiday to Aruba.

He asked how my winter had gone.

"It's not *gone* yet," I said but added that I couldn't complain too much because I'd halved Arnold Palmer in the Kings Crown and then gone to Rye, England, to watch the President's Putter, the annual winter golf competition of the Oxford and Cambridge Golf Society, and then soldiered on to Pebble Beach where my Dewsweeper buddy Jon Sager and I came in nearly last in the Friends Classic.

"So you've managed to *play* a little golf this year already," Dugan said. "That's good. Get a nice jump on Terry."

Terry Meagher was the third member of our standing Brunswick group, the current golf and hockey coach at Bowdoin College, a thoughtful Canadian who hit his tee shots indecently far, putted like Ben Crenshaw in his prime, but used any old crappy ball he could find and, frankly, couldn't tell you who was vice president of the United States. To say Terry was *cheap* was like saying Jesper Parnevik likes primary colors. Terry insisted that I was a ball *snob*, but he was unquestionably a ball *slob*. Still, we played off an identical handicap, were exactly the same age, had the same divisible number of children, and always played our matches with a million-dollar (American) running side bet. Did I mention that he was my best friend in town and *still* owed me a million dollars (American) from the final match of the previous season?

"I could get an even bigger jump on him if I figure out where to take the Dewsweepers next week," I said to Tom, explaining that a spring golf trip to Myrtle Beach I'd carefully worked out for the boys from Syracuse was suddenly in jeopardy due to a pending airline strike. The Dewsweepers all had tickets on the same airline and if I couldn't come up with a decent alternative where the sun was shining and the grass was growing and the first tee was invitingly standing open, we'd be enjoying Easter in the snowbelt.

"I want to meet those guys sometime," Tom said, adding, "you know, Terry, Sid, and I could get jealous—you spend so much time over there in Syracuse these days."

"Yeah, well, you get to spend winters in Florida without me," I volleyed straight back at him. "How is coach Sidney J. Watson?"

Sid Watson was the fourth member of our hometown four-some and Terry's old boss at Bowdoin, a legendary NCAA Hall of Fame hockey coach and college athletic director who also spent winters doing nothing but playing golf down in Florida not far from Tom Dugan. Sid had a short game to *die* for and a short fuse that was really fun to light. Once upon a time, he'd been Johnny Unitas's roommate and one of the NFL's top punt and kickoff returners, in an age when only sissies or pretty boys wore protective facemasks. At sixty-nine or whatever he was, Sid kept himself in great shape and still carried his bag à la Tom Dugan.

"Oh not good, I'm afraid," Dugan said, his face suddenly darkening. "Didn't Terry tell you?"

I replied that he hadn't, reminding him that from November to April Terry and I communicated through two inches of safety glass girdling the Bowdoin hockey arena. He sometimes actually telephoned to chat, but only if his team wasn't winning, which was pretty rare in Terry's case and meant we mostly had to resort to goofy hand signals through the glass at home games. Currently the Polar Bears were on a scoring rampage and Terry was happily in another world.

"Last week Sid couldn't even get up the steps of his condo without having to rest. Henrietta finally made him go in and have some medical tests. It's his heart. They say it's growing weaker. They don't know why exactly. There's apparently no blockage or anything. It's just giving out for some reason. That's the scary part."

This concerned me greatly to hear. The idea that Sid Watson's heart could simply be "giving out" seemed as incongruous as, say, Terry Meagher suddenly announcing he would only use Titleist Pro-V1 golfballs from now on. Sidney was the toughest bird I knew, with or without a face mask, and this was difficult news to take with another golf season not even remotely close yet.

Switching on his dapper Dugan smile again, Tom said: "Speaking of hockey, how's young Jack doing this year?"

Once upon a time, Bunny Dugan had been the greatest schoolboy hockey player in the city of Boston, maybe the greatest ever produced in Beantown. Thirty years later, and working as a top sales rep for Brine sporting goods, thanks to his buddy Sidney Watson, he agreed to coach youth hockey and spent the next two decades doing that; so it wasn't the least bit surprising that Tom took an unusual interest in my son Jack's progress in Mite League hockey.

"He just scored his first goal of the season. Unfortunately the season only has two more weeks to run. So he probably won't win the scoring title."

"Does he show any interest in golf yet?"

"Not much. I'm not pushing it. He did ask me to go to the Ryder Cup, though. So I took him."

"How was it?"

"Speaking purely as a fan, awful. Too many people and outrageous prices. But Jack loved it because he got to see Tiger play a little bit. That's really all he wanted. I guess it pays to be a kid. Maybe I'll talk about that tomorrow night."

"What are you planning to talk about? What Arnold Palmer's really like?"

"Haven't a clue. He's really like you, by the way—a nice guy who doesn't feel a bit of remorse at taking the lunch money of guys half his age."

Our soup arrived and we started eating.

"Say, what are you doing up *here*? It's only March," I remembered.

Dugan, who had been smiling, stopped smiling.

"It's Tommy," he said. "He's having another operation."

Tommy Dugan, Tom's oldest son, had been gamely battling melanoma for almost four years. Tommy was my age and the last I'd heard he had finished a tough round of chemo but was putting on weight again. That had been, I suddenly realized, many months ago. Funny how time flies when someone else isn't having fun.

Tom shook his head and said, "The tumors keep popping up all over his body, Jimmy. It's terrible. They keep opening him up and cutting parts away. The kid amazes me—he just won't give up."

Tom picked up his spoon and then, as if his appetite had vanished, turned his handsome old Irish face to the window and stared at the slushy street.

· · ·

THE next afternoon in Boston, on the heels of a lawyer talking about the legal ramifications of the well-chronicled Haverhill case (involving a prominent Bay State club that was being sued for denying equal access to its female members) and a guy from the National Golf Foundation who wondered why the game's participation boom of the past decade had suddenly leveled off, I walked up to the speaker's podium and explained that I didn't wish to talk about what kind of monster year Tiger Woods might be poised to have, or relive the highs and lows of the recent Brookline Ryder Cup, or even tell tales about Arnold Palmer's amazing professional career and private life.

I thought I might talk, instead, about my golf buddies.

Golf buddies struck me as the very best thing about the game of golf because they involve uncomplicated friendships that span summers, decades, even lifetimes, enduring through the best and worst of times, providing comfort and cheer through the Darwinian trials of a funny old Presbyterian game that makes suffering fools of us all.

Golf buddies, whether they are men or women, link us as if by a golden thread to the great traditions and heroes of the game—and therefore each other—in the most unexpected ways.

One of my regular golf buddies up in Maine, for example, I explained, had once upon a time been Denny Shute's caddie at Brae Burn Country Club in Boston, the place where Walter Travis won the U.S. Open of 1919. Native son Shute, as everyone in the room knew or at least should have, not only captured back-to-back PGA championships in 1936 and 1937, but also won a British Open in 1933 and nearly took the U.S. Open in 1941. Shute was a bona fide hero of American golf, a spiritual heir of Francis Ouimet himself.

But it was Shute's amazing caddie I wanted to talk about. His name was Tom Dugan, though most people around West Newton simply called him "Bunny," a nickname planted on him by his older brother Jimmy.

Bunny Dugan liked golf but he *loved* ice hockey. Golf in those days, after all, was purely a rich man's pastime and Bunny Dugan was a poor Irish kid, so he lettered in three different sports instead at West Newton High and became the schoolboy terror of Boston's hockey arenas, a prolific-scoring center who once nailed three goals in the span of a few minutes.

One afternoon in 1942, Bunny Dugan walked into a U.S. Army recruiting office and enlisted in the Army Air Corp, wanting to do his part for the war effort in Europe. He said good-bye to his parents and was shipped to North Dakota for training as a radioman, then on to gunnery school in Texas. A short while later, he made the rank of gunnery sergeant and was shipped to a squadron of B-17s just outside London, England.

Bunny's first mission—a bombing raid over Stuttgart, Germany—nearly ended in disaster when his plane ran out of fuel and he almost had to ditch it in the English Channel. On his sixth mission twenty days later, he was wounded in action and returned weeks later in time to survive one of the most costly air battles of World War Two, the infamous Allied raid on the ball bearing plants in Schweinfurt.

When Gunnery Sergeant Bunny Dugan came home on a twenty-one-day leave to West Newton in March of 1944, he was something more than a local hockey star who'd done his patriotic duty. His uniform bore five air medals, a Purple Heart, three oak leaf clusters, and the Distinguished Flying Cross. He was the first radioman in his squadron to complete twenty-five missions over enemy territory and he was interviewed for United Press International by a correspondent named Walter Cronkite. Headlines in the *Boston Evening Traveler* called him "Newton's Man Over Germany."

After the war, Bunny Dugan went on to skate with the first U.S. national team that toured Europe and preceded the start-up of the Winter Olympics. He came home and got married and found a job selling hockey, soccer, and lacrosse equipment for a famous Boston sporting goods company, a job he would keep almost forty years. He relocated to Maine and started a family and rediscovered his childhood fascination with golf.

Bunny Dugan was a war hero and a living link to golf's golden days but it took me almost a *decade* of playing with him, I told the congregants of the Mass Golf Association Spring Conference, to learn these amazing facts. That not only said a lot about the character of Bunny Dugan, I'm pretty certain I said— it said a lot about the game he now loved more than any other.

Denny Shute's old caddie, my golf pal Bunny Dugan, war hero and son of West Newton, I added, once told me golf really isn't about greatness—it's about goodness. Good shots. Good friends. And ultimately, good memories.

With that in mind, I told my audience, I was devoting the

year to getting back in touch with those fundamental values of the game—spending more time with my friends on the golf course and less time around Tour stars. I admitted that I needed a "time out" from the pro game and a chance to recharge my batteries and play golf for fun with my friends—including a swell group of guys I was supposed to lead on a spring golf trip to South Carolina in a matter of days. They called themselves the Dewsweepers, I explained, because they played at the crack of dawn every weekend and they'd more or less adopted me and, because of the impending airline strike, if I could only find a place to take them to play golf down on Cape Cod, let's say, I might become a real hero of golf in their eyes.

I thanked the golfing sons and daughters of Francis Ouimet and the Bay State and wished them a fun and prosperous new golf season.

An older man marched straight up to me after the speech, glaring like a mongoose, thrusting out a wiry arm. For an instant, I thought he was taking a swing at my chin.

"I like that business about playing for *fun*," he declared, clamping an iron hand on my sore elbow so I couldn't get away.

"That fellow you mentioned—Bunny Dugan. By any chance did you mean young Tommy Dugan?"

I said it was probably one and the same, though young Tommy was now almost eighty.

"Well I'll be damned. So he's still alive and kicking, is he?"

"As of lunchtime yesterday."

"Good man. Knew him in his hockey glory days. Boy could he ever skate! What's his golf like?"

"Make sure you get strokes."

Someone else tried to get a word or two in edgewise but the old guy wouldn't give me up.

"Hey, before you run away," he said loudly. "Here's a bit of history trivia I bet even a golf buff like you doesn't know. You belong to Brunswick Golf Club way up in the wild and wooly state of Maine. Right?"

I admitted that I did, though frankly he made Maine sound like it was an outpost of civilization where golfers wore polos made of caribou skin and ate whale blubber sandwiches at the halfway house instead of a pretty green vacation spot just sev-ently miles and a couple turnpike booths up I-95. Once upon a time, in fact, Maine had even belonged to Massachusetts, I was sorely tempted to remind him, which, as I figured it, more or less made me eligible for full membership under some kind of hard-ship rule or grandfather clause of the MGA bylaws. (For the record, unlike some Mainers, I also seldom if ever referred to sui-cidally aggressive summer drivers from the Bay State as *Massholes.*)

"Ever hear of Pops Erswell?" my captor demanded.

I said of course I'd heard of Pops Erswell. Pops was my club's first golf professional. Brunswick Golf Club was supposedly founded in 1889 by Bowdoin College professors, ship captains, and maybe even a few golfing Civil War veterans—or so the tale went. The truth was, the history was so murky nobody knew for sure when the place got rolling. Anyway, Pops Erswell was probably there when the first ball was hit, or showed up shortly afterward.

"Here's something important about Pops Erswell very few people know." He paused for dramatic effect, glancing around to make sure others were listening. "He invented the pull cart!"

I hear lots of interesting stories on the golf hustings. But this one seemed even wilder and more outrageous than Sager's ac-count of the mythical Al Devendorf inventing the original Ping putter in a Syracuse television factory. Naturally, I didn't want to tell this sweet old fella that he was full of Boston baked beans, so I politely pried loose my arm, grateful for the sudden rush of blood to my fingers, and promised I'd investigate the story as soon as I returned to the wild and wooly state of Maine.

"You don't need to investigate what I'm telling you!" he shouted at me. "It's completely true! By the way, we're the hanging nuts!"

"I'm sorry?"

"Those guys you mentioned who play every weekend morning. At my club north of town, we go out every Saturday morning no matter what the hell the conditions are—rain, snow, bad tickers! My wife once said we were all nuts. And I told her she didn't know anything. We're all *hanging* nuts! That's how we got our name!"

A man named Dan thanked me for coming and offered me his hand. He also smiled politely and asked me if I'd ever played Kittansett Golf Club down on Buzzard's Bay.

"Are you *kidding*?" I replied, "That's just about my favorite golf course on this earth."

"Maybe you'd like to bring the Dewsweepers there to play," he suggested.

"If you're taking them to Kittansett," another man said, leaning into the conversation. "You really ought to have them see Hyannisport Country Club, too." He presented his card and my head began to swim. Hearing this, a distinguished bow-tied gent beside him tilted forward and smoothly observed that if we were headed out that direction anyway, we definitely shouldn't miss cute little Eastward Ho!, where Jess Sweester used to play. He added that he would be pleased to see about arranging a visit.

"Wow," I think I must have said articulately at this point.

Tom Landry, the MGA's polished executive director who presides over a low handicap and the organization's 360 or so affiliated clubs, stepped in at this point to prevent me from slobbering all over my complimentary MGA striped necktie out of awe and simple bovine gratitude.

"Give me a day or two to work on it," he said with a custodial wink that would have done Bay State native son and PGA Tour impresario Fred Corcoran very proud indeed. "We can probably put together an itinerary that will make the Dewsweepers forget their striking airline and Myrtle Beach."

We shook hands to seal the deal and he smiled as if a little devil on his shoulder had whispered in his ear.

"Do you think," he added almost as an aside, "the Dewsweepers might be up for a friendly little Ryder Cup–style match at Kittansett? Nothing too serious. It could be kind of . . . fun."

I smiled back and assured him we would like nothing better.

• • •

I<small>T</small> was late when I got back to Maine. My mom's light was still on at the Highlands, though, and she invited me in for a nightcap and placed a small glass of sherry in my hand.

"You look so nice dressed up like that," said Mrs. Congeniality. "Have you been to church?"

"Yes ma'am," I replied and explained that I'd made a speech to the congregants of the mother church of American golf, the Mass Golf Association. I told her that I would be going to Cape Cod instead of South Carolina with the Dewsweepers.

"I love Cape Cod," she said fondly. "Your father took me there once. I love all those little gray houses. We looked for the Kennedys but didn't see them." She sipped her sherry, glancing at the TV where some frighteningly muscled guy with a head the size of a cabbage was peddling an abdomen-flattening machine before the conclusion of Mom's Spencer Tracy movie came back on.

"I miss him," she said simply, still staring at the TV screen. I was fairly certain she didn't mean either Spencer Tracy or Mr. Cabbagehead.

"I know you do. I do, too."

She sighed and smiled and looked at me again.

"I was thinking I might go home to North Carolina," she said. "Just for the summer."

I sipped my sherry.

"Mom," I said gently, "you can't go home to North Carolina. Your home is here now."

She smiled sweetly. "Why ever can't I? I still have my house there. I mean, darling, Maine has been lovely. I adore seeing Maggie and Jack regularly. I just want to see everybody in Greensboro for a while."

"That's the problem," I said, wondering if I should open up this topic once again. We'd already had several versions of this conversation—though she'd apparently forgotten them all. "You no longer *have* a house there anymore. You gave it . . . away."

She searched my eyes with her sky-blue ones and then laughed like that was the funniest thing she'd heard since Pat met Mike or Tracy met Hepburn.

"Don't be *ridiculous*, Sugar. Why on earth would I do *that*? And to whom?"

I sighed, falling silent, doffing off my sherry. Her memory was leaking away like old bath water. I looked at her, took her hand, and gently told her for the umpteenth time that she'd given her house to my brother's new wife. I couldn't say why she'd done that. But she had.

"I certainly did *not*," she declared indignantly, pulling back her hand like an angry child. "All I signed was a piece of paper that allowed your brother and her to live there and fix up the house. We *all* own that house. It's yours too! That's the way your father wanted it."

"Well," I said, "not anymore, Mom. The paper you signed was a legal document transferring ownership of the deed to Miss Clairol. Don't ask me why."

"That's absurd," she added primly, switching her attention to the television where we'd missed the end of the movie and now the late news had come on. "I'll just call them and tell them it was a silly mistake on my part. I want my house back."

I watched the news with her for a few moments, wishing like hell that my father was still alive. My horse in the presidential race, John McCain, had been slaughtered by Bush Minor in the South Carolina presidential primary and the airline strike was definitely happening. At least the Dewsweeper trip was still happening, too. The idea of going to Kittansett after the idles of a long hard New England winter almost made up for the family madness of recent weeks.

I finished my sherry and said good night. Mom walked me to her door.

"First thing in the morning," she instructed sweetly, "please call your brother and tell him I want my house back."

"Mom," I said with a note of exasperation. "I've done that already."

"What did he say?"

"He said nothing because he has nothing to say. He doesn't even *own* the house. None of us do. Don't you understand? You *gave it away!*"

Unfortunately, I said this with an angry whisper through gritted teeth and she began to cry. I hated making anyone cry, especially my own mama.

"This is terrible," she said. "What have I done?"

I put my arms around her and kissed her downy white head. Her hair was remarkably soft. We stood in the doorway for a moment and I assured her things would be fine and asked if she wanted Maggie and Jack and me to come for dinner at the Highlands tomorrow night. We just happened to be free.

"Oh yes, please," she said like a little girl, almost pleadingly, sniffing gently and lifting her gorgeous old face from the breast of my sports jacket, looking up at me with her movie star eyes. She gave me a bit of the Mrs. Congeniality smile.

"But only if you promise to wear that same necktie."

"Agreed."

"By the way," she said. "My new friend Stan might wish to join us. I think he wants to ask me out on a date. He says I'm the best looking babe in the place and wants to show me his fishing rods." She laughed like her old self. "Can you believe *that?*"

"Absolutely," I said, realizing she didn't want any part of what was going on down south. Her mind either couldn't or wouldn't process it.

"Tell him that your son says you're not old enough to date yet," I said, wondering if we would just gently go in circles until one or both of us returned to the womb.

My mother laughed gaily. And then, she sneezed.

"Are you okay?" I asked, peering at her. The last thing we needed about now was for her to get ill.

"No problem," she assured me, spitting into a Kleenex and briskly waving me off into the night as she shut the door.

"Spring allergies. I'll be fine in the morning, babe."

SIX

THE ROAD TO KITTANSETT

BUT she wasn't.

A week later, Mom was in strict isolation in the intensive care unit of Parkview Memorial Hospital, suffering from bacterial pneumonia and barely clinging to life.

I phoned my brother to let him know the news. He said he was starting another new job and couldn't come visit but would check up on her daily via phone. It was not a lengthy conversation.

Finally, after a few touch-and-go days, Mom's doctor permitted me to put on a blue cotton surgical gown and mask and sit for a few minutes beside her bed. She looked pale and remarkably small, her lustrous hair white as the inch of late spring snow lying on the hospital lawn outside. Someone had thoughtfully brushed Mrs. Congeniality's hair back. I took her hand and sat there watching her. Eventually she opened her eyes and blinked at me as if trying to remember who I was.

"Hello, Gorgeous. How are you feeling?"

"Fine." Her voice was slurred, dreamy. She cleared her throat. "How are you?"

"Better now."

I watched her calmly studying me. Her eyes were bluer than

normal, though it could have been the window light making them that way. It occurred to me that she really was trying to remember who I was.

I lowered my mask.

"Hi. It's *me*," I said, sounding a little like the Scarecrow farm-hand speaking to a dazed Dorothy after she's returned from Oz.

"I know, *silly,*" she said, and smiled.

Opening a paper bag, I explained that I'd smuggled her favorite comfort foods past the hospital ward matron—a thick chocolate milkshake and onion rings from Ernie's Drive-in, our weekly grease stop.

"Thank you," she said. "Maybe you'd better eat them, babe."

"I tried to sneak Molly up here but the surgical gown kept falling off her. She's waiting out in the car."

"*Molly.*" At least she remembered her beloved dog. "How is Molly?"

"She's fine. She'll be delighted to eat your onion rings. But I'll have to fumigate the car later."

"You're funny," she said.

"Just doin' my job, ma'am."

"I'm sorry I ruined your week," she said. "I should just go home."

I wasn't sure which home she meant—the home she had at the Highlands or the home she thought she had in North Carolina. I was growing weary of reminding her she was, in fact, already home.

"You didn't ruin my week. On the contrary, you brightened it up."

"You're nice to say so, Brax," she said, apparently mistaking me for my father. I was flattered she thought I was Opti.

With that, she shut her eyes as if she were drifting off to sleep again. I sat looking at her for a few minutes and then got up to go.

"Are you still going to Cape Cod with your friends?" she said. I paused by the door.

"I don't know yet. Somebody's got to keep an eye on you. And the only other person who volunteered is Stan the fishing guide. I don't trust that rake."

"I love Cape Cod," she said. "Your father took me there once."

"Really? Did you look for any Kennedys?"

"No."

"I'll see how you are tomorrow," I said.

"Good," she said, and drifted off to sleep for sure this time.

I left her room and went outside and fed the onion rings to Molly and drank my mother's milkshake in a patch of late March sunlight, savoring the drip of melting snow and my first undramatic day in at least a week.

On Monday, Mom had nearly died and her doctor informed me that if she did pull through, because of her greatly diminished memory skills—he actually referred to it as permanent *dementia*— the chances were good that she would require full-time assisted medical care from now on and could no longer manage her current apartment at the Highlands. That would cost, I roughly calculated, approximately twice what she was paying now and took the shine right off my day.

On Tuesday, while driving slowly through the town square on my way to visit my mother, a woman in an SUV with Florida tags cut me off and suddenly stopped at the main intersection. The light was still green but my mind was preoccupied. I crunched her rear bumper, a minor fender-bender, my first accident in over thirty years. The woman phoned her husband and then asked to be transported to the hospital. She was released a short while later with no discernable injuries but the cop who declined to cite me for the accident smiled and assured me that my insurance company would soon hear from her lawyer. He was right, too.

On Wednesday, Tom Rohr phoned from Hawaii to inform me that my Buddhist golf pal Bill Kimpton had been diagnosed with a powerful form of bone cancer and had flown to Houston for a cutting-edge procedure that destroyed his entire immune system and meant he would be confined to an air-tight germ-free room for several weeks. The prognosis, Tom said, wasn't particularly encouraging. But on the plus side, Bill and Isabel had immediately gotten married—proof he intended to fight the good fight.

On Thursday, while picking up my kids at school, a woman I scarcely knew sidled over in her designer jogging suit and, blushing intensely, relayed the startling news that her estranged husband might wish me acute bodily harm. Months before, she'd phoned me out of the blue for advice about helping children adjust to a family going through a divorce. I'm no expert on the subject, please understand, but I'd written a book about my family's experiences in this terrifying realm where no responsible parent hopes to find himself; in lieu of advice, I frequently gave out copies of a book of spiritual meditations based on the Book of Psalms that I'd found extremely helpful under such circumstances and urged the troubled parent to seek a good family counselor. That was the extent of my involvement with this woman, but she now explained that her estranged spouse was under the impression she and I were "having a thing" and he was roaming around town with a loaded pistol, mad at her, mad at me, mad at the world. Fleeing like the madwoman of Chaillot, she apologized again and said she thought I really ought to know. After dropping my kids off at church choir practice, I calmly drove home and phoned a cop who came out and took down my statement. "This sort of stuff happens all the time," he attempted to reassure me, failing spectacularly. He smiled and shook his head, closing his pad. "I guess that's what you get for trying to be a good Samaritan. By the way," he added, "didn't I hear that you had a fender-bender downtown on Monday?" I didn't deny it. "Tough week," he commiserated. I didn't deny that, either.

By Friday, I'd decided I'd had enough of life in general and springtime in Maine in particular. The Tournament Player's Championship was on TV and my club's formal opening was *still* a week or two away but my veins were surging wildly with what I call *golflust*—a preternatural desire to hit a golf ball, any golf ball, even one of Terry Meagher's X-out rocks—so I took a ball out to the first nice patch of grass I could find and dropped it there, prepared to perform a strange little ritual I've done for almost a decade now—my version, as it were, of the swallows returning to Capistrano. The patch was in my front yard. Setting up with a sand wedge, I took dead aim at my chimney, the objective being to loft the ball neatly over my roof and dramatically herald the arrival of official golf season on my one-hole golf course. I swung smoothly and skulled the ball straight through my bathroom window. I went in and cleaned up the glass, patched the hole wondering if spring rituals were really worth the trouble, warmed up a cup of day-old soup, and sat down to catch the end of the TPC on the tube. The third round had been canceled, alas, because of heavy thundershowers. So I phoned Wendy, looking for a little tea and sympathy, only to discover she was zonked out in bed, according to her mother, with the first flu bug she'd had in twenty years.

On Saturday morning, I drove Jack to his final hockey game of the season. The Polar Bear Mites were playing a fearsome team from Lewiston, a handsome old mill town that specializes in unemployment and youth hockey. The Lewiston team had already beaten us once that season, 18-zilch. Mercifully, Jack had missed that particular slaughter of lambs. This time, approaching playoff form, the Lewiston squad brought a dozen cheerleaders and three dozen enthusiastic spectators on a bus. They all arranged themselves around me at midice, bearing blankets and bullhorns, screaming encouragement even before the opening puck was dropped.

Jack, playing center, made me think of a young Bunny Dugan. The puck fell and he deftly flicked it toward a teammate and started down the ice toward the Lewiston goal. As he pulled up to shoot, a pair of Lewiston players body slammed him from behind, sending him hurtling into the boards of the same arena where B.U. star Travis Roy—the kid who was paralyzed during the opening minutes of his first collegiate game—played his youth hockey. The Lewiston loyalists cheered lustily and a woman drinking coffee screamed, "Great *hit*, Joey! That'll teach the creep!"

"Hey," I said to her. "These are *kids*. And that's my son. He's a nice boy and not a creep. Do you mind?"

"Screw *you*," she said, and laughed merrily.

Lewiston was up by only a 3-1 margin with five minutes to play. The Lewiston loyalists were out of their minds and Jacko, if a proud papa may boast a bit, had played his best game of the year, scoring once, fouling up several Lewiston power plays, repeatedly getting slammed to the ice for his efforts. With forty seconds to play, he had another opportunity to score, a break-away that was basically meaningless. As he raced past me, the leather-lunged woman aft yelled, "Catch that little shit!" and a Lewiston player crossed the ice and cut Jack's legs out from under him. He hit the ice very hard, his helmeted head bouncing. I stood up, my heart freezing. The horn blew. The Lewiston fans cheered and congratulated each other as if they'd reached the Stanley Cup finals.

"Maybe by next year your kid will know how to skate," the woman offered in lieu of *Have a nice day!* as she departed the bleachers.

"Maybe so," I agreed. "And maybe next year you'll remember to take your medication."

She tossed her cold coffee on me. On the drive to pick up flowers and go visit Jack's grandmother at the hospital, feeling very damp and even more foolish, I told Jack how proud I was of him. He'd never had a better game and behaved with much more class than his old man. Mr. Dugan, I added, would be proud of him, too.

"Dad," he said, after a few minutes of thoughtful silence, "would you mind if I took golf lessons?"

When you least expect it, the sun suddenly emerges from the gloom.

"Of course not," I replied, scruffing his sweaty head.

• • •

"**W**HY is golf much better for a man than sex?"

The chatter at the dinner table was so loud I wasn't sure any of the Dewsweepers had even heard Jon Sager's curious philosophical question.

Russ King and Lester Austin were busy talking about the great spring skiing in Vermont, Bill Tuck was telling John Zawadzki about his new consulting gig in the business school at Syracuse University, and Peter Marshall was outlining, to anyone who cared to listen, which was basically nobody except Tom Cahill and me, his suggestion that the Angry Yoots play the Hostile Elders in something called "Quota" tomorrow at New Seabury and Eastward Ho!

That afternoon, in the opening round of the Cape Cod Caper, as the trip had officially been named, the Hostile Elders had surprisingly routed the Angry Yoots 3 and 2 and 5 and 4 in a pair of opening fourball matches over a fine but deserted Woods Hole course where, according to the lonely assistant professional, Brad Faxon's grandfather was a member but never showed up until the average afternoon high matched his grandson's Tour stroke average—in other words, about mid-June. We now had fifty-four holes to play on our own before meeting our hosts from the Mass Golf Association for the best-ball Ryder Cup–style finale at Oyster Harbours and mighty Kittansett.

Peter's game of Quota, at least from where I sat, sounded impossibly complicated—something to do with subtracting your USGA handicap from the number 36 then determining the square root of the number of times a TV analyst says a tournament leader is "playing beautifully within himself" during an average season of PGA Tour telecasts, multiplied by the earnings-to-profit ratio of your favorite golf IPO, minus Fluff Cowan's estimated pre-tax annualized income for the year 1999, minus something else that would ultimately determine one's personal "quota" target number, which you were supposed to achieve, if I heard correctly, before accumulating actual points.

Frankly, to be blunt, still mildly afflicted with spring golflust and dazed by events of the previous week, I was personally more interested in why golf may be better than sex for a man.

"Golf is better than sex for a man because if you're having trouble with your game," Peter replied crisply, apparently able to describe the world's most complicated golf game *and* ponder such profundities, "it's okay to go see a trained professional to get help with your technique." He quickly got back to describing Quota to anyone who cared, which was basically nobody now because everybody suddenly had a theory why golf might be better for a man than sex.

"Because you can't possibly go blind if you play by yourself," chipped in Friar Tuck, smaller but fitter than ever beneath his great bushy eyebrows and glowing Domincan stogie.

"You can play with a perfect stranger and your wife won't even get upset," suggested the ever-sunny Tom Cahill, perhaps thinking about the feelings of his beloved Nancy Who?

"You guys are going to get us thrown out of this place," Russ King, Dewsweeper Dean of Protocol, warned the table, to little or no avail.

"Nobody's *here* anymore," Zawadzki accurately pointed out. "They already got offended and left."

The waitress appeared bearing a final bottle of wine, demanding to know what was so funny. We really were the last patrons in the place and Zawadzki, always the soul of decorum, asked her if we'd managed to chase off the restaurant's other patrons. She laughed, pouring the wine.

"No. It's spring, honey. Nobody really comes here until June anyway."

Someone asked her if it was true that golf was better for a man than sex.

"I dunno," she admitted somewhat guardedly, "but maybe that

explains why my husband is always on the golf course on week-ends. *Is* golf better for a man than sex?"

"Absolutely," Jon assured her, as if he were summing up to the jury. "Consider this. You'll never hear a loyal golf partner complain, 'What? Sweetie we just had a round of golf last week! Is golf all you *ever* think about?' "

· · ·

THE next morning on the Green Course at New Seabury, a fine resort course where the grass had yet to become green for the season, Russ King, a 21 handicapper, shot a brilliant 39 on the front side to earn, under Peter Marshall's inexplicable Quota scheme, his quota and accumulate fifteen insurmountable points on the first side alone. Tom Cahill, his partner in crime, finished the outward march with an equally dazzling 40, to earn fully two thirds of his quota—effectively finishing off Zawadzki and me before our games even got properly unpacked.

I apologized to Z-Man on the 10th tee for my deplorable play, noting that any minute now I fully expected to duck hook a drive into the fairway and begin playing golf. I assured him I was, historically speaking, your basic back-nine player and gamely pre-dicted that I would at least shoot my age if not my handicap on the back nine, though it was highly doubtful even a score of 46 would do us much good at this point.

"That's okay," Z-Man politely attempted to cheer me up. "I knew you couldn't be as bad as you seem."

There is no worse feeling in golf than letting down a steady partner in team match-play, especially one who seldom misses fairways, never resorts to unseemly language, and maintains per-fect hair posture in any environmental situation. As Russ and Tom rang up point upon point, chatting about the uncommonly nice weather and their wives and the approaching Opening Day at Onondaga, I wandered around the New Seabury course like Chip the Teenage Tennis Star or a bloke who didn't quite know which end of the club to grip properly, leaving Z-Man to carry our team.

At least he made his quota. I didn't come within a mile of making mine, causing me to question seriously whether golf really is better for a man than sex.

Every now and then, I glanced back to see how our team-mates on the rear flank were faring and saw Peter Marshall gesticulating at the sky or Jon Sager wandering disconsolately by himself in the rough, a sign that their squad was doing about as well as we were in their battle against the formidable Hostile Elders Tuck and Austin.

That afternoon, the weather and the golf course were even more spectacular at Eastward Ho!, the short but rugged seaside track in Chatham built by acclaimed British architect Herb Fowler in 1922, the only North American course Fowler, creator of London's Walton Heath, managed to do before his death.

In a bold strategic move aimed shamelessly at rattling our opponents, the Yoots switched partners and Peter and I followed Sager and Z-Man out in the afternoon matches, hoping for better luck against Tuck and Austin. Our host, a very proper Boston-looking horn-rimmed lawyer who worked in some capacity for the Red Sox and went by the name Peter Lyons, explained that Eastward Ho! was built as a tribute and American sister club to Royal North Devon Golf Club, also known as Westward Ho!, said to be the oldest golf course in England.

I was pleased to hear this because Westward Ho! meant something to me even though I'd never set foot on the course.

That had been the favorite course of David Earl, the former editor of the USGA's *Golf Journal*, the man most responsible for bringing me into the brotherhood of golf writing. The Duke of Earl, as several of us he kindly mentored affectionately referred to him, was a nearly scratch player who seldom bothered to keep a formal scorecard—the result, he once told me, of having been a reconnaissance pilot in Vietnam. He had a plane or two, I believe, shot out from under him and promised himself that if he survived the ordeal he would never complain about a bad golf shot again. "Luckily, golf ain't real life," he liked to say, a prominent gold tooth flashing. "It's much better."

Shortly before becoming the top dog at *Golf Journal*, Duke got married and I had the distinct feeling that he'd never been happier when we met for lunch and a round of golf in Far Hills one afternoon just before he took off on a golf trip to France. It was there, while playing the game he thought was better than real life, Duke suffered a massive heart attack and died. He was just forty-six years old.

I told Peter Marshall this story as we played along the high and beautiful windy ridges of Eastward Ho! with its glorious view of the Atlantic and fragrant chilly breezes off the salt water of Cape Cod Bay. Peter was forty-six, too, and nothing stimulates a man's philosophy glands like hearing of another son of the game's premature departure.

"You know," he mused, "just hearing that story reminds me how fortunate I was to hook up with the Dewsweepers. They keep me laughing through the shittiest days. I never thought I'd have friends like these guys."

He explained why.

Peter was the second son of a Dupont textile executive who grew up in Delaware but summered on Squam Lake in New Hampshire, followed an older brother to boarding school at Phillips Exeter, and rebelled against the custodial life of prep school with a vengeance. After Exeter, he ran a YMCA youth camp in Georgia and went to college in England, where he had Ted Hughes for an English Lit professor. Hughes, poet Sylvia Plath's husband and England's future Poet Laureate, turned Peter, a self-described party animal and dedicated underachiever, into a genuine student. He returned to New Hampshire and met his wife, Cynthia, moved to Colorado and earned a degree in public accountancy, finished second in his class and was hired by a Big Eight accounting firm in Boston.

The firm eventually transferred him to Syracuse—"the Very Edge of Civilization as we know it," as he joked later.

After relocating, he joined Onondaga Golf and Country Club, where he soon met a group of golfnuts who went out on the heels of Onondaga's maintenance crew every weekend morning, chasing golf balls over the dew. "Given the club's reputation," he remembered, "I thought they might be major league golf snobs. My golf game frankly wasn't all that good and the last thing I wanted was to feel like I was trying to qualify for the U.S. Open. Who needs *that?*"

During one of his first tee shots, though, someone relieved himself of excess intestinal pressure and everyone burst out laughing. "No fair clearing your throat while the man is trying to hit his shot," Jon Sager sharply rebuked the others—and Peter Marshall knew he'd found a home.

Five years later, his career with Dover Industries was going gangbusters and he now commuted an hour to an office in Binghamton rather than give up life in Zerocuse with the Dewsweepers. It was Peter who'd first proposed that the 'Sweepers form a bowling team so they could see each other regularly during the city's long winter months, the same Peter who faithfully showed up with hot sticky buns during the weeks he was out of action due to a strained neck muscle. It was also Peter who brought John Zawadzki to the group, the nice guy with bowling in his blood.

I sometimes thought Peter would be a good fourth for the manly rigors of the Blarney Cup competition, the season-ending, no-prisoners-taken, seventy-two-hole, last-man-standing, politically incorrect, unapologetically vulgar challenge-cup competition that determined winter bragging rights between Jon Sager, Pat McDaid, and myself.

Thus far, we'd conducted two Blarney Cups—the first, aptly, in Southwest Ireland, which I'd won going away, and the second on Kiawah Island, which Sager had miraculously tied with a shot in the dark he had yet to stop talking about. The third installment of the Blarney was scheduled to take place sometime that September, at a site yet to be determined but very possibly in England—maybe even Westward Ho! if I could swing it. The other Dewsweepers were far too dignified to be exposed to the dogged competition and crude badinage of a Blarney Cup. But Peter Marshall definitely had blarney in him and therefore definite Blarney Cup competition potential.

This became apparent when Peter and I managed to win our match with Tuck and Lester by a one-hole margin at Eastward Ho! then waited beside the eighteenth green in the fading sunlight to watch our Yoot-ful comrades in arms finish against Elder Cahill and King.

From thirty yards down the hill, Jon nipped his ball beautifully onto the putting surface and sent it loping toward the hole as if it had eyes. The ball touched the stick and nearly dropped in for a birdie. Watching it halt, comrade Sager did a passable imitation of *Dying Gaul*, then snatched up his ball and stalked off the green, looking over at Peter and me for a gentle word of consolation. The Angry Yoots were now officially 4 and 1, advantage Hostile Elders. Both the sun and our hopes were sinking fast.

"In case you guys are wondering, that was for a halve," Jon declared tragically. "I sincerely hope *you* idiots carried your weight. Which isn't inconsiderable, by the way."

"As a matter of fact," Peter advised him primly, "we *won* our match. But cheer up, Jon. Without that magic wedge of yours, you might be just another twenty handicapper."

· · ·

AFTER that, as old Ted Hughes himself might have said, we hastened to a lively Chatham roadhouse, aptly called the Squire, for balm and sustenance. A loud rock band was playing something undistinguishable and the place appeared to be full of pretty college girls straight from the 1960s, blond and braless, and I was surprised to glance over and see that Peter Lyons, our proper-looking host at Eastward Ho!, had come along for the ride.

A beautiful college girl walked slowly past me and I smiled at her and Jon leaned over and whispered in my ear, "Forget it, Ace. We're so old we're *invisible* to them," and then he chortled and wandered off to sit with Peter Lyons.

A short while later, we paid the bill and assembled on the pavement in front of the Squire, where someone had determined that the Hostile Elders were going home to bed in Peter's Navigator and the Angry Yoots were going someplace else in Karen Sager's minivan.

"Nothing like sleeping on an insurmountable lead for a good night's rest," Jon teased the Dewsweeping Elders.

Zawadzki and I climbed in the back of Karen's van. Peter and Jon rode in front. Yawning, I asked Jon why we weren't going home to bed, too. My legs were aching from our thirty-six-hole march and my eyelids were beginning to involuntarily shut themselves.

"Our team needs a little team inspiration," he declared.

"It's all over but the shouting," Z-Man said. "But I'm too tired to shout."

"Never say die," Jon replied. "Besides, remember the famous words of Teddy Roosevelt . . ."

"Walk softly but carry a big stick?"

"No. You're only young once. But you can be immature forever. Now *those* are words to live by—at least on a golf trip."

"I don't think Teddy Roosevelt said that," I pointed out to him from somewhere beneath my closed eyelids. "That's *your* motto, Ace."

"You're right," he said. "I *knew* some brilliant guy from New York said it."

"Where *are* we going?" wondered the sleepy bank president.

"For an evening of high culture," said Peter in a fruity Englishman's voice that probably would have caused Ted Hughes to summarily flunk him.

"What *kind* of culture?" I asked suspiciously.

Jon glanced over at Peter and both men smiled.

"The kind you find," Peter said, "at the Mashpee Performing Arts Center."

• • •

ON Sunday morning, Lester Austin rode alone with me to the grand finale at Kittansett. A gorgeous spring day was spreading over Buzzard's Bay, presenting a teasing but unmistakable hint of summer's reluctant approach.

"Having a good time?" I asked him.

"Oh, man," he said, smiling pleasantly, glancing at the glittering bay. "This has been *wonderful*. Great course, terrific guys. Just what the doctor ordered."

Though I didn't say so, I couldn't have agreed more. Even Zachary's—a.k.a. the Mashpee Performing Arts Center—the lame exotic bar Peter and Jon had somehow found out about from Peter Lyons and dragged us into for a quick nightcap after the Elders went home to bed, had provided a moment's diversion. The place was packed to the rafters with golfers and businessmen in suits and early season vacationers and probably a Kennedy or two ogling bare naked ladies frolicking to bad rock music on a stage. Call me a complete rube, but I found the scene of wiggling wraiths more vulgarly amusing than exotic, thinking how far the art of burlesque, like most art forms, must have sunk since its glory days in the Roman Empire, remembering that I really hadn't been in a strip joint since the Madison Mayodan county fair in 1972. At one point, in fact, I admitted to my mates that I was surprised, legally speaking, that the home of the Puritan ethic permitted such full exposure of personal assets. "This is an Indian reservation," Peter Marshall enlightened me. "The white man has no authority here." "Which explains," added his sidekick Jon Sager, "why all the white men are in here." We stayed only long enough to doff off a longneck beer, admire the Venusian agility of a pretty blonde who looked as if she modeled Talbots outfits by day, and unanimously rededicate ourselves to the Augustinean proposition that golf is at least safer, if not better, for a middle-aged man than sex, then toddled off sleepily to the bunks ourselves.

The next day, we wandered around a handsome Oyster Harbours course with eight officers of the Mass Golf Association, managing to be swept in four of four matches. Afterward, though, in the true spirit of Ryder Cup sportsmanship that hadn't been seen in years, the Dewsweepers treated the boys from Massachusetts to a marvelous dinner at a place called Winpys where there were lots of hearty fraternal toasts to golf, life, new friends, old adversaries, Pedro Martinez's fastball, and the dancing maids of Mashpee, among other things.

Lester glanced at me. "How about you?"

"Absolutely. Just what the doctor ordered, Doctor."

"Good," he said, resuming his bay watch. "Frankly, we're all a little worried about you."

"I'm okay," I said, adding after a moment: "But thank you."

"Tough week, I hear."

"Yeah."

I smiled and admitted it might be one for the personal record book—nearly losing my mom, my first car wreck since the week of my high school prom, the crazy woman at school, Kimp's unimaginable ordeal, the Titleist zipping through my bathroom window, and Jack's coffee-stained hockey finale. At least my mother was out of the woods now.

"Jon told us a bit about your brother. Families can be so messy. Were you guys close?"

I replied that we once had been, but I didn't have a clue now.

"The hardest part isn't the money. Somehow I'll figure that out and take care of my mother. The hard part is loss of faith and betrayal of trust—figuring out what the hell happened to my brother."

"Maybe he did it for love," Lester speculated. "Men do crazy things because of women."

I smiled, realizing that was certainly a possibility. If anyone would know about that sort of thing, it was probably Lester, who was wise in the ways of the world. Jon sometimes kidded him about the years of bachelorhood between Lester's divorce and remarriage to Sheila, his so-called "Wonder Years," a time when he played as hard as he worked, a tale made all the more poignant because nobody any of us knew had worked as hard and come as far in life as Lester Austin.

His story was almost the stuff of a Horatio Alger story: the scrappy young son of a poor Long Island land surveyor grows up thinking he'll become a bay clam digger like his grandfather and instead wanders into an elementary school basement where local kids are learning the ancient sport of Greco-Roman wrestling; Lester jumps in, gets hooked, and—a wrestling version of Bunny Dugan—within five years is the Amityville champ, the 140-pound horror of Long Island's schoolboy wrestling mats, earning all-scholastic honors, all-state recognition, and even an appointment to the U.S. Military Academy.

As in the Alger myths, Lester's story takes an unexpected turn when his high school girlfriend gets pregnant. The West Point scholarship vanishes. The lovers get married, the baby comes, and Lester goes to work as an electrician's apprentice, supporting three mouths on forty-nine dollars a week. He still faithfully goes to the gym and works out. "Staying in shape," as he put it one afternoon when he told me this story during a round at Onondaga, "for I don't know what to come along."

Something, of course, *does* come along. Fate intervenes when his old high school coach points him out to the wrestling coach at Syracuse University, who likes what he sees—a hardworking, clean-cut kid, a married teenage father who is basically going nowhere—and offers him a full-ride athletic scholarship that covers books and tuition. Fifty bucks a month for food and housing also comes from an anonymous source that later turns out to be the physician that birthed his son Jay . . . Lester digs in and works hard, cleaning faculty houses and mowing lawns on weekends, lifeguarding at Jones Beach in summer, figuring he may someday be a phys-ed teacher at some school on Long Island.

But Lady Fate has other plans. Over the next four years, Lester never loses a *single* wrestling match in regular competition. He is tied only once. He becomes the top-ranked wrestler in America the same year the Syracuse Orangemen reach number one in the final coaches NCAA football poll of the 1959/60 season. At an institution where Ernie Davis and Jim Brown are already living legends, the coaching staff votes Player of the Year honors overwhelmingly to a skinny, rawly barbered, undefeated wrestler named Lester Austin.

But the story doesn't end there, of course. It really only gets better. During his freshman year, a biology professor plants in his head that Lester should seriously consider a career in medicine. He obviously has a keen mind, the professor says, but also an extraordinary work ethic. Lester is startled by the suggestion but promises to give it some serious thought and ultimately decides *Why not?* "My parents actually laughed when I told them," he explained that day at Onondaga. "They thought I was joking."

So, in addition to his all-America honors and Syracuse's most coveted athletic award, he graduates Phi Beta Kappa and a straight-A student and heads straight for the university's medical school. Two more children, Wendy and Terry, come along and Lester finishes med school in 1964, then completes his internship at Saint Joseph's Hospital just in time to be drafted for Vietnam. He's shipped to Fort Bragg, in North Carolina, where he runs the intensive care unit at the base hospital for two years, getting on-the-job training in anesthesia in the process. Sometimes, when he has a rare idle moment, he slips away to break the tedium of work and family with a new pastime—golf.

He's terrible at golf. But golf is a loner's game and a scientific game, he thinks, where your body and mind can shape the outcome of the shot. There are good breaks and bad break and no such thing as *fair*. His next-door neighbor at Bragg, for instance, a fellow doctor and father of five, a pretty close buddy, got shipped to 'Nam, and, ironically, killed in a plane crash while returning from his tour of duty. Lester realizes this fate could have been his own, how narrowly he may have missed it. Nothing is fair in love and war and maybe golf. He got a decent break after all.

After the war, he completes his residency at Peter Brigham Hospital in Boston, and is invited to join a distinguished practice in Syracuse.

Anesthesiology suits his personality. It is intensive, a little bit on the edge. "Hours of boredom interspersed with moments of terror" is how he jokingly sums it up that day at Onondaga, and elaborates why. "Slipping that needle of Pentothal into a patient's vein really takes you by the lapels because you're placing them about as close to death as a human being can come. It's a strange kick, to be honest—the responsibility is so huge, the stakes so high. It's really more art than science. I loved it."

One day after he returns to Syracuse, his old friend from graduate housing Tom Cahill invites him to go play golf at a local public course. Lester gets some cheap clubs and tries golf a second time. For the first time in his life, he finally has the time and money to play a game of his own choosing. He is a thirty-three-year-old father of three robust and growing teenagers, a good-looking doctor who is loved by all the nurses and sometimes can't believe how far he's come in life.

"That's when my life really went crazy," he said that afternoon at Onondaga.

. . .

STRANGELY enough, I'd never asked Lester to finish the story. But the road to Kittansett seemed as good a place as any to find out more. So, given the opening presented by my own brother, I asked him to tell me why some guys did crazy things for love.

"I can only speak for myself," Lester said, picking up the story where he'd left off. "I was getting paid decent money and I had a little time for myself. The kids were in high school, my wife, Carol, had the big house she always wanted. I was still a cocky little shit. And . . . there were so many pretty nurses around."

He smiled ruefully. "Basically, I tried to find a youth I felt I'd never been able to have."

His wife eventually divorced him. He found an apartment near the house, determined to try and repair the damage and remain a vital part of his kids' lives. I knew Lester had excellent relationships with two of his children, as a result of these efforts—with Wendy, the graphic designer in Boston, and Terry, who was married and had two small children, and was thriving in his job as the executive VP of a highly successful West Coast high-tech start-up company specializing in manufacturing logistics. The firm was called Manugistics, which regular viewers of the PGA Tour might have seen advertised on the visor of surprising upstart player Franklin Langham. His relationship with Jay, his oldest son, had been strained for a while as a result of the divorce, but after many years it was on the mend, too.

Marrying Sheila, he said, had settled his life in the best possible way. They had the same keen loyalty to family, the same unpretentious tastes, a deep love of the outdoors, and ultimately a shared passion for golf and a wild dog named Woody Austin. I knew Lester was completely devoted to his children and granchildren, and I knew that despite the relentless ribbing he took from Jon Sager about his weak bladder and short stature, there was no Dewsweeper Jon admired more. I seconded that opinion.

"Thanks for finishing the story," I said as we turned down the pine-girdled coastal road leading out to the sandy peninsula where mighty Kittansett's wind-swept links jutted dramatically into Buzzard's Bay. "It helps to know your friends have gone though tough times, too, and lived to not *whine* about it."

"That's what friends are for," he said with a smile that grew even wider as the trees ended and the turf of New England's greatest golf course suddenly appeared.

• • •

A FRISKY breeze was whipping off the ocean and the distinctive blue and white scallop shell flag of the Kittansett Club was fluttering pleasantly on the kind of glorious sabbath morning when P. G. Wodehouse would have said Madame Nature herself was crying *Fore!*

As the participants of the 1953 Walker Cup discovered, playing Kittansett in any weather is a pure and unadulterated joy, but visits there for me—this was my eighth and counting—always evoked a special reverence even before I learned, through the kind auspices of a member, that Kittansett struck a similar powerful chord in Henry Longhurst when he visited to cover what is often described as the most memorable Walker Cup on record.

The most compelling thing about that competition was not, after all was said and done, the final score. The Americans, presenting perhaps the greatest team of players ever assembled—and I'm including Ryder Cup squads here—ran away with the contest, nine wins to three, to retain the gigantic filagreed challenge cup donated by George Herbert Walker, USGA president, member of the National Golf Links and devoted patron of the game, and maternal sportsman grandpappy of the forty-first President of the United States.

What's most recalled by those who were either there or read about the Kittansett Walker Cup was the extraordinary spirit of sportsmanship that prevailed from opening swing to final toast—a level of competitive goodwill that has probably never been achieved in any international golf competition since.

Queen Elizabeth was in her first year of her reign and Augusta National golfnut Dwight Eisenhower was beginning his first term as president. In golf, Ben Hogan, just four years away from the disfiguring car crash that nearly killed him, became the only player in history to win three of the four championships in the same calendar year. Meanwhile, a few blocks from the White House, where Ike was practicing his putting on the oval office rug, in the maternity ward of Columbia Hospital for Women, I was also born—but that's another story, best told around Groundhog Day.

At Kittansett, the vaunted American squad included five present or past U.S. Amateur champions, two future ones, and a pair of future U.S. Open champions: Dick Chapman (U.S. Amateur 1950), Charlie Coe (U.S. Amateur 1949,1958), Sam Urzetta (U.S. Amateur 1950), Jack Westland (U.S. Amateur 1952), Gene Littler (U.S. Amateur 1953, U.S. Open 1961), Harvie Ward (U.S. Amateur 1956), Bill Campbell (U.S. Amateur 1964), and Ken Venturi ((U.S. Open 1964)—captained by Charlie Yates, Bobby Jones's old Atlanta chum, a wily two-time Walker Cupper and former British Amateur champ.

Bob Jones, patron saint of sportsmanship, also showed up to watch what most London oddsmakers believed was sure to be a quick American whitewash of a strong British and Irish squad that included the great Joe Carr and reigning English Amateur champ and legendary Oxfordian Gerald Micklem.

One of the great moments of golf occurred when American James Jackson, paired with Navy golfer Gene Littler, arrived on the second tee already one down against formidable Scotsmen Jimmy Wilson and Roy McGregor. Jackson looked in his bag and discovered an extra brassie and wedge, sixteen clubs in all, a serious infraction of the rules and two beyond the legal limit. The American authorities, led by the ageless rulesman Ike Grainger, voted on the spot to disqualify the Americans and award the match to Britain. But British team captain Tony Duncan strenuously objected to such a harsh penalty, claiming the remedy far exceeded the crime. The rule was waived, a two-hole penalty imposed, and the Americans still managed to win going away, two and one. But British sportsmanship won the day, and I shall now move aside to allow Henry Longhurst to pick things up from there:

No better evidence could be cited of the spirit in which golf used to be, and should again be, played than the incident that became known as BrittaniaWaives the Rules. Under the rules as they then stood the proper penalty for this terrible offense would have been so savage as to turn the match into a farce. It was thereupon decided to waive a Rule so ridiculous as to spoil the purpose of the game . . . This seemed to me absolutely in keeping not only with the spirit of amateur golf but with the general atmosphere of Kittansett.

Of all the places where I have played or watched golf, the Sage of Augusta's 16th hole concluded, *Kittansett, as we came to know it during theWalker Cup match of 1953, remains my favorite.*

•   •   •

And so, it should come as no particular surprise to anyone, inspired by the history and rugged beauty of the place, at least from the outset, marching out to do battle in full regalia with my buddy Tom Cahill in our match against Bill Van Faazen and MGA president Cary Jubenville, I felt I might even be the recipient of a bit of Longhurst luck.

I birdied Kittansett's opening hole, the long par-four tester, then proceeded to fashion birdie three on the doglegging par-four second. We stood two up at the beautiful if dangerous par-three third, the famous one-shotter over the sand beach and lapping salt tide that some say is the course's premier hole. I played first and landed my seven-iron shot on the small, slightly elevated putting surface, which looked about the size of a billiard table.

Suddenly, in my mind, golf's holy choirs were singing, Father Longhurst was stepping forth to give the morning homily, and I felt almost giddy as the result of the place, the companionship, and perhaps the fact that Doc Austin had shared so much of him-

self and had made me feel even more of an honorary Dewsweeper on the road to Kittsansett.

"If I'd known this was what we were up against, I would have
asked for strokes," quipped Cary Jubenville, and promptly placed
his ball ten feet inside mine—for a tap-in birdie that won the hole.

After that, the wind picked up. Tom Cahill played gallantly
against the onslaught of Van Faazen's brilliant iron game and
President Jubenville's precision driving. Kittansett, especially as
the track turns inland and begins to alternately resemble Pine
Valley and Britain's Sunnydale old for whole stretches, is said to
be first and foremost a driver's course, meaning the accurate
placement of tee shots is critical to a score that will later glow
warmly in your memory.

If I may say so myself, I was working on just such a score going into the ninth, making the turn in thirty-seven and then par-
ring the shortish uphill tenth, good enough to hold us dead level
with our insurgent opponents. Unfortunately, as we trod confi-
dentially to the eleventh tee, I committed the cardinal sin of golf
by remarking to my partner that in all likelihood my best play
was yet to come because I adored Kittansett's back nine and was
your classic back-nine player.

One should *never* tempt the golf gods in this manner.

Kittansett's eleventh is an ingeniously devious hole, essentially
a blind par-three where you strike your tee shot two-hundred
yards over a high cross bunker to a huge undulating green guarded
by traps. Tom made bogey. Our opponents both made textbook
pars. I buried my tee shot under the lip of a bunker and recorded
triple bogey. Suddenly, the choirs in my head stopped singing and
Father Longhurst gave the benediction—or was it *Last Rites*?

I won't trouble you with what came next, far too many bogeys and doubles to be worth mentioning. In a nutshell, I col-
lapsed like a cheap beach chair in a gust of cold spring wind.

Suffice to say that by seventeen, the daunting four-par where
the Kittansett golfer once again hovers in view of the glittering

sea, our match was essentially over and safely in the able hands of Van Faazen and Jubenville.

Up by the edge of the final green, the other four matches had finished ahead of us and twelve players thoughtfully waited to see how our group finished—grown men who'd been complete strangers not twenty hours ago but were now standing and shooting the breeze in the sea breeze and laughing at each other's jokes beneath Kittansett's perfect blue and white scallop shell flag.

The Dewsweepers, for the record, didn't win a single match that magnificent spring Sunday at Kittansett. Like our British forebears, we got thoroughly trounced by a superior team. But once again, all anyone would later remember was the uncommon sportsmanship of the place.

After saying good-bye to my friends and starting home to see how my mom was feeling, and feeling much better myself, I realized one more thing that really does set golf apart from every other sport.

The truth was, I probably couldn't have played worse that day. Or had a finer time.

SEVEN

CAROLINA BOYS

HARVEY Ward, one of the heroes of Kittansett, sat with the Carolina sun on his face. We had been talking for much of the warm May morning, on the Donald Ross porch by the main practice putting green at Pinehurst, about his spectacular amateur playing career—and the sad episode that ended it. This was the kind of work that made my job at times seem more like child's play, conversing with players from what I considered golf's greatest years, in this instance maybe the greatest player who never was.

After coming out of nowhere to beat Frank Stranahan for the North and South Amateur Championship as a baby-faced Carolina fraternity boy in 1948, and going on to capture the British Amateur Championship at Prestwick in 1952, Ward anchored two Walker Cup teams and won back-to-back National Amateur titles in 1955 and '56.

With a signature short swing that produced unusually straight tee shots and a lethally wielded wooden-shafted putter he'd used since caddying for his pharmacist father in a cow pasture golf course in Tarboro, North Carolina, Ward, most observers felt, was on his way to an unprecedented third National Amateur in a row, when the bottom fell out of his world.

The nightmare began when he was summoned to answer accusations that he accepted, in violation of his amateur status, travel and living expenses from his employer, Eddie Lowery of Brookline caddy fame, Francis Ouimet's pie-faced kid looper who grew up and moved to San Francisco to make a fortune in the automobile business. Lowery's lavish spending on golf—he was generous patron to both Ward and Ken Venturi—attracted the attention of federal and California revenue agents, who ultimately prosecuted him for tax fraud and prompted the USGA to examine the rules and practices of amateur patronage that were scarcely governed by more than a wink and a nod in those days.

"The mistake I made," Ward, now seventy-one and silver-haired, said in his soft Mayberry drawl, "was I went in to face the USGA executive committee alone, thinking if I spoke from the heart and told the simple truth and apologized for any honest mistakes I made, everything would be just fine. That would end it. Eddie *had* given me money for plane tickets and hotels, that much was certainly true. And it was a mistake, though I didn't realize it was so at the time. The rules, you've gotta understand, were pretty loose in those days—every player I knew got free clubs and was helped out by somebody financially—and I was also doing some legitimate business work on those trips, seeing prospective customers and so forth. And so I thought, foolishly as it worked out, that if I admitted my honest mistake and promised never to do it again, they would forgive it and move on. A top lawyer from Philadelphia later told me that if I'd gone in there with a decent lawyer, they never would have touched me." He fell silent, shaking his head. "They never would have done what they did to me."

What the USGA did to Ward was make an example of amateur golf's golden boy by suspending his playing status for one year, rendering the reigning National Amateur champion unable to defend his crown and thereby causing him to forfeit an opportunity to make golf history. On a recent *Golf Magazine* list of the game's most notorious scandals, the Ward affair was still ranked in the top five.

Worst of all, the decision sent E. Harvey Ward, maybe the most promising player to come along since Bobby Jones, into a forty-year tailspin. Despite a third appointment to the Walker Cup team in 1959, his personal rage at the perceived injustice deepened as his relationship with Lowery soured. "I got a real bug up my ass," he remembered, "and decided to show them I didn't need golf. So I just *quit* the game, almost like that, walking away cold turkey. Hell, I even started playing tennis! Of course, that was a huge mistake—my vanity and wounded pride. The truth was, I really needed golf. It had given me so much pleasure in life, so many friends, taken me so many places. But sometimes, as a young guy who feels life has given him a raw deal, you go a little crazy.

"After that, nothing really worked out very well for me. My marriage came apart, I started drinking too much. In retrospect, the only person I really hurt was me."

What followed, he elaborated with a rueful smile, squinting into the sun where several teenagers were conducting a putting game on the nearby green just days ahead of the latest edition of the North and South Amateur and yards from where the campaign tents of the 100th U.S. Open had recently stood, were what he calls the "Lost Years"—promising jobs that didn't quite pan out as planned, three more marriages that failed, a patented swing that slowly disintegrated, a golf career that never quite got back on track from too much booze, not enough perspective, and precious time slipping away.

At one freezing Crosby Clambake at Pebble Beach, leaning over to line up a putt, a pint of whiskey slipped out of Ward's jacket and slid across the rock-hard green. He followed it and wittily marked it the way you would a golf ball, breaking up the gallery. Golf's Golden Boy had become a court jester, the Gomer Pyle of golf, a living parody of himself.

"As you look back, you realize it all comes down to the choices you make at a critical moment in time," he mused, watching the boys, who perhaps reminded him of himself long ago—and made me think of my endless competitions with Pat McDaid, whom I was scheduled to meet for golf later that afternoon at a new golf course just out of town.

"Some things can be repaired," he said, "and some things can't."

Ward "repaired" his life a few years ago by coming back to Pinehurst to teach the game, kicking the booze, and marrying a woman who understood his demons. One of his better moments occurred during the 99th Open Championship when he approached his old pupil Payne Stewart and they reconciled their differences, an encounter that took on deeper significance after Stewart—who'd "repaired" his own life by rediscovering his faith and rededicating himself to his family—went on to win the Open and perish in a bizarre plane crash that stunned the world just days after his Open triumph.

As we walked out to his car, I asked the star of Kittansett if he ever wondered what he might have been in terms of the golf promise he never fulfilled.

"Oh, sure," he admitted. "There's a time when your eyes are blue and your pecker is red you feel like you can do anything. I was going to be the greatest player since Bobby Jones, that's for sure. But I don't have nearly as many regrets as I used to think I did. And I feel blessed to have just survived it all and be as happy as I am now. Golf is a healing game that way. Look at Payne. When he finally figured out what was really important, golf or God or both healed something in him. My wife and I now play golf with friends just for fun. Now that my eyes are red and my pecker is blue," he added with a chuckle, a mischievous glimpse of the golden golfing fraternity boy, "I believe I've finally figured it all out."

· · ·

I DROVE to meet McDaid thinking how similar Ward's story was to Lester Austin's—and, for that matter, perhaps every man's, including my own. We make choices and sometimes spend years trying to undo the consequences. My brother had made his choice and I'd made mine and only time would tell if golf or God or something else would fill the rift that lay between us.

My friend the Irish Antichrist was patiently waiting for me on the Tobacco Road putting green, studiously rapping balls with his new See-More putter, ironically the same putter Payne Stewart used to win the 99th Open.

We shook hands and then hugged and I realized Pat had a peculiar look on his aging leprechaun face. He pulled a folded newspaper clipping out of his hip pocket and, wordlessly, handed it to me. It was an obituary for Aubery Apple, the feisty old cigar-sucking head professional from Green Valley Golf Club, where I grew up playing in Greensboro.

"I thought you would want to see this," he said. "In case no one called to tell you." The *no one* he meant, of course, was my brother. But not only did my brother not play golf, he didn't read the newspaper much. The truth was, we hadn't spoken in more than eight weeks, and after calling off the lawyers, I'd decided to leave him alone with his life and get on with my own, trying to forgive if not quite managing to forget.

Apple had been my first, and really only, golf teacher, a richly profane character who sent a lot of fine players into the world of amateur and professional golf, a member of the North Carolina Golf Hall of Fame and an old war horse I checked up on fairly faithfully whenever I was passing through town. I knew Aubery's health, which was based on a steady diet of cheap cigars, wasn't great, but his death nevertheless came as yet another jolt to my jolt-weary senses. We'd spoken via the telephone only a few weeks ago, when Aubery called me to demand, in his inimitable charming fashion, that I get my *bleeping* hind-end to town because he had a "great story" for my column in *Golf Magazine*. Most of Aubery's story ideas were unusable or simply unprintable. I sometimes got the impression he used these brainstorms just to say hello. *So how the hell are you?* he barked into his end of the phone. *Stayin' outta jail up there in Yankee country?*

"Oh, wow," I sighed, reading his obituary.

"I know," Pat agreed.

The starter at Tobacco Road slotted us in behind four middle-aged men who behaved as if they were attempting to qualify for the North and South Amateur—lots of solemn male preening, soulful stares at the opening fairway, exaggerated pre-shot routines, lengthily consulted yardage books, and faces that looked as if they'd had morning facials in industrial cement. They clearly had no interest in allowing a twosome of hackers to play through them.

While we waited to play, seated in a riding cart, Pat asked me with a whisper how the Cape Cod Caper had come off. I whispered back that, despite misgivings about leaving my mom in the hospital, the trip had been just what the doctor ordered—awful golf but lots of laughs and a bunch of new friends made.

"You should have been there," I said.

"You didn't invite me," he pointed out.

"That's true," I said, "but there is serious talk of a Dew-sweeper trip to England or Scotland in the fall. Sager and Marshall wish to see if there are any decent exotic bars in golf's Holy Land. I'll make sure you get invited."

"Good," he said. "Hey—maybe we could even settle the Blarney Cup over there."

"Not a bad idea," I agreed. "I think I may even know the course—Royal North Devon. Sometimes called Westward Ho!"

"Shhhhhhhhhhhhhhhhhhhh."

One of the well-dressed contenders was glaring balefully at us from the rear championship tee, where he was about to go into a lengthy pre-shot minuet that eerily reminded me of Marie Kluttzenhooper's strange peacock dance at Pebble Beach.

"Stop talking," I whispered loudly to Pat.

"I'm not talking," he said, "I'm whispering."

"Well stop that, too," I said. "You're bothering people."

"They can't hear us," he correctly pointed out because our riding cart sat fifty yards from the teeing area and it was probably just the idea that we *might* have the temerity to be talking while a guy who loved golf more than his own family was hitting that was bunching up this guy's boxers.

"Well, I can," I replied. "You're bothering me."

The guy pounded a drive that hooked wildly over a sharp sandy ridge, and he issued a stream of blue words that would have immediately endeared him to old Aubery Apple, may he rest in peace beneath the Old North State sod. We watched his mates all hit horrible shots, reload and fire again, then finally drive off.

"You would think, if we're so annoying," I said, "they would have been happy for us to play through. We won't have this problem at Westward Ho!"

"Why?"

"Because you have to *walk*. And if you walk too slow, a sheep will run over you."

"I like that," Pat said. "That's the way golf should be played."

"That's how we played as kids."

"I know. And it was great. Except you won all the time."

"I won at golf," I reminded him. "You won at everything else."

"True," he said with a smile, as if remembering those distant innocent days that probably, upon fuller reflection, weren't so innocent. "But I always planned to someday kick your butt in golf, too."

• • •

Pat was the Dewsweeper in my life long before I heard the word or even had a clue what a dewsweeper did. We met the summer morning my family moved into the house on Dogwood Drive. Someone's old English bulldog showed up to supervise proceedings, and when he finally got bored of watching the movers do their job and wandered down a narrow path directly across the street from my house, I followed him, swinging an old sand wedge at the honeysuckle bushes that grew there. I happened upon a scrawny little kid shooting hoops in his driveway.

"Wanna play one-on-one?" he challenged me.

He was, as I say, a tiny little cuss—looked like a real-life Irish leprechaun.

"Sure," I said, putting down the golf club. "Make it, take it?"

He took the ball out first and I scarcely touched it again during the game. He beat me so badly I immediately demanded a rematch, which he won by an even larger margin, followed by a game of "horse," the game at which nobody beat me. Whoever he was, he beat me at that, too.

Following these humiliations, we went into his house to play a game of Risk and his mom invited me to stay for lunch. He beat me at Risk, too, so we switched to Chinese checkers—same story, I'm afraid. On the plus side, Pat's older sister Jane sauntered past his open bedroom door in her underclothes and, seeing us, shrieked and ran away. We turned and smiled at each other, bonded for life. As it happened, my new friend had three very pretty sisters, all green-eyed and Irish, and Pat informed me he was more or less expected to someday become a Catholic priest. His claimed his hands had been "blessed," whatever the heck that meant, and I assumed this might be one reason he'd beaten me so badly at basketball and vaguely wondered if he was expected to become a priest because he lived in a big house where pretty girls strolled around in their underwear.

After beating me at Chinese checkers, we went down to his basement to play billiards and listen to the Four Tops. Pat ran the table. Then we went outside and played "Around the World" in basketball followed by a game of croquet, followed by a game of darts at the back of the garage. You guessed it: three more wins for the leprechaun. By then it was starting to get dark. Pat's mom stuck her head out and asked me if I wanted to stay for supper. I offered to stay, hoping to beat Pat at *something* and possibly see more of his undressed sisters. After dinner, we listened to the Temptations and played Monopoly—don't bother to ask—and out of sheer athletic desperation I was about to challenge him to Indian leg-wrestling when my own mother appeared at his door, casually inquiring if I had any firm plans to come home before, say, Easter.

This was just the *first* day I lived in the neighborhood.

Basically, over the next decade, year after year, season upon season, sport upon sport, from Motown to the Grateful Dead, McDaid remained my best friend and managed to find a way to beat me in just about every game we played save one—golf.

I *killed* him at golf.

By the time we reached our respective state universities in the early 1970s, the Vietnam War was winding down and I was reading Hemingway novels and fantasizing about expatriating to Montparnasse with a dark-eyed beauty and my sticks in tow, in the meantime skipping most of my Friday afternoon classes to play golf with fraternity brothers. My best friend, meanwhile, was a hundred miles away reading Schopenhauer and Kant and going to anti-war protests, occupying administration buildings and plotting how to kidnap Richard Nixon and exchange him for a bale of marijuana from his slate-roofed attic dorm room aerie across the street from Charmichael Auditorium.

Thus began, shall we say, the "quiet" period of an enduring friendship, a philosophical schism best symbolized by our respective definitions of "good" grass. I loved the kind that imparted a perfect roll to a balata golf ball. Pat loved the kind that came from the peasant meadows of the Yucatan Peninsula. We didn't see each other for almost six years.

One spring afternoon the year we both turned thirty, I was passing through town on my way north, driving down Dogwood Drive when, suddenly, there he was—the same old Pat, cocky as ever, headed God knows where.

I pulled over and and he climbed in and we drove to our old high school haunt Ham's Pub for a cold beer, which turned into a couple of pitchers and a three-hour conversation, both of us ultimately realizing how stupid we'd been to let a little thing like Richard Nixon and the Vietnam War get in the way of a great friendship.

Pat was hoofing it, I discovered, because he was without a car and a job. He had reached one of one of those crossroads of life Harvie Ward would talk to me about fifteen years later.

Pat's father—Big Pat, as he was affectionately called—owned the most successful electrical supply house in town and Pat had worked for him almost five years at this point, more or less being groomed to take over the family business.

Big Pat was a charming Irishman in every way save for the fact that he had a nasty habit of getting drunk and firing his son in front of the other employees—then later phoning up to wonder why Little Pat was late for work.

The day Pat and I reunited to Hams, he'd just been through another row with Big Pat and, having had enough, walked out before Big Pat could humiliate him again.

"I quit before he could fire me," Pat said, shaking his head. "I love the guy. But he's killing both of us."

I knew how much this decision hurt him. The truth was, I felt bad for both Pats, too. Pat's mother, Big Pat's wife, who was called *Mary* Pat, had just moved out of the family house to her own condo, leaving Big Pat to fend for himself in their big family house on Kirby Drive, and Pat's sisters had all grown up and moved to Washington and Boston. Big Pat was completely alone and his only son was walking down Dogwood Drive, hoofing straight out of his father's life.

A year passed before we saw each other again. By then, Pat had gotten divorced and I'd gotten married. Unable to afford the plane ticket to Boston, he'd sent me a couple of sleeves of golf balls with the UNC logo on them as a wedding gift and a note suggesting we play golf next time I was through town.

I suppose he felt we had unfinished business. Golf was still the only game at which he'd never beaten me.

I learned Pat had taken a job selling light bulbs to apartment complexes and the city's schools and governmental offices, a crummy door-to-door selling job he did so well he was soon offered a regional sales position with the company.

The next time I saw him in Greensboro, about a year later, he was working as a sales rep for several original equipment manufacturers in the plastic and automotive fields, being mentored by an older man who would soon offer to make him a partner in his company; he was also engaged to marry a pretty grade school teacher named Terry and pulling down a handsome income. We went to a municipal course and had our first golf match in over a decade, which I won handily.

"How's your dad doing?" I asked him sometime during the round.

"Same old Dad," he answered and laughed it off—then explained that the two hard-headed Irishmen were at least finally speaking again. He also admitted he was worried about Big Pat's drinking. He knew Big Pat paid local taxi drivers to pick him up and drop him off at his favorite bars in town. Nobody had been inside the house on Kirby in years.

The next year, Pat's daughter Emily was born and Pat's mentor retired and he decided it was time to start his own repping business. He drove by his father's house to break the news to him.

The door was locked but his father's Buick was in the driveway. He looked through the window and realized the place was trashed. He phoned the police. When they arrived, he broke a window to get inside. Pat found his father lying on the floor unconscious in the master bedroom upstairs. "The place was a filthy mess, the carpets ruined from urine, the wallpaper coming off, the entire floor was covered with wine bottles, beer cans, and vodka bottles." Several prescription pill bottles sat on a small dresser, mostly empty, tops missing. His father had a very shallow pulse and his breathing was scarcely detectable. An ambulance was summoned. One of the policemen, Pat remembered, went outside and threw up on the lawn.

Big Pat was in the hospital for weeks. The complete alcohol and drug workup Pat ordered the hospital to conduct showed something startling. Big Pat was suffering from spinal meningitis contracted from birds nesting in the window fan in Pat's old bedroom, where his father had taken to sleeping in recent years, the symbolism of which wasn't lost on either my best friend or me. If Pat hadn't found him that afternoon, Big Pat would have been dead by the next morning.

Big Pat was never quite the same. He recovered enough to go back to work, resumed his drinking, being his grand jolly self when sober, and basically drove what was left of his once-successful company into the ground. He was soon back in the hospital suffering from a strange immune system disorder that caused frontline cells to be replaced by inert or dead ones—the body of the victim literally calcifying itself.

The excruciating disease typically claims its victim in a matter of months. Big Pat astounded everyone, however, by lasting almost five *years*, confounding his doctors and driving his daughters crazy with worry, making Pat's life a living hell at times. Big Pat was still an Irish charmer. "I would get a phone call that he was missing from the nursing home and I would find him at the Red Lobster, sitting at the bar with his nurse, happy as a clam, hollering cheerfully for me to pull up a stool and have a beer. I don't know if he even remembered who I was." Another time, Pat discovered a pistol in his father's room.

Little by little, Big Pat drifted away. He had no idea who the man was who looked a little bit like an aging leprechaun and came and sat by his bed to chat and feed him scrambled eggs by the spoonful. "Hey," Big Pat would say to this friendly stranger, "I have a great idea. Why don't you and me go over to the Red Lobster and get a beer or two!"

Big Pat had a heart attack and died one day in November of 1997. He was just seventy-four years old. By then, Pat had become one of the top industrial and commercial reps in the South—and he'd even finally beaten me at golf. As the end of the

nineties approached, not only had Pat torn apart his swing and
rebuilt it into a thing of beauty, but he'd also started seeing another woman on the side—a talented former teacher and LPGA
player named Melissa Stockton.

Big Pat, I think, would have been mighty proud of his son's final sales job. When the supervising priest informed Pat that he
wouldn't be permitted to take communion at his father's funeral
because he and Terry now regularly attended Grace Methodist
Church (where Pat taught the eighth-grade Sunday school class)
and he'd therefore "fallen from a state of Grace" and wasn't officially listed on the church's rolls anymore, Pat made him an interesting proposition. "I tell you what, Father. I'm going to hold
out my hand and you just place the host in it and if God decides
I'm unfit to be taking communion here in honor of my father's
life, He'll make sure I join him pretty quick."

The priest, it should come as no great surprise, accepted
the deal.

*   *   *

THE broiling Carolina sun had rendered the sand pits of Tobacco
Road one big outdoor sauna, if not hell itself. Almost two hours
had elapsed since the start of our round and we'd only covered
six holes that felt like a full eighteen. Pat held a one-hole lead but
even his pretty LPGA swing was beginning to wilt under the
staggering heat and tedium of hit-and-wait cart golf. It didn't
help that the course was a wild moonscape of a design that severely penalized players for the slightest mistake, the kind of New
Age modern architecture that leaves me cold no matter what the
weather.

"How's your mom?" he asked as we waited by the sixth tee.

"Better now, " I replied and explained how the previous three
weeks had been almost surreal. When it became apparent that
Mom would require full assisted care, I'd phoned my brother to
explain the situation and suggest that we split the additional two

grand a month it would require to keep her in the Highlands. He'd informed me that he "really wanted to help" but was going back to school to get his teaching certificate. He could "maybe contribute in the autumn."

I'd hung up the phone and driven into town to look at the Steven Homes in town, a pretty, sunny rest home that we could afford, not far from the Bowdoin campus. That afternoon, I'd even taken Mrs. Congeniality on a walking tour of the premises. She was now having to use a cane to get around. "Very nice," she said, eyeing the pretty floral curtains and the attractive common dining room. "But I think I'll just stay at the Highlands, honey. Or maybe I'll just move home to Greensboro."

"Mom," I'd said to her, struggling to keep a cheerful face on my growing sense of panic and frustration. "You can't go back to Greensboro. This is a *very* nice place. People say it's great. I think you'd love it here."

"If you like it so much," she snapped, "then *you* move here."

The next afternoon, wondering what the hell I was going to do, I began moving Mom's furniture out of her old apartment and into a spare room at my house—figuring she could live with my children and me with a visiting nurse until I came up with a suitable alternative we could afford.

"Maybe you reached this point with your father," I said to Pat as we sat there waiting interminably to hit. "All your noble plans have come to zilch and you basically realize you have little, if any, control of the situation. The gods of chaos rule."

I admitted to him that I'd run completely out of ideas—and, even scarier for me, most of my cockeyed optimism as well. That's when something happened that proves that God must be a golfer after all, at least a Sunday duffer with a nice mom, or so it seemed to me.

"As I was carrying out Mom's furniture, the secretary of the man who owns the place stopped me and said that her boss wanted a quick word with me. I went to see him. His name is John Wasaleski. He wondered if I might take a look at something."

It was a topographic map and rudimentary sketch for a golf course he wanted to build in the forest adjoining the new phase of the ambitious senior community he planned to break ground on that next spring.

"People here have really enjoyed getting to know your mother," John said. "I understand she is quite the Southern belle charmer. Frankly, we'd hate to see her go."

I thanked him and said that made two of us—maybe *three* counting Mom. But, due to circumstances beyond our control, she'd lost a major sustaining asset and we simply couldn't afford the more advanced level of fully-assisted care the Highlands offered. Without airing too much of the family's dirty laundry, I explained that I was in the process of trying to make other suitable arrangements.

"We don't advertise this," John said, "but the Highlands has a special program for certain residents who have a sudden change in their financial circumstances. In your mother's case, we might be in a position to make some kind of adjustment to help cover the additional expenses."

I'd thanked him again but said we really couldn't possibly accept that kind of generous assistance. Perhaps my pride or vanity was simply too strong, or perhaps my anger at my brother was just too intense.

"In that case," he said, smoothing a hand across the golf course plans, "perhaps you would consider an arrangement? What if we agreed to cover your mother's additional expenses for full assisted care in exchange for your ideas about the golf course we want to build. I understand that you've traveled pretty extensively in the golf world."

I admitted that I'd traveled a bit and thought about it for a moment. We stood and shook hands on the unorthodox barter, and the following afternoon, to her delight, my mother moved into the memory-loss assisted care wing of the Highlands, to a homey and secure hall where a staff of nurses and a friendly man named Norm looked after four other delightful ladies there who couldn't remember what they had for breakfast.

Mom had never seemed happier, I told Pat—at least in Maine. Of course, she *still* maintained that she planned to spend time this summer "at my house back in North Carolina" but we'd cross that bridge, so to speak, when we came to it.

"Wow," he said, shaking his head. "Just when things look darkest . . ."

"Tell me about it. This came out of nowhere. Manna from Heaven."

He got out of the cart and pulled out a 3-iron and began limbering up with it. The Irish Antichrist still had honors, though I fully intended to take them back—though, in truth, neither of us felt much of a competitive fire in the belly. Maybe the weather was too hot or the game too slow—the course too modern or the moment just not right for one of our fabled *mano y manos*. For me, at any rate, it was just enough to trundle along poking balls into the short grass, two old Carolina boys enjoying a chance to catch up and shoot the breeze, if not our handicaps.

"I guess, in that case, I can safely tell you the other bad news." Pat paused and glanced down the fairway, then shook his head, smiling lazily. "Terry drove down Dogwood yesterday and saw a for sale sign in your mom's yard. They're obviously selling the place."

I told him it didn't surprise me to learn this. Nothing my brother or his new wife did was beginning to surprise me at this point. That's why I was taking Wendy to Paris to play golf and see the sights—to quit worrying about what my brother did or didn't do and get on with my own life and Mom's. I was going there to research a travel piece and thought I might hike Wendy to the top of the Eiffel Tower and propose to her just for kicks.

"You're getting *married*?"

"I don't know yet. I'll let you know after Paris."

"This calls for an official ruling of the Blarney committee."

Pat pulled out his cell phone and dialed Jonathan Sager, Esq.

"I *knew* it was coming," enthused Counselor Sager all the way from his leather chair in Zerocuse. "I told Tuck and Lester the other day that it was only a matter of time till you popped the question. When's the date? The Dewsweepers will all want to come."

"Who says you're invited? Besides, she hasn't said yes yet."

"Of course we'll be invited! You two never would have met without the Dewsweepers. Maybe we'll *all* give the bride away."

"In that case, we'll probably elope."

"Do you have a ring, Ace?"

I admitted that I didn't and conveyed Wendy's charming view that she would much rather have a new set of custom-made golf clubs than an expensive diamond ring.

"Well, take it from me, pal," Jon said, "regardless of what she says, *every* woman wants a diamond engagement ring. You better not get on that plane to Paris without one or you'll be walking down the Eiffel Tower alone. If you don't believe me, ask the Irish Antichrist."

So I did. He shrugged and then nodded his head as if he hated to agree but did.

"Maybe you're right," I said.

"Damn right we're right."

• • •

THE next evening, I took my mother to her favorite dinner place by the sea in Maine. We sat on the wooden deck overlooking Harpswell Sound, soaking up the salt air and the spring sun.

"Your father loved this place," she said, sipping her chilled California Chardonnay and glancing at a family that had obviously just arrived into Maine for the annual tourist occupation. Parked in the gravel lot next to the deck was the family Ford Excursion, where half of everything they owned appeared to be tied to the roof—bikes, suitcase carrier, canvas tenting, lawn furniture. A friend of mine calls May the official start of "Luggage Rack" season in Maine.

"I know. He loved cheap fresh lobster. The lobsters used to put out a special security alert whenever they heard he'd crossed into the state."

"I miss that man," she said, turning to the sea.

"I know," I repeated. "I do, too."

I asked how her new apartment was working out.

"Oh, it's *fabulous*," she said, switching on a genuine smile. "Those girls come by constantly and can't seem to do enough for me. That Norm is *so* charming. I can't remember all the other ladies' names in there. But they all seem terribly nice. We're going on a van ride up to Boothbay tomorrow. Want to go?"

I smiled and told her no thank you. I had a column to finish so Wendy and I could get on an airplane Friday night and go to Paris for a week.

"You two are going to *Paris*?"

"Yes, ma'am. Remember? I mentioned that last week." And the week before that.

"How *thrilling!*" she declared and laughed like a girl who'd just been named Miss Congeniality. "Are you going to *propose* to her over there?"

"As a matter of fact," I said. "I might."

"That's wonderful, babe," she said, tilting her wineglass toward me. We touched glasses—my beer glass to her wineglass. "I'm *so* happy about that."

I told her it made me so happy to see her so happy.

"May I see the ring?" she asked with a conspiratorial grin.

I admitted that I didn't have a ring. Yet.

"How can you possibly propose without a *ring*?"

I repeated the bit about Wendy being more interested in custom-made golf clubs than a second diamond ring.

"Don't be *silly*," my mother said, laughing as if that was the stupidest thing she'd ever heard. "You'd better get a ring, buster. And a good one."

I told her she sounded like my buddies McDaid and Sager.

"*Who?*"

"Pat and Jon."

"Oh," she said. "Well, they're right." She set her wineglass on the table. "Here . . . ," she said.

And then I realized what she was doing—wiggling off the large diamond solitaire that had been on her finger for over five decades.

"Mom," I protested, "what are you *doing?*"

"Giving you a ring for Wendy," she said. "Your father gave me that."

"I know. That's why I'm not about to accept it. Put it back on . . ."

"*Take* it," she declared, and placed it in the palm of my hand. "Your father and I *both* want you to have it."

We politely haggled for a few minutes and then I gave up and placed the ring safely in my shirt pocket. Maybe my mother and my best friends were in cahoots on this matter of the heart; maybe I'd give Wendy a custom-made set of golf sticks and a diamond ring.

"I miss your father so much," she repeated, looking at the water again.

"I know," I said, admiring her pretty profile, realizing how lucky both the folks at the Highlands and I were to still have her.

"Well," she said peacefully, "at least I'll see him soon."

I didn't think much about this remark at the time, I confess. She said it so peacefully, so pleasantly and without the slightest trace of concern, it was impossible to believe that she was either wrong or that anything would be given up in the process.

"There *is* something you can give me in exchange for that ring."

"Name it." I'd more or less decided to at least get the ring cleaned and boxed—and would decide later whether to keep it and give it to Wendy.

"You could take me golfing."

I laughed a little. "You want to play golf?"

"No, sugar. I want to watch *you* play golf again. The way we used to when you were small."

"That could be arranged. Maybe you should drive the cart, though."

I was pleased to see she smiled at this. Perhaps she remembered the time thirty years ago when I accidentally tossed her out of a golf cart and broke her arm. Perhaps she didn't.

"My elbow still hurts from that tumble," she said, as if reading my mind, proving that even when short-term memory vanishes the distant past often remains as clear as a photograph.

"Mine hurts, too, which may be one reason my golf ain't what it used to be," I remarked, finishing my beer before we ordered.

"I'll risk it," she said with that fabulous beauty pageant smile of hers.

. . .

THAT next Friday, on my way to Logan Airport, I stopped by the Highlands to say good-bye and thank her again for the ring. I found her in the common room with the gang of four ladies who'd lost their memories, watching a Humphrey Bogart movie. She introduced me to her new friends for the third time—but that was just fine with me.

"Honey," she said quietly, "may I have a word with you in private?"

I suggested we walk down the hall to her apartment.

Once inside, I asked her what was up.

"I feel *terrible*," she declared, her pretty blue eyes puddling with tears. "I've lost something so near and dear to my heart. I can't find my diamond engagement ring *anywhere*. I must have taken it off somewhere and forgotten it. I'm losing my mind, I guess . . ."

I smiled and took her in my arms, removing from my zippered jacket pocket the ring I'd had cleaned just that morning. I'd even had it placed in a beautiful new rosewood box. I opened the box and presented it to her with a flourish.

"Hey, you *are* getting forgetful," I gently needled her. "Don't you remember giving it to me the other night at Cooks? You asked me to get it cleaned for you. Well, here it is."

She immediately placed it back on her finger, where it obviously belonged, and as I watched her fiercely admiring it, I suddenly realized that maybe my mother really had given her house to my brother the same way she'd given me her diamond ring, and both "gifts" had simply slipped from her memory. At the end of the day, she couldn't emotionally let go of her house any more than she could part with her engagement ring. That possibility, in my view, didn't exonerate my brother from his disappointing actions of late or repair the shattered trust that lay between us, but perhaps it was at least a step toward fixing what was broken.

"It looks like it's been there forever," I commented to Mrs. Congeniality, admiring the gorgeous ring on her finger.

"I know. Your father gave it to me. I love it *so* much."

She looked up at me and smiled hugely, childlike, those great blue robin's egg eyes leaking gratefully, unable to say any more than that.

EIGHT

DIVOTS OF THE GODS

THE Golf Club de Chantilly was home to ten French Opens and had once been ranked the number two course in all of Europe by Britain's *Golf World* magazine. Set on the edge of a royal forest in the rolling countryside of Picardy, approached through a medieval village where the narrow streets wander whimsically around a famous racetrack and a breathtaking château, France's greatest golf club sat drowsing in the warm Impressionist sunlight of a lazy Friday afternoon, with—*sacré bleu!*—nary a soul about and only cuckoos calling dreamily from the surrounding forest.

"Maybe it's closed," Wendy said, admiring the lush vast lawn and beautiful timbered clubhouse, clearly feasting her eyes on the place.

"Nope," I said, "look," pointing to a pair of golfing *madames* who had just appeared, wobbling out with trolleys to the first tee of Parcours des Longères, the less famous of the club's sister courses. Both tracks, I knew, had been recently dressed up by my friend Donald Steel, the dean of British architects, who had agreed to give some thought to an autumn Dewsweeper trip, perhaps steer us to some lesser-known British clubs where most civilian American golfers never set foot. Places just like Chantilly.

I'd been there once before, five years ago, playing the vaunted Parcours de l'Ancien Vineuil, or old course, through a thick November rain and Picardy fog bank, seeing only enough of the place to guarantee that I would hasten back some distant day when the sun was shining. Happily, that day was finally here and so was my favorite golf girl, to share the experience. Unhappily, there was probably only two or three hours of sunlight left at most, and the club—like many across Europe—was closed to outside visitors come the weekend. It was either play today by sundown or perhaps wait another five years.

"I'm not sure we could get in a full eighteen," I cautioned, checking my watch. "But shall we give it the good old American try?"

"Why not? I think I might hate to miss *this*," she agreed, reminding me why I was so nuts about this woman.

Frankly, Wendy would have been well within her rights to beg off politely because we'd already had the kind of day that inspires Visa commercials and travel posters. We'd commenced just after dawn up the road at Aprément, dewsweeping a beautiful John Jacobs parkland course in just shy of three hours, then pushed on to the ancient stone village of Senlis, twenty kilometers away, where we lunched in a fabulous *pâtisserie* and hoofed through the medieval cathedral where Joan of Arc once rallied her troops and dozens of feature films have been made, then followed a tunnel of magnificent sycamores along the picturesque River Oise to the market town of Compiègne, where my father had been stationed following the *Libération de Paris*, home to a decent little golf club that was creatively woven into the turf of a famous steeplechase course—which just happened to be running its final race of the day when we serendipitously ambled up. On a lark, we plunked twenty francs on the number eight horse and watched it gallop from dead last to win, thus sending an unexpected windfall of 144 francs back at us through the betting window, which we promptly squandered in the local farmer's market on truffle-flavored vinegar, fresh raspberries, three kinds of cheese, and two bottles of the locally wrung cabernet.

Now at Chantilly, with no further ado, we fetched our golf bags from the car's boot, presented eight hundred francs to a girl named Marie doing her nails, and strolled out to the empty first tee of the championship Vineuil course, which was a little bit like paying fifty-five bucks apiece and being pointed to the opening hole of Merion or Winged Foot while the members are away at Rich Persons Camp.

"This is like an antidote for that goofy dream I had so often last year," I confided to Wendy as we walked to the tee with only the sound of our footsteps and the cuckoos audible. "Instead of arriving late and finding McDaid and Sager already out on the course and you consorting with a convicted killer, we've got nobody around, a gorgeous day, and real live cuckoo clocks in the woods. Does it get any better than this?"

"Too much work and not enough play," she said. "That's what *that* dream meant. The only way this day could possibly get any better is if there is a nice French supper waiting somewhere for us afterwards."

"We'll find one of those, too."

Created around the turn of the century by Tom Simpson, one of the lesser-known but true masters of early golf design—a crusty tempered, beret-wearing British aristocrat who earned a law degree from Trinity Hall, Cambridge, only to ditch his budding law career and become a course architect instead—Simpson's Vineuil merely topped the list of his acknowledged masterpieces, which included Morfontaine and Fontainebleau in France, Royal Antwerp in Belgium, England's Sunningdale Old, and a popular little golf spa on the Southwest coast of Ireland called Ballybunion Old, site of the first-ever Blarney Cup competition (a tale meant for proper airing when there are no small pets or impressionable children present).

Simpson worshipped the Old Course at Saint Andrews and wrote that no architect worth his salt should ever look anyplace else for inspiration, subscribing passionately to the gospel of design subtlety encountered there in the birthplace of the game—hazards that are typically within view, fairways that place emphasis on strategetic shotmaking, putting surfaces that are firm but quietly dangerous.

Most of all, Simpson seems to have adored bunkering, especially daunting cross-bunkering of the type you encounter straight off at Vineuil's opening hole, a sweeping four-par of 412 meters that plunges downhill and back up and lustily encourages you to swing for the outfield fences. I did just that and found my tee ball half buried in the face of the opening cross-bunker, still 170 meters to go to the green.

"Now *that's* a sand trap," Wendy said with a laugh, surveying the damage and admiring the way the ancient turf of the bunker's grassy brow naturally heaved like a smooth Atlantic roller far at sea.

"No," I pointed out politely, mindful she was still a delicate newcomer to the game, "that's a *bunker*. Only Americans call these sand traps. If you called this a sand trap around Tom Simpson, he'd sneer at you beneath his beret and smack you with his shooting stick."

"He carried a shooting stick?"

"He also traveled in a chauffeur-driven Rolls and wore a cloak," I said, being something of a walking authority on Simpson thanks to Donald Steel and his design protégés, Martin Ebert and Tom Stewart, not to mention Father Longhurst himself, who held the eccentric Simpson in the highest esteem due to his unwavering hostility toward greens committees and governmental meddling in any shape or form.

"He fervently believed the element of luck was an essential part of any golf examination and that every golf course *must* have an out-of-bounds," I pointed out, somewhat didactically. "Furthermore, he advocated banning the sand wedge and halving the

number of clubs you're allowed to legally carry in competition—
a way to return shotmaking to the game. Talk about a cure for
what ails modern professional golf. That would be a good start."

Wendy smiled charmingly and wondered if I intended to
stand there lecturing on the brilliance of Tom Simpson or try and
get my ball out of the sand.

"You're right. Stand back, love. This could get ugly."

I climbed down in the bunker with a sand wedge and an
8-iron both in hand, fully aware that the only reasonable play was
blasting out sideways, which was obviously what that crafty old
beret-wearing bugger meant for me to do.

"You know," she mused pleasantly, "these bunkers look like
they were left by a giant sand wedge or something."

"Yep," I agreed, trying to calculate if I could somehow lay
open the face of my wedge and *pound* the ball just over the lip
and at least advance it a few meters toward the hole. Playing out
sideways, after all, is like asking road directions when you're on
the verge of being lost or watching Rosie O'Donnell for fun—
something most men are constitutionally unprepared to do. Besides, with all due modesty, I submit that sand play is one of the
few strong parts of my game.

"Like a divot of the gods."

"Right. Very poetic. Brace yourself."

"Why don't you play it out to the side?" she wondered pleasantly, as if that unmanly strategy *hadn't* occurred to me already
and been quickly discarded.

"Because," I said patiently. "I don't want to do that. Watch
this."

I swung hard and drilled my ball into the bunker's sneer-
ing upper lip. The ball richocheted ten feet straight up in the air
and fell, give or take the length of a noble Gallic nose, directly at
my feet.

"Uh oh," Wendy said, and covered her laughing mouth with a
gloved hand. "It looks like the gods, or at least Mr. Simpson,
won."

"What do you expect from a guy who wore a cape, for Pete's sake? The devil wears a cape, you know," I pointed out. "Probably a beret, too."

I made double bogey on the first hole and wondered if maybe one more loop that day was really one loop too many. When I get tired I get lazy and when I get lazy I hit truly awful golf shots that make me think I'd be far better off taking up backgammon, a game that strikes me as utterly pointless unless you are either rich, French, or so bored out of your skull you would consider watching Rosie O'Donnell.

Par failed to heed the call *pour moi*, in fact, until the difficult fourth hole, and not again until the magestically cross-bunkered par-five eighth. Chantilly's front nine concludes with rare back-to-back five-pars, which I parred to finish the outward march in a woeful 43, having spent all of my USGA handicap and then some on just the opening nine holes.

Wendy Anne, on the other hand, finished the front halve with her best nine-hole score ever, a nifty 54. When I suggested we repair to the clubhouse bar and have a valedictory pastis or glass of Château de Golfball, she would have none of it. "We've still got an hour of sunlight," she chirped enthusiastically. "Can't we *please* try and get in the final nine? Please, please, *s'il vous plaît?*"

What kind of heartless beast could possibly say *non* to that tender beginner's entreaty? Maybe it was the fact that, despite my disappointingly mediocre score, I genuinely felt more unexpected *peacefulness* than I'd felt in months, due perhaps to the knowledge that all I had to do was contribute a few Simpson-esque ideas to the creation of a golf course back home and my mother could spend her remaining days in safety and comfort, remembering only the good and forgetting the bad.

Or maybe it was simply because, after months and months of trying to make sense of the ways of the world and handle "grown up" problems I'd foolishly once assumed only visited other people's lives but never mine, suddenly and inescapably, here we were, lost together in the green vastness of French summer, exact whereabouts known only to ourselves and some French girl with nice cuticles named Marie, a pair of Dewswept lovers who'd wandered into a golf Eden of almost incomparable serenity and beauty—just us, the reddening Van Gogh sun, Simpson's amazing bunkers, and those dreamy sounding cuckoos. Whatever the true source of this unbidden happiness, the divot-making golf gods said *play on.* So we did. And, *mon ami,* am I ever so grateful for that little decision.

I birdied ten, another cross-bunkered beauty, in a most unorthodox manner, wedging into the cup on a razorback green from 110 yards, causing Wendy to whoop, applaud, and even dance a little Picardy jig. On the next hole, no doubt from all that jumping about, she was suddenly looking around for the ladies' loo and didn't hesitate more than a moment when I suggested she answer the call of the wild and mark her trail à la Lester Austin, thus nullifying the only marginal physical advantage men have over women on the golf course. "This is the first I've done this since a Four-H hike in eighth grade," she confided demurely with the top of her pretty head just visible above a flowering bush. "This makes me feel like a kid again!"

"You're only young once." I heard myself giving her a bit of the Sager motto from the heart of the fairway, discreetly averting my gaze. "But in the right setting you can be immature forever."

"I think *that's* why men love golf so much!" she said with a giddy laugh. "They can pee anywhere. It makes them boys again!"

"More true than you know."

We reached the sixteenth tee on the edge of a descending blue twilight, the skies to the west pleated with faint pinks and dusty yellow. At that point, we stood right next to the clubhouse and I saw through an open doorway several men drinking, smoking, and rolling dice at a table. My feet were killing me, I must confess, and I was certain Wendy's must have been hurting, too. It was really too dark now to continue, so I wondered if *now* we should simply call it quits and go wet our whistles.

"I think we should finish," Wendy said matter-of-factly, even though her back nine wasn't going nearly so well—numerous sevens and a couple eights bloodied her scorecard. I told her she didn't have to be brave, and she gave me the look she uses on Liam when she catches him sketching reclining nudes in permanent marker on the wall behind the den couch.

"Brave *nothing*," she said. "I want a complete score this time."

Whatever else was true, you had to admire her work ethic. Men have their will, said some wag who probably was carried to glory in the club's annual mixed-team championship on the slim but steady shoulders of his wife—but women have their *way*. I parred the next two holes and finished with a birdie for an even par score of 35. Wendy shot sixty for a final total of 114—no small accomplishment, as I told her, for a rank beginner on the second toughest course in Europe. The light was gone and the stars had come out over Picardy. But Chantilly's clubhouse door still stood invitingly ajar and fraternal male laughter spilled out into the night. I put my arm around *ma chérie* and limped her in that direction.

As I once attempted in vain to convey to a suspicious French customs official who got a bit peckish when I wondered if he knew the proper translation for "French virgin" (answer: *pièce de résistance*), I like to think I handle the theatrical language of France pretty darn well, all things considered, for a guy who doesn't even speak it. I only wish people there understood what *I'm* trying to say to them.

The six chaps hunkered around the dice table, alas, were no exception.

They looked up and—seeing that one of us was young, attractive, and female—warmly greeted us like long lost kin, but looked completely stumped when I wondered if they could recommend a nice cafe in the village. One *homme* pushed a couple clean tumblers toward us and threatened to fill them with pastis until I made an eating motion with my fingers.

"*Ah, oui.*" He glanced solemnly at his table mates and they began an earnest discussion that could have been, for all we knew, a general debate about the fate of the battered euro or a discussion about which conniving tribe member should to be voted off the next episode of *Survivor*.

On the other hand, next to sex, food is probably the most serious subject a Frenchman contemplates, and luckily for us a pair of dice-rollers who spoke English returned at that moment from the loo, or as they properly refer to the facility in France, *zee place du peepee*.

One was a handsome teenager named Stéphane who spoke beautiful English, the other an older man named Nicholas who had a wild shock of thinning gray hair and reminded me of Angelo, Jack Nicklaus's old caddie.

"Here is what you must do," Nicholas proclaimed, quickly sketching a road map on the back of our scorecard. "Go to Guillaume's—it is there, *ça va?* In the Rue de Connable. Ask for . . . the *beeg* Egyptian. They call him Naba. Tell him Nicholas sent you. You wish a table in the back. Very important!" He lifted his glass and dramatically polished off the last milky ounce of his pastis. "We shall come along!"

Everything in France, it's said—weddings, christenings, duels, burials, maybe even golf—leads to dinner. Apparently, we were either taking them to dine or they were taking us. Dutifully, a short while later, we drove into Chantilly and found the bistro and Naba the big Egyptian, dropped Nicholas's name, and were promptly escorted to a great long wooden table in the rear of the rapidly filling-up restaurant, whereupon we were immediately presented crusty bread and an enormous platter of chilled *asperges blancs* as well as a chilled bottle of the local red Sancerre.

"You eat and *like*," Naba commanded with a confident, nononsense smile of a man who knows his clientele, flinging the stunning appetizers before us. We dug in like starving legionnaires just as our new mates from the golf club entered the

place, smiling and smoking, scraping up chairs, calling urgently
for more wine.

Nicholas had gone home and fetched his pretty wife, Dominique, who spoke little or no English but hunkered down next
to Wendy as if they were old college roomies intent on swapping
a decade of gossip, the two of them quickly plunging into a remarkably complicated female dialogue involving lots of endearing hand motions and passionate references to children, men, sex,
boyfriends, dogs, and, I believe, something about garden rakes.

Truthfully, I had all I could handle just keeping up with chatty
Nicholas, who was busy telling me about the golf shop he owned
somewhere in Paris near the Champs-Elysées and grieving about
poor Jean Van de Velt's historic collapse at Carnoustie and wondering if a Frenchman would could ever win a major golf championship, and Stéphane, who wished to go to America and either
find a job, a girlfriend, or attend college—or possibly all three.
Meanwhile, Naba placed a *steak au poivre* the size of a Michelin
tire before me, along with a mound of golden-fried *frites*, and
suddenly I realized that I was eating one of the best meals I'd ever
tasted.

"You must come to my shop," Nicholas insisted over the din,
and then laughed. "But of course I may be away playing golf somewhere, you know. This game addicts me. Will you go to Paree?"

Dominique pulled a face. "Gulf, gulf, *gulf*," she complained,
briefly leaving garden rakes behind, deeply inhaling her Gitane
and simultaneously rolling her lovely round eyes at her husband.
"I work in zee shop all day. All I hear about is about . . . *gulf*!" She
dismissed Nicholas with a weary wave of her hand and turned
her attention back to Wendy.

I explained to Nicholas that we did, indeed, plan to slip into
Paris—right after I finished my research on a few golf courses
around the City of Lights.

"You write a book about this?"

No, I explained. I was writing my final travel column for a
magazine called *Departures*.

"You quit?" The idea seemed utterly incomprehensible to him.

"Oui," I said, neatly deploying some of my fluent French. I explained that I'd written this column for almost ten years. The job had taken me almost around the world but all good things must end and perhaps it was time to move on and try new things.

"This season I plan to work less and play more." I tried out my new philosophical approach on him. "That's what a guy named Arnold Palmer said is the true way to happiness. So I'm trying it out."

Nicholas, dumping more Sancerre in my goblet, fixed me with a Gallically raised eyebrow.

"You meet *Arno Pal-mere?*"

I said yes. We'd met.

"He comes to France. He loves France."

Actually, I *almost* corrected him, it was Winnie Palmer who adored France and almost anything French—Arnold just sort of tagged along for the swell chow and memorable golf. During his first visit after the British Open in 1960, the Palmers checked into a posh hotel in Paris and drove straight to the site of the French Open only to learn that Arnold—the new United States Open Champion—had been denied entry into the field because of some minor administrative screw-up. When Arnold politely asked to be allowed into the field, he was brusquely informed that "not just anybody, *monsieur,* can enter the French Open." He got so mad, he stomped back to the club dining room, where Winifred was just tucking into her crème brûlée, ordered her to her feet, and drove straight back to the hotel in Paris. An hour later, they were on a TWA flight headed back to New York, and Arnold wouldn't return again for several years.

I thought of telling this amusing little tale to my host but feared I might come off as a name-dropping ugly American. As it happened, touchingly, one of Winnie's final requests was to take a "serious" vacation to France, which she and Arnold and Helen and Russ Meyers had done the summer before her death. She'd taken great pleasure later in telling me how Arnold had spent approximately *four* minutes viewing the famous Tapisserie de Bayeux and then wandered on outside "to get some air." An hour or so later, when Helen, Russ, and Winnie emerged from the exhibit, deeply moved by what they had seen, they had to laugh at the sight of Arnold sprawled on a patch of park grass not far away, happy as a clam, chugging beer and chatting animatedly with a old Frenchman who had no idea he was hanging with the *Roi du Golf*.

Well, both Winnie and Arnold were right. Life, I was finally beginning to realize, *was* way too short *not* to play golf and taste the glories of France and make new friends all at once.

I leaned over and confided to my new golf pal Nicholas that I was thinking of marching Wendy to the top of the Eiffel Tower in a couple days and proposing matrimony to her—just the sort of thing Winnie Palmer would approve of. First, though, I had to somehow lay hands on an engagement ring. Did he have any ideas in this department?

He pinched his lips and nodded thoughtfully.

"I know a place in St. Germain. I write it down for you. Very old rings but very nice. Why do you wish to take her to zee Eiffel Tower? Too many tourists there, you know?"

"I know," I said. "But Arnold Palmer once hit a tee shot across the River Seine from up there. I'm thinking that's the perfect spot."

"Could be," he agreed, shrugging like a human question mark, clearly indicating it wouldn't be his choice. He wondered what other golf courses we were planning to visit. I mentioned a few—Valecoeurs, Belesbat, St. Cloud, and St. Nom la Breteche, where the Trophée Lancomb is conducted every year.

"You are a most fortunate man, *ami*," Nicholas observed, peering solemnly with his large spaniel eyes down the table at his wife, who was deep in conversation and dangerously waving her cigarette, or my possible future one, who was drinking wine and smiling at whatever secret of domestic life Dominique was revealing. "Your Win-*dee* likes to play zee game."

Looking that way, I agreed I was indeed a fortunate *homme*, maybe in more ways than even I fully appreciated at that moment, lost in rural France with the woman I adored, if not quite a king of golf at least one reasonably contented *roi du* something.

"Oh," Nicholas said as if a passing thought occurred to him. "If you have time, go to play Fontainebleau. You will very much enjoy, I think."

"*Bon?*" I wondered, making a mental note.

"*Très bon.*"

. . .

W<small>IN-DEE</small> slept in on our final designated "golf" day in the countryside around Paris. After walking around six courses in five days, she opted to rest her weary feet for a full sightseeing assault on the City of Lights, and I slipped out just before sunrise from the lovely Château Belesbat and followed the signposts through waving wheat fields toward Milly-la-Forêt, where, eventually, a couple kilometers past the grand palace at Fontainebleau where Napoléon bade his troops farewell en route to exile, I pulled into the empty gravel car park of the ultra-private club of the same name on the edge of the royal town, home of another Tom Simpson gem.

The sun was up but the clubhouse gate was locked and nobody but a small gray cat was loitering about. So I followed it into a green shed where I discovered an elderly caretaker about to attack a lawn-mowing machine with a large rubber-headed mallet. He stared at me, unshaven and a bit wild-eyed, like a character from *Les Misérables*, but then spotted my Ping golf bag and realized I meant him no harm other than unforced entry to his golf course. He nodded, grunted something, fetched a ring of keys and let me in, waving in the general direction of the clubhouse. He lit a cigarette and studied me for a moment, gave his large bald head a small shake when I said "Merci. Par-lay vous Ang-lays?" then shrugged and went back to the comfort of bludgeon-ing his lawn mower.

The cat and I were alone. The cat meowed at me and padded up some crumbling stone steps toward one of the most enchant-ing clubhouses I'd ever seen, an adorable green and white Tudor-style manor house with vast Pavillion windows overlooking a spectacular first tee covered with a quicksilver of morning dew.

Golf in France is a gentrified pastime, a true rich man's sport played by only about 300,000 souls in a country that has 70 mil-lion people and 246 different kinds of cheese, which is why most private courses like Chantilly and Fontainebleau are frequently as empty as churchyards through the week, meaning you can often walk straight onto some of the finest golf courses on the Continent—assuming you can find somebody to pay your green fee to.

I walked to the elevated first tee for a wider look around the premises and a closer look at Fontainebleau's captivating opening hole, admiring the way the early sun filtered through pine boughs to a rough and sandy terrain that distinctly recalled both Pine-hurst and Pine Valley, causing tendrils of mist to rise off the wet grass. Fontainebleau sits on the edge of the largest forest in all of Europe, but instead of cuckoos all I heard this time was the serenade of contented doves, the steady thump of a rubber mal-let getting down to business, and the faintest hiss of a distant motorway.

A young red-haired woman suddenly bounded up the club-house steps behind me, smiling hugely and swinging her large shoulder bag.

"*Bonjour, monsieur,*" she sang pleasantly.

"*Bonjour,*" I replied, probably dazzling her with my command of the language.

"You are Amer-i-can?" she asked in deeply accented English.

"*Oui,*" I said. "By the way, that's French for 'yes.' "

She laughed and offered to make me coffee. Cely was the

clubhouse manager. She'd lived in Manhattan for a couple years and spoke English well enough to convey that she knew nothing whatsoever about golf, had no clue about the club's visitation policy or what the green fee structure happened to be, but thought I should just "go and play the golf" and settle up with the club authorities afterward, before the local *gendarme* hauled me off to jail for trespassing. I thanked Cely for French roast and hoofed straight to the first tee before anybody could appear and raise the alarm to stop me.

That's when I saw them—footsteps in the dew.

Someone, a French Dewsweeper, was already out ahead of me.

The opening three holes of Fontainebleau ascend a dorsal of sandy turf into the forest and feature all the usual Simpson trademarks—bunkers that look as if they've been there since Napoléon said good-bye to the troops, challenging approach angles, and subtle putting surfaces that must be respected to avoid *catastrophe*!

On the first green, the footsteps reappeared and I studied the helpful line where the French Dewsweeper's ball had crossed the wet green and just grazed the hole from thirty feet. Whoever he was, *monsieur* could putt. I birdied the first hole and parred the second and realized my swing suddenly felt as good as it had felt in a very long time.

I must confess that I love playing golf alone, especially on the edges of the day. If that sounds a tad antisocial, well, maybe it's simply that walking alone after my golf ball, taking time to set up and experiment with new shots and so forth, affords me time to wander around in my own head, sort though problems, ponder lots of things or nothing whatsoever. Goofy as it sounds, sometimes I actually hum favorite bits of church hymns, other times recite favorite bits of poems. Invariably, I think about the things I love and cherish most on this planet—my children, who are growing up much too swiftly to suit my tastes, my garden that is growing much too wildly back home in Maine. I count frequently overlooked blessings, take quiet inventory of stuff in general, and marvel at how things really have worked out pretty well despite my best-laid plans. I regard these moments of golf solitaire as walking meditations, opportunities to find useful bits of my true self if not my old game.

From the summit of the hill, where the third tee overlooked a beautiful fairway valley maybe a hundred feet below, I spotted him—a dark figure just walking over the hill with his trolley, vanishing behind another matched set of beautiful Simpson cross-bunkers.

It was the fourth hole before I managed to catch up with him. The Dewsweeper was an older man with large tortoiseshell spectacles and a frizz of gingery hair, sweating lightly in his red plaid pants and a matching navy sweater that read "GOLF." He stood discreetly off the green as I putted out and then asked, in very fine and proper French-accented English, if I wished to play through him.

"Perhaps we could play together," I suggested, pulling off my own windshirt due to the rising warmth of the day. "We could sweep away what little there is left of the dew."

He smiled, jerking his trolley gently along the path next to me. "That would be most enjoyable," he said, offering me his hand. "My name is Marcel. But only if you don't mind my game. It is very poor, I fear."

"Have no fear," I assured him, shaking his hand. "Mine is, too, I'm afraid."

Marcel was a novelist and a filmmaker, as well as one of France's leading screenwriters. I learned these surprising details over the next three holes of play, as we slipped deeply into an easy stream of conversation. He'd been a student at Oxford in the fifties, where he fell in love with the writing of Joseph Conrad, met and married an English girl, had a child, and first got acquainted with golf. In the late sixties and seventies, he'd written screenplays for several prominent directors in Hollywood, and in the eighties and nineties he'd alternated between New York and Paris, writing novels and films for television. He'd written thirty

TV movies, he explained under gentle cross-examination, and twenty feature films.

As we played the fifth hole together, I asked him what his movies, generally speaking, were about. Dramas? Comedies? He smiled and shrugged.

"Ah, well, the usual thing. They are about being young and idealistic, lonely and in love, terribly misunderstood, perhaps gay with AIDS, politically disillusioned with modern life, living in a country where there is a large component of unemployment and the bureaucrats run everything and nobody even writes decent poetry anymore."

"They're *all* about that?" I couldn't avoid smiling at his bleak artistic vision.

"More or less."

Despite his protests, Marcel had a nice swing for an aging Oxfordian who took up jogging when he moved to America and ran in ten New York Marathons and didn't come back to golf until he was nearly sixty. He thumped the ball quite respectably down the fairway, only slightly over the top with his downswing, which produced a squirting slice at times. After watching me hit a long draw on the par-five eighth, which featured the kind of brilliant "blind" approach to the green you seldom see in the *Etats Unis*, Marcel asked me if I could teach him how to work a draw. We stopped together in the middle of the sunlit fairway, surrounded by monastic-like silence, and I strengthened his grip, closed his stance a touch, and showed him how to sweep the club back and through on a slightly flatter plane. He tried it once and topped the ball. At my urging, he dropped another ball and hit a beautiful little draw, positively lighting up his intelligent Gallic face.

"Marvelous," he muttered with touching wonder. "Simply marvelous."

I asked him what he'd thought of America.

"Oh, in the sixties and seventies it was magnificent. Everyone was young and beautiful. America was on the go. Ideology existed! Even French intellectualism meant something! Thanks to the war in Vietnam, people had real causes! By then I was a widower. I particularly loved the American women! They were so *alive* and curious. It was possible, for example, to walk along Fifth Avenue in New York and your eyes would meet a beautiful woman. I do not mean street hustlers. I mean a *beautiful* woman, walking in her own glory. And she would look back at you and maybe you would go and have a coffee and speak for a while about this and that and maybe you would wind up in her arms later. It was so easy, so pleasant." He strolled along in silence with his creaking trolley, perhaps remembering someone in particular. "I do miss that."

I wondered, in that case, why he'd left America. We were standing at the ninth tee now, and out of simple habit I'd casually totaled up my front-nine score in my head. If I made a par at nine, I would go out in even par 35. I was playing the kind of effortless, unthinking golf my friend Laird Small would have loved. I'd achieved the blessed state of *stupid happy* and finally reached NATO. The Dewsweepers would be proud to claim me at last.

Marcel peeled off his golf cap and scratched his head. "I came back because I have a grandson in England and because, for better or worse, my work is very well known in France. There was a very good living to be made here, despite the fact that most of the young directors here today have no idea what they are doing behind a camera. They have no creative ideas because they have no genuine experience, no history. They are all nineteen—in soul if not years. They are the equivalent of Sunday painters."

"Sunday painters?"

"Manet painted every day of his life. Painting *was* his life. It was his discipline, his art. He lived for it. He didn't just paint on Sunday, like everybody else. Today, I'm afraid, these directors are Sunday painters. They have no story to tell."

Marcel paused and smiled. "Sometimes I think I should have

stayed in California. Perhaps I would have won an Academy Award. You never know." He glanced at me. "How about you?"

"A United States Open would be nice," I said. "But then again, I'm pretty much a Sunday golfer any day of the week."

He laughed. We played. I hit one of the sweetest seven-irons I've ever struck to the ninth green. The ball bit the soft flesh of the green and stayed put inches from the cup.

"Watching you play is exhilarating," Marcel remarked calmly, sounding as if he really meant it. I thanked him because nobody, including my mother, ever told me *that* before.

Several children were mustering with putters on the club's practice green, as if a junior competition were about to commence. So we hurried straight past the clubhouse to the tenth tee and played on.

Seeing them made me ask Marcel about his grandson. Did he play golf like his *grand père*?

"His name is David. He is ten. A very bright boy who takes after his mother, my daughter. Perhaps someday he will play golf. I do not know. He knows everything there is to know about computers."

"Small world," I said, and told him my son Jack who was ten as well, also a computer whiz who could probably get a weekend job.

"Does he play golf?"

I explained that Jack played hockey but had recently asked out of the blue for golf lessons.

"You will give them to him of course . . ."

"Not a chance. We have an old pro at our club who is in the state golf hall of fame. He's great with kids." As I said this, I thought about good old Aubery Apple. How ironic that he'd slipped away the same summer my own son asked to take up the game. Or what perfect timing.

"I think you are wise not to push the game on him," Marcel concurred. "He will show you if he truly loves it. And if he does"—here a quick, sweaty grin—"he will keep you safely young for many years. And how about you? With that game of yours, you surely must play in competitions?"

I liked that . . . *safely young for years*. But I had to laugh at the question, replying that golf was so damned confounding I seldom managed to play in tournament competition the way I played with my buddies or happened to be playing at that moment. Perhaps I got too nervous or tense or something like that. More often than not, playing in serious golf tournaments usually placed me in a state of *stupid unhappy*.

"Perhaps you should just play for the pleasure."

"Yeah. It's only taken thirty years for me to figure that out."

We played on through the doves and the warm piney morning, seeing not another living soul, striking shots and pausing here and there to chat about everything from Joe Conrad to the state of Parisian food, the approaching American presidential election and the woeful free fall of Frenchman Jean Van de Veldt.

Marcel had extremely strong views on his countryman's historic collapse at the 1999 British Open.

"It was disgraceful what he did—or should I say *didn't* do," he observed as we came off a par five where it took me a moment to realize I'd made my first eagle of the year—actually the first in almost two years. "Van de Veldt could have performed a great service to the schoolchildren of France if he hadn't played so stupidly at Carnoustie. Consider that you are Van de Veldt. This is *your* week and you will probably never have another one like it. You have one hole to play and a three-stroke lead in the British Open! My *God*. You choose what? A driver? Are you *mad*? Well, obviously so. You *must* be mad. Otherwise you would play three-iron shots to the green and become the first Frenchman to win golf's oldest championship! *C'est magnifique!* You will be a hero forever back in France!"

Marcel shook his head sorrowfully, rubbing a scuff on his golf ball with his blunt thumb.

"No. Instead, with the entire world watching and wondering what the *hell* you are doing, you attempt some gloriously vain shot and blow the lead and lose the tournament! You are schmuck! A *dog*!"

For a moment I was hoping my companion might spit on the ground in disgust, the way they always do in French movies. But he didn't. He started walking with his trolley creaking behind him.

"An honorable man would at least have had the decency to hang himself," he added thoughtfully over his shoulder and then smiled as if to say he was only partially kidding.

After I'd settled up my green fee in the club office, my new dewsweeping pal and I shook hands by the iron gate where I'd entered the premises three or four hours before. He wondered how much longer I would be in France and I explained only long enough to march my girlfriend all over Paris and up the Eiffel Tower to see if she would agree to become my wife. My only regret, I added, was that she'd missed Fontainebleau and him.

"I would love to meet her," Marcel declared and then pulled a scrap of paper from his pocket and began writing on it. "I tell you what," he said. "Do you fancy steak tartare? This place has the finest steak tartare in Paris. I have an important director's meeting in the morning. But perhaps I can meet you there shortly after noon."

He handed me the scrap. The note said La Closerie des Lilas on the Boulevard Montparnasse. I knew the place. It was one of Hemingway's favorite haunts. We shook hands again and I assured him we would be there.

Back at Château Belesbat, I found Wendy reading a book on a sun-splashed terrace near a four-hundred-year-old moated guardhouse where one of the Sun Kings kept his mistress comfortably stashed for many years.

"How was the golf?" she wondered, looking up drowsily and shielding her eyes from the sun.

"You wouldn't believe it if I told you," I said. And then told her anyway about Cely and Marcel and the stunning empty golf course and the cooing doves and, almost incidentally, about making an unthinking eagle and recording my first score of even par in almost ten years.

• • •

ON our last full day in France, we walked the equivalent of seven championship golf courses around the City of Lights. We spent the morning hoofing through the Louvre and knocked off most of the Left Bank, including Notre Dame, St. Germain, and Place St. Michel by noon, arriving at Edvard Munch's personal table at La Closerie des Lilas with five whole minutes to spare.

In honor of my new golf *ami*, who must have been unable to free himself from his director's meeting and thus failed to appear, as well as the father of German Expressionism, whose violent woodcuts once shocked the sensibilities of the formal art world and whose table we temporarily occupied, I ordered the steak tartare anyway, on the rough theory that when in Paris you go with the flow and the *plât du jour* and throw up later in the municipal begonias if you have to.

That afternoon, we saw Montmartre and Pigalle, moseying from Le Sacré Coeur to the Folies Bergères, traipsing from sacred to profane in a matter of a few blocks, then walked down the busy Rue Blanche to the National Opera, thence to Place de la Madeleine and a welcome snack at Fauchon, the great *maison délectable*. We just avoided getting killed crossing Place de la Concorde and hiked *all* the way up the Champs-Elysées and *all* the way down to the Trocadero. And suddenly, we were there—at the base of the biggest golf tee in the world. The Eiffel Tower.

Unfortunately, as warned by Nicholas of Chantilly, so were a few thousand other *touristes*. The elevator lines at the Eiffel Tower resembled a Ryder Cup crowd, save they were better behaved. While Wendy went to ask how long the wait might be, I spotted a guy from Cameroon selling nipple rings, cheap sports jewelry, and authentic faux Rolex watches from a battered suitcase. I quickly purchased a nice Nike sports ring for twelve francs.

Suddenly Wendy was waving at me, indicating I should follow her. It took me a few moments to realize we were evidently *walking* up the Eiffel Tower. Well, *Wendy* was—bounding enthusiastically up the iron steps of the 984-foot structure among hordes of rambunctious body-pierced German teenagers, while I more or less staggered along a dozen yards behind her, gripping the rail with one hand and the Nike ring with the other, idly wondering if any nine-handicap American golfers had ever expired of exhaustion on the world famous structure.

That's when it happened. A large, loud American teenager blasting *down* the tower slammed into me and the Nike ring went flying. I saw it suspended in midair for an instant, spinning like a Tiger Woods lob shot, reached out to grab it, and saw the ring flick off a student's backpack. Miraculously, it bounced off the steel-grate steps at my feet and was briefly in my grasp again before slipping away and vanishing down a hole.

When I *finally* caught up with Wendy at the west side of the second platform, she was admiring the stunning view across the Seine, skin aglow from the exertion, looking as if she'd merely performed a light aerobic workout. I slumped heavily on the rail and let out a sigh of relief.

"Would you mind if we don't go any higher?" she asked, blushing a bit. "I'm feeling a little weirder up here than I thought I would. Guess it's the heights."

"No problem," I said, gasping for air. "By the way, would you mind marrying me?"

"Holy crow!" she said, laughing. "What took you so long to ask?"

"I dunno," I said. "I needed a ring. Unfortunately, I dropped it on the way up here."

Wendy looked horrified, peering over the rail.

"Don't worry. I got it cheap. The guy even threw in an attractive set of nipple rings with it."

We kissed and I placed my arm around her and we gazed romantically across the Seine at the setting sun. It was the perfect moment to reveal another important detail to the dewsweeping heart.

"This is the sacred spot," I pointed out tenderly, "where King Arnold du Golf hit a Big Mamoo clean across the river."

"You know," she admitted after thinking for several seconds, "I believe I'd like to try that sometime."

I pleasantly agreed, strengthening my grip on *ma chérie*, though for an unsteady moment perhaps due to the unexpectedly dizzying heights, I wasn't quite sure whether she meant golf, the nipple rings, or marriage to me.

NINE

CROP CIRCLES

W HAT'S the worst thing that can happen to a man our age?"
Jon Sager asked. "Something that emphatically says, *Okay,
pal. Your youth is gone forever.*"

"You've lost the rest of your hair, begun to smell like an old
sofa, must get up to urinate five times a night, and Karen is making you sleep in the laundry room due to your awful snoring?" It
was just a wild guess on my part, I admitted. But I was displaying
some of the same worrying symptoms myself.

We were having our weekly phone conversation about golf
and life, more or less in that order, swapping all the news and
gossip that was fit to print between Syracuse and Maine. He'd
called to let me know the Dewsweepers were wondering if I ever
planned to come back to town and that his game was approaching
mid-summer form; he'd been dispatching good players right and
left in his evening league matches, tuning up nicely for the annual
Onondaga member-guest in early July. I wasn't a bit surprised to
hear Jon's game was growing as sharp as his wit. Unfortunately,
the only single-digit player I knew who had a history of collaps-
ing in big tournaments that could match mine was Counselor

Sager. Clearly, one of us had to develop a tournament game—and fast.

"Worse than all of that, Lump. *Much* worse, I'm afraid. I'm selling the chick magnet to buy a car for Sarah."

This was *big* news.

The "chick magnet" was a vestige of Jon's younger and slightly carefreer days as a rising attorney-about-town, an aging BMW convertible he kept tuned and polished and safely stored under canvas in his garage except when he dared to take it out for a Sunday spin with Karen or drive it downtown to work on perfect summer days. I called it his "automotive codpiece" because the two-person sports car was the spiritual descendent of his first set of wheels, an aging yellow Opel Jon fondly nicknamed "The Golden Gonad," in which he batted around Syracuse and Fayetteville cruising for chicks and adventure with his sidekick and high school buddy Eddie Eagan—*his* Pat McDaid. Though Eddie and Jon weren't as close as they'd once been—Eddie was now an industrious born-again businessman with three small daughters—they remained good friends through their charity work together, and Eddie would smile and shake his head if you mentioned their teenage sorties in the Golden Gonad.

"Look at the bright side," I commiserated with Jon. "Pretty soon you'll be eligible to have the senior citizen's van pick you up right at your doorstep."

"Not one bit amusing, Jimbo."

Of course, both of us knew it was completely hypocritical of me to tease Jon about his ridiculous little sports car. Every man has his hedge against mortality, and I, too, had my own fanatical devotion to a set of luxury wheels—in my case a John Deere deluxe lawn tractor (with rear bag attachment!) that I loved to climb aboard and spend hours mindlessly riding, hewing beautiful corridors of northern fescue, white clover, and Kentucky bluegrass in my yard and one-hole golf course with the care of an Augusta National greens attendant. I affectionately called this seasonal pleasure "mowing crop circles."

The reason I hadn't been to Syracuse, in fact, was precisely because it was the heart of crop-circle mowing season in Maine, and I didn't want to miss any of the action. I'd also been slipping away most afternoons to play nine holes at noon with Terry Meagher, Sid Watson, and good old Bunny Dugan, and taking my mother and children out to dinner by the sea whenever her busy social schedule with the Gang of Four at the Highlands permitted.

Jack's golf lessons with Mal Strange had also commenced and, according to Mal, the lad showed more than ordinary promise, though frankly the proud papa hadn't worked up the courage to sneak down to the club's practice area, called the Bullpen, to take a discreet peek for himself. My plan was to keep safely out of sight and wait for Jack to ask me to play a full eighteen, which Mal assured would happen any day now. Instead, during these tutorials, I always waited for my son at the putting green, dutifully practicing my own short game, which suddenly showed, post-Fontainebleau, more promise than it had in donkey years, so much so that I dangerously began to wonder if I dare try to qualify for the Brunswick club championship and maybe even the state amateur. One afternoon while I was out there chipping and putting, waiting for Jack and pondering these chimerical matters, Chris Doyle, our club's taciturn head professional, wandered out to join me.

"Did you hear Robert Trent Jones died?" he asked, dropping a ball and putting it toward a small white post.

I hadn't. I was saddened to hear this even though I knew from my friend Rees, his younger son, that his father's health had been deteriorating rapidly for years and Papa Jones had basically been in a coma-like state for months. Still, no one's passing leaves us untouched and especially so in the case of Trent Jones.

The four hundred or so golf courses Jones authored between the Great Depression and the 1980s revolutionized golf course design, introducing such novel ideas as multiple platform teeing grounds as long as one hundred yards, huge greens allowing for multiple pin placements, the strategic deployment of water hazards in place of bunkers (reasoning that the sand wedge had rendered sand hazards all but obsolete), the concept of a "signature" hole, and his famous conviction that every golf hole worth its grass should be a "hard par, easy bogey."

English-born and Cornell-educated, hopelessly hooked on the game since he saw Walter Hagen driving up a dusty lane in his gleaming white Packard to the Country Club of Rochester and soon afterward began caddying both there and at nearby Oak Hill, Jones abandoned a promising amateur playing career due to a nervous stomach and decided instead to pursue the unpromising career of golf course architecture. At Cornell, he essentially created his own academic program of studies melding the principles of classical landscape architecture with golf course design, and even built a couple contract courses before graduation—both of which went belly-up and never paid him.

One of his first paying jobs and most engaging designs, at least in my estimation, reposed in a glorious hardwood forest above a deep green glacial lake a couple miles down the road from Onondaga Country Club. Green Lakes State Park came about in the darkest days of the Depression when Jones convinced the legendary state parks czar Robert Moses to allow him to build a golf course there with the use of Civilian Conservation Corps workers. After routing and shaping the course, Jones had so many native evergreens and other species of trees brought in from the Adirondacks, as it turned out, that crews hauled the extras up the road to Onondaga, where today they sit like Druid elders guarding the fairways. On May 27, 1936, Green Lakes Golf Course opened with an exhibition match between Gene Sarazen and Sam Snead, watched by a gallery of one thousand paying customers who paid half a dollar for the pleasure of seeing the two finest golfers of the day.

In lieu of a fee, Trent Jones paid a symbolic dollar lease on the property to the state and operated the course himself for years, before an increasingly busy design life forced him to give the lease back to the state. He went on in short order to collaborate with Canadian designer Stanley Thompson, and later, after they split, to earn the moniker "Open Doctor" for rebuilding Oakland Hill and half a dozen more U.S. Open venues, creating over the next forty or so years more Top One Hundred courses than any architect in history, including signature tracks for the Aga Khan and several kings.

But his original little masterpiece at Green Lakes, where Wendy and I and sometimes the other Dewsweepers slipped away to chase the game among the gloriously mature evergreens and admire the long views over a dark blue glacial lake, to the very foothills of the Adirondacks themselves, remained just about my favorite Trent Jones course of all—and all the proof I required that golfers everywhere are linked by the attractions of a royal and ancient game, distanced from each other by only a few degrees of separation.

I mentioned this theory of spiritual linkage to Chris Doyle and explained the Trent Jones–Dewsweeper connection, and he smiled and said he fully agreed on the degrees of separation, reminding me that he had been Gene Sarazen's pro at Lake Sunapee for many summers and that Sarazen, who recently passed on to golf's greener pastures as well, was one of the game's true gentlemen.

He complimented me on my putting, said he heard from Terry and Tom that I was striking the ball pretty well. I admitted I was suddenly hitting it decently and thinking of maybe taking a shot at qualifying for the club championship and—what the heck—even the State Amateur.

"You could do it," he said. "Just remember the way to Carnegie Hall."

I looked up at him to see what he meant and found him smiling at me.

"Practice, practice, practice. That's what I tell Joe. Practice and it will pay off."

Joe was Chris's thirteen-year-old, the club cart boy.

Just then, Jack and Mal Strange rolled up in Mal's cart. Jack followed Chris into the pro shop to purchase a new sleeve of Nike ("Tiger's brand, Dad") balls and Mal said to me, "Have you seen Jack hit a ball yet?"

"Not really," I admitted. "Haven't had the courage to have a look."

Mal shook his head. "Well, I think you're going to be surprised— and I really mean that."

Jack came back out and shouldered his bag and we started for the car. I put my hand on his shoulder and told him that his golf teacher was pleased with his progress and wondered if he, Jack, might be interested in accompanying me to Scotland to host a father-son golf tour for a top golf travel company called InterGolf.

"When? This week?"

"No." I had to smile at the worldview of a boy like Jack— which extended only slightly beyond lunch tomorrow. I explained that the trip was in the autumn, middle October, near the end of the golf season—which gave him some extra time to work on his game. If he wanted to go, I said, I just might be able to convince his mother to let him miss a week of school to go play golf in the land of his ancestors.

"Wow. That would be *cool*, Dad," he said enthusiastically beneath his Bay Hill ball cap.

"You might not be old enough to play every golf course we visit," I warned, "because Scottish clubs have very firm rules about minimum age limits. But I think I can promise you'll get to play on the Old Course at Saint Andrews and a fabulous new links course called Kingsbarns. I know the folks who own it. There will be three or four places where you might have to just caddie for me. We'll still be a team, though."

"I'd like to caddie for you," he said, simply. "The best golfers start as caddies, you know."

I had to smile at this insight and told him I'd heard that somewhere, too.

Jack's natural enthusiam was one of his great assets. He was exactly Trent Jones's age when he saw Hagen's heavenly Packard tooling toward the golf course and, as I pointed out to him, was getting a two-year head start on his own old man. I hadn't taken up golf until I was twelve.

"If that's the case," I added casually, "how would you feel about caddying for me in the club championship—maybe even the State Amateur, assuming I manage to qualify. That's a big if."

"What do you mean by qualify?"

As we buckled up and drove off, I explained to him that only a limited number of players who recorded scores low enough in a "qualifying" round make it into the field of the championship itself. They earn their right to play for the championship, so to speak. In the club championship, for instance, I explained, I'd basically have to shoot no worse than my usual 77 in order to make the field. State Amateur qualifying would be considerably tougher. It was being held over at a club named Martindale in Auburn, a hilly track with small fast greens. The rule of thumb in the Amateur was that aspirants needed to shoot no worse than the mid 70s to have a decent shot of making the field. Plus, I explained, there was the nerves factor.

"*You* get nervous?" He seemed surprised by this.

"Oh heck yeah." I told him Bob Jones's famous line about there being two kinds of golf—golf and *tournament* golf. "Don't you get nervous before a hockey game?"

"Sometimes," he admitted. "But I'm okay when the game starts."

I told him I wished that were true in golf—at least for me. Taut nerves did funny things to golf shots, in my case. But that wasn't any reason not to take a shot and give it my best—especially with him on my bag. *That* would quell my nerves.

I told him about my friend Bob Kingman, whom he'd briefly met once on the putting green. On the heels of a bitter divorce and protracted custody battle for his children, Bob, a gifted

family therapist who long ago played on his rural Minnesota high
school golf team, had picked up his clubs and returned to golf after almost a thirty-year absence. Golf became Bob's own form of
personal therapy—and his holy grail. He managed to hack his
handicap down to single digits only to cruelly discover that he
had cancer, a huge tumor wedged against one kidney. Months of
aggressive chemotherapy ensued, weakening his body and steal-
ing his hair. One thing helped get him through the ordeal, Bob
later confided to me: a vision of returning to golf and maybe
getting good enough to qualify for the State Amateur with his
teenage son Eddie caddying for him. By early summer Bob was
back on his feet and I saw him fairly regularly down at the Bullpen, diligently hitting practice shot after shot, chasing his little
dream. With only a few holes left to play in the qualifier, he knew
he probably needed at least one more birdie and nothing worse
than pars to have any hope of making the Amateur's field. But
he felt himself faltering, growing impatient, giving up. "That's
when Eddie handed me a club and looked me in the eye and said,
'C'mon, Dad. Don't quit. You can do this.' " Bob parred the rest
of the way home and made the Amateur field with one stroke to
spare.

"Oh, man," Jack said, clearly impressed. "That's really cool.
Did he win the Amateur?"

"No. I believe he came in next to last. But he told me it was
one of the most fun things he and Eddie ever did together."

"Sure," Jack announced, fingering one of his new Nike balls.
"I'd love to caddie for you."

"Assuming I qualify, of course."

"Right. Don't worry, Dad. You will."

. . .

I MENTIONED these pleasant domestic developments to Jon
Sager during the weekly phone update from the Sager abode in
Dawley Farms to a forested hill in Maine, and he filled me in on

what new and exciting was happening around Sagerville: He'd traded in the "chick magnet" and used the proceeds for a down payment on a new Nissan Altima for Sarah, who was headed off to Washington and Lee come fall. Becca, number two daughter, meanwhile, was almost fully recovered from her knee surgery, talking of returning to the track team and stringing two boyfriends along. Billy was winning swim meets and setting records in the process and young Charlie, who was Jack's age, was still in mourning over the loss of the sports car.

Speaking of dream cars and Dewsweepers, Jon added, Lester's new Chrysler PT Cruiser had finally arrived and Jon had once again urged him to enter it (and himself) in the Munchkin parade at the annual Oz Festival in nearby Chittenango (birthplace of Frank Baum); Peter Marshall had recently shown up for a Dewsweeping session astride his Harley Davidson, wearing Tommy Bahama shorts and Swedish clogs, with his stand bag riding dramatically on his back. "I told him he looked like a gay Dennis Hopper, an embarrassment to badly dressed, grossly unenlightened Harley owners everywhere." Bill Tuck had dropped another five pounds and recently shot his lowest score ever—an 80 for eighteen holes—but was in a mild funk due to the annual Red Sox slump and seemed to be losing his standing dollar bet to Russ King more than he was winning it. On the plus side, Tuck had recently spotted the mythical Al Devendorf, which meant the man who may or may not have invented the Ping putter was back in town. Russ and Jiggy King, meanwhile, had taken their six grandchildren for a big trip out west and now had their new English threshing barn up—they hoped I would come by and see it soon. Tommy Cahill was now officially retired, playing a lot of golf, and wondering if there was any validity to all the gabble about a possible Dewsweeper trip to England in the autumn.

I explained to Jon that I'd already placed calls to friends in Britain, including Donald Steel, and hoped to hear something promising on that score by British Open time. I asked him to convey this news and my abiding best wishes to the Dewsweepers and inform them I would join them on the first tee at dawn any day now. I'd be the guy dressed like Peter Marshall's lumpy but slightly more enlightened brother, which was still a far sight better dressed than Jon Sager, whose golf shirts appeared to be made from old clown costumes and Mafia hotel draperies.

"Hey, *careful,* pal," he snarled. "You sound like a real clothes snob. I can't help how I look. Karen bought this shirt for me. You're one to talk. Looks like you're wearing a hospitality tent from the GGO.

"By the way, how's your mom doing?"

I was pleased to bring him up to speed. "Safe and sound and happy at last. Still thinks she owns her house in Greensboro but apparently what she doesn't remember won't hurt her anymore. Frankly, I never even mention it. Thanks for asking."

"And your brother?"

"Don't mention it. In this case, ignorance is bliss."

"Oh, one more thing," he said before signing off. "The guys all want to know. Are we coming to Maine for a wedding anytime soon?"

I apologized for not having filled him in on events after Paris. Wendy had enthusiastically said yes to my ringless proposal, I explained, and, to that end, was in the process of filing a relocation petition with the family court of Onondaga County, the procedural first step in moving with her sons to Maine. As I understood the situation, because she already had complete physical custody of her boys, it was simply a matter of negotiating a new fair and equitable visitation agreement with her former husband, a busy real estate lawyer. In the greater interest of the boys, Wendy was preparing to offer him a deal that would provide him with even more quality time with his sons than he currently enjoyed. Neither of us could see how he could possibly turn it down.

While she took care of that task, I explained, I was already investigating Irish string bands and planning to surprise her with a honeymoon trip to the land of *her* ancestors and the inaugural Blarney Cup. I would probably take her to Ireland before or after the Dewsweeper trip to England, assuming it came off.

Jon snorted and laughed.

"In other words, you're going to take her on a golf trip. What a *romantic*."

"Hey," I pointed out. "The winters are just as long in Maine as they are in Syracuse."

• • •

THAT next Friday morning, days after Tiger Woods won his first U.S. Open at Pebble Beach and appeared to be having the most dominant year anybody'd had on Tour in thirty years, my friend Rollin Ives phoned out of the blue to invite me to Portland Country Club for a round of afternoon golf. Once upon a time, Rollin was the human services commissioner for the state of Maine and many pundits had him cruelly condemned to the governor's job, but Rollin, to his credit, realized that his wife, Martha, and teenage sons Lucas and Jake meant far more to him than any life in the political footlights. These days he worked as a consultant and administrator for a large health care organization and occasionally met me for golf at our respective clubs over the course of a far-too-brief northern summer.

Rollin explained that he had a "mystery" guest he thought I would really wish to meet, noting that the "golf journalist" in me would be "*very* intrigued."

I explained that, much as I would dearly love to see him and hand over all my spare pocket change, I had a column to finish and a large lawn to mow and was scheduled to pick up my children at day camp at five and then meet my mother at the Highlands for an early dinner. After that, I planned to turn in early because Brunswick's two-day club qualifier started at dawn on Saturday, followed by the State Amateur qualifying round early Monday morning. In all three events, I'd craftily finagled to tee off in the first groups out, dewsweeping for a little bit of tournament glory.

"Okay," Rollin teased, sounding only slightly like a good politician spurned. "Maybe next time you can meet Hughes Norton."

Hughes Norton was Tiger Woods's recently fired super-agent, the controversial IMG rainmaker who negotiated the legendary $60 million-dollar deal that made Nike balls so appealing to Jack and Elderick Woods, wealthy beyond anyone's dreams before Tiger ever swung a club in professional competition. Norton had a reputation for being a tough and cynical cuss, one of the most feared and disliked men in golf. He'd recently vanished from sight, reportedly with the assistance of a golden parachute worth millions.

"Okay," I relented, thinking I might at least sneak a column from the encounter *and* lose some money to Rollin, the only five-handicapper I know who regularly breaks par. "Let me make a few phone calls."

"You're sure?" Rollin said, ever the diplomat. "The last thing I want to do is come between a father and his kids—or, for that matter, his mother."

"The kids will be fine," I assured him. "And I'll meet my mother in time for dessert."

• • •

HUGHES Norton was a trim, darkly handsome bloke with a rich tan and thinning hair brushed stylishly aft. He was exceedingly friendly when Rollin introduced us, and we shook hands on the first tee at Portland Country Club, but he seemed either slightly keyed up or maybe a bit wary of having to play golf in close proximity to the kind of chump he used to beat up regularly on behalf of IMG and his clients.

To my way of thinking, at least at that moment in time, Hughes was a perfect symbol of how professional golf had dramatically changed and, as Father Longhurst himself might have put it, sacrificed no minor amount of its sporting soul in recent times. When I'd begun golf writing about 1985, for example, it was still possible to meet the top players and spend more than a few unhurried moments talking about the direction of their lives and their private passions for the game and anything else that crossed their minds.

As purse money and the Tour's corporate profile grew to *Brobdingnagian* proportions, though, so did the presence and custodial influences of super-agents like Hughes Norton—whose principal jobs became negotiating bigger and better endorsement deals and muzzling players to prevent them from revealing anything their sponsors might later regret.

As we ambled along Portland's first fairway, I asked Norton how he'd been getting along since leaving the fast lanes of sports super-agenting. It was sad to think of the guy being just fifty-three years old and washed up—even if he did have millions in the bank.

"Doing very well, thank you," he replied crisply. "Been able to do a number of things I always wanted to do. I work out every morning, for example, and read a lot of books I've always wanted to read. I even get to actually play golf now, as well."

He politely injected that he really wasn't free to discuss the terms of his departure from IMG, nor discuss his former clients in any depth, due to a contractural agreement with his former employer that prohibited him from competing or writing a book about his experiences for an unspecified period of time. Tough-ass world, big-time sports agenting.

I replied that was okee-dokee with me, as we were just having a little friendly round of golf on a swell Donald Ross course on a perfect summer afternoon with pals. My tape recorder wasn't running, I joked—only my mouth. I birdied the opening hole, to put Rollin and me one-up on Hughes and his partner, a nice man named Chris Pierce, Hughes's childhood buddy.

"You must play a lot of golf, by the looks of it," Norton remarked, as we headed for the second tee.

I was flattered. But then, I'm easily flattered when someone says *anything* nice about my golf game.

"This year I'm on a mission from God and some guys called the Dewsweepers to just have more fun playing golf."

"The Dewsweepers?" he wondered.

"Yeah. They play the game for the *opposite* reasons Tiger Woods plays it. This year I'm hanging with them."

Norton, who grew up in Portland and was a former club champion at PCC, possessed a flat and powerful golf swing that loaded up far past parallel and sent his tee shots flying on a low and dramatic drawing trajectory. Somehow he managed this unconventional swing, reminiscent of Hogan before he cured his hook, quite handsomely, and soon started knocking off pars right and left.

Portland, an original Ross layout, is a terrific course but one I seldom manage to navigate very well. While I foozled along with pars and bogeys, slipping back to my usual game prior to the glories of France, Rollin and his reliable old-style "pro's" swing—the kind where the abbreviated backswing and forward thrust are so smooth and natural they almost appear to be one adroit movement—kept us safely in the match against Hughes and Chris. We finished six holes tied and swapped partners. Chris and I became partners. Chris's son Eddie, he explained to me, was an incoming freshman at Bowdoin College, a fifteen handicapper who hoped to try out for the Polar Bear golf team.

"Small world," I said and I explained that one of my regular golf pals in Brunswick was Bowdoin's golf coach, Terry Meagher. I offered to put in a few good words about Eddie with the coach.

"I hear Terry's wonderful with the kids," Chris said.

"He is," I assured him. "Unfortunately I owe him a couple million dollars at the moment."

Chris looked confused until I quickly explained how we play our matches. As it happened, Terry was presently up two matches, hence my children and I were living rather hand-to-mouth until I could manage to beat him again, hopefully thrice so my kids could go to college, too.

Chris laughed.

"I love this nutty game," he said, and explained how he and Hughes, then college students, hopped a cheapo flight to England and hitchhiked across the Blessed Isle to Royal Birkdale, where they arrived just as Lee Trevino was putting out to win the 1971 British Open Championship.

Chris amplified: "The Open finished in those days on Saturday, as you probably recall, and Trevino hung around for what seemed like *hours* talking to fans, signing autographs, posing for photographs, really enjoying himself. He couldn't seem to get enough of it all, the atmosphere, the appreciative people, and neither could Hughes and I. It was so, I don't know . . . *magical*."

"I think that moment may have been why I became a sports agent." Hughes joined in the dialogue, visibly relaxing his guard. "I mean, being so close to someone who plays the game you love better than anybody else. That was special. I was hooked."

Rollin slipped me a smile and a wink. Perhaps he was thinking the same thing I was—namely how ironic it was that Hughes Norton would grow up to become the super-agent who cut the sixty-million-dollar deal for a guy who played the game better than anybody else perhaps in history.

In any case, with a skin of ice apparently broken by the social ease of pasture pool, by the time Hughes and I were partnered over Portland's final few holes, I felt comfortable enough to ask if he agreed with the view that Tiger Woods was the most dominant player in more than a generation. Talk about a *stupid* question, I thought.

"He's the most gifted I've ever seen in *any* generation," Hughes replied. "And I'm including Palmer and Nicklaus in that group. Nobody has a work ethic like Tiger's. Maybe Hogan's was slightly stronger. He loves hitting golf balls. He'll do it all day long. So many of them out there don't. To them, golf is a job. A great job, maybe, but still a job. Tiger's different. Concentration that's unique. You can see it. As far as I can tell, only one thing can hurt Tiger Woods."

He paused as if waiting for me to try and guess what that might be. I almost guessed *Having a really crappy agent?* but realized, in the nick of time, that Hughes Norton might not find that particularly funny.

"Only Tiger can hurt Tiger," he said. "If he chooses to get married and have a family. Right now he only has golf in his life. Hitting golf shots and playing video games. Everything else is secondary. That's what it takes to perform on the level where he is. Nobody's ever been there before."

I asked if he reckoned that fact made Tiger Woods happy, at the end of the day. Talk about a *softball* pitch of a question. I was a regular Larry King in softspikes.

"I can't say," Hughes admitted. We were standing on the eighteenth green, both a little winded from the steep final hill. "But I know *I* am. I was paid to be a rainmaker and I made it rain. I never knew what that life was like, though, until I left it."

Jake Ives was waiting for his father by the putting green. Jake's grandmother, Sally, Rollin's mom and his favorite golf pal, was standing with him.

Seeing Sally reminded me of a lovely tale involving Jake, Rollin, and the ghost of his late father. In 1999, Rollin reached the final thirty-six holes of the PCC club championship, coming to the dangerous uphill fifteenth with the lead and a Maine nor'easter howling around him. Jake was caddying for him. A rare snaphook caused Rollin to triple bogey the hole, dropping him two strokes behind his opponent. His opponent, though, doubled 16 and, following a couple pars at 17, the pair arrived at the final hole all square. A crowd of fifty people huddled beneath umbrellas around the final green. Rollin holed a gutsy uphill six-footer to halve the match as the rain came down in torrents. The play-off lasted four holes and ended with Rollin lipping out a five-footer to lose the championship.

Jake came and gave me a bear hug, he wrote in his personal jour-nal afterward, permitting me to read it sometime later. *I knew he was exhausted and disappointed . . . what felt good was that I'd not given up . . . and I had really done my best . . . I may have lost but that really wasn't as important as having given it my all.*

That evening, as he relates in the journal, he relived the match with his mother. *She always had a passion for the game and in fact probably had more to do with my loving golf and returning to the game after my father's death than anyone in life.*

As I finished, she said she thought I might like to know something she had decided not to tell me for fear that it might be a distraction . . . that fifty-three years ago to that very Sunday in August (she checked this with her diary) she walked with my father the same eighteen holes I had walked with Jake a few hours earlier . . . in the same tournament . . . when he won his last club championship. That was 1946, a year before they married and two years before I was born.

Rollin introduced me to his mother. The resemblance be-tween the three of them was unmistakable. I told them about my conversation that week with Jack, about the possibility of him caddying for me in my own club championship the way Jake had ushered his old man around Portland. This remark seemed to please Jake.

"Jim's even planning to try for the State Amateur on Mon-day," Rollin felt obliged to reveal, smiling at me as if there's no fool like a proud papa.

I told them I planned to give it my best shot, partly because of Jack and partly because my mom was dying to come out and watch me play one more time before her wheels gave out. That's exactly how I put it. If I somehow managed to qualify, I would make sure she came out to watch me play.

"Good for you," Sally declared. "Take it from me. She'll never forget it."

"Don't count on it," I replied with a laugh, and then apolo-gized for having to run. I was terribly late for dinner with my mom.

· · ·

I FOUND Mrs. Congeniality having her lemon meringue pie and coffee with her Southern buddy Marie in the Highland's main dining room.

"Marie's daughter is moving her over to my wing," Mom confided when Marie went back up to the buffet for a slice of watermelon. "Marie wants me to keep her booze in my room because she's not supposed to drink alcohol. If her daughter finds anything, she pours it straight down the drain . . . glug, glug, glug."

She grinned at me impishly.

"Hey, sweetie, you look like you've been mowing the lawn. All *sweaty* and rumpled," she said.

"I came here straight from the golf course," I explained, finishing the last bite of the pie she offered me. "Getting ready for tomorrow. By the way, I resent being called *rumpled*. Jon Sager calls me Lumpy. As I tell him, big guys have feelings, too, you know."

"Tell him you're just *my* big lump of sugar, then."

"I think I'll just leave it alone. Good pie here . . ."

"So what's up tomorrow?"

"Club championship qualifying. Two rounds, tomorrow and Sunday. Figure I need to average no worse than seventy-seven to get in. Good news is, my game feels pretty good right now. State qualifying is on Monday. Jack's agreed to caddie for me if I make the field."

"Wonderful," she declared. "And I'll come root for the home team."

"What's wonderful?" Marie wondered, taking her seat with her melon slice.

"Golf," I said, smiling at her. "Life's greatest four-letter word."

"Goodness me. I just don't know why men like that silly game so *durn* much," she drawled, starting down a familiar road.

"Well, I *do*," my mother declared loyally. "And I just might take myself out to that golf course tomorrow and watch my son play!" She smiled and winked at me.

I reached over and patted her hand and swiped a slug of her coffee while I was at it.

"Mom," I reminded her, "it's just qualifying, not the actual tournament. You just sleep in tomorrow and I'll come pick you up after lunch. We'll take the kids and drive up the coast to Boothbay. I know a place Dad would have loved."

"Okay, babe," she chirped. "Anything you say."

.   .   .

I SHOT my worst round ever at Brunswick that next morning, a big fat 86.

As I was standing over my final approach shot on eighteen, with a seven-iron in hand, wondering if anyone had thought to get the license plate number of the truck that flattened me, my golf bag began to ring—again. I looked at it with numb detachment, finally unzipped the side pouch, and took out my cell phone, realizing I'd once again left it there in violation of my own rule about phones on holy ground.

"Jim," a familiar Southern voice said sharply, "where the hell *are* you?"

"A golf course in Maine," I replied vaguely, not quite placing the voice. "Who is . . . this?"

It was my brother, sounding really annoyed. "It's *Mom*. She's had a stroke. The people at the Highlands had no idea where to reach you."

Fifteen minutes later, I walked into the ICU of Midcoast Hospital. Mom was in a private room, lying serenely beneath a cool white sheet. I sat down and touched her hand. Her skin felt soft and cool. After a few seconds, her eyes opened and she looked at me.

"Hey, Gorgeous. What's cookin'?"

She mouthed *Hi*. The duty nurse had informed me that her

right side was completely paralyzed from the stroke but her speech was okay and she could wiggle her toes. They were waiting for other tests to try and assess the extent of the damage.

"Did you play?" she asked me very slowly.

I smiled and shrugged. "Sort of. It wasn't pretty. But *you* are."

She smiled back and squeezed my right hand with her left one, her only hand with feeling.

A machine was monitoring her heartbeat, gently bleeping. I sat holding her hand and assured her she would be fine. The doctors had everything under control.

"You'll do better tomorrow," she said with some difficulty, though strangely she didn't seem at all uncomfortable.

"I'm not playing tomorrow," I replied. "I plan to be here bothering you all day."

She shook her head, little tiny shakes.

"Go," she managed, clearly tiring, "play."

I stood there for a minute and thought about how my father and I would find time to play together whenever one of us needed to talk or get through a difficult time. It was almost a Dodson tradition to let the golf course help us grieve, and then help us heal.

"Okay," I said. "But I'll be here before that. At dawn."

. . .

I DROVE home and climbed on board my John Deere lawn tractor and mowed crop circles for the next two hours, disappearing into my own head, trying to figure out if uprooting my mom and hauling her to Maine had been the very worst, or very best, thing I could have done for her.

Mowing grass helps me much in the same way as playing a round of golf by myself. I chug along thinking how nice it would be to have a job cutting grass at a golf course, boss of my own gang-mower, permitting the pungent smell of cut grass and the precise geometry of mowing to absorb my thoughts for a little while. In this instance, when I switched off the mower and sat for a moment to assess my labors, I realized I was looking at the last peonies of the summer blooming gloriously against the white fence. Peonies were mother's favorite flowers—and mine as well.

The next morning at dawn, Jack and I brought Mrs. Congeniality a bundle of freshly cut white peonies in a vase. She looked better, sitting up slightly, lucid and composed.

She smiled when she saw the flowers.

"Don't worry about a thing, Mom," I said to her again, taking her hand. "You'll be home soon."

"I know," she replied, sounding as if she had no doubt about that whatsoever. Her blue eyes shifted from me to the peonies to Jack and back to me. She smiled at us both.

I dropped Jack off at church, where his mother planned to meet him, and then drove straight to the golf club figuring I needed to shoot an improbable even-par 71 or better to make the field. I'd done that only once in fifteen years at Brunswick, but at least I'd done it.

On eighteen, almost exactly where I'd been standing twenty-four hours before, pointlessly struggling to make par and finish with 85, my golf bag rang again. Once again, I was holding my seven-iron and staring at it dumbly. And once again I unzipped the side pouch and reluctantly took out my cell phone. I'd fallen into a bad habit of keeping it in there and would soon have to submit my own digit to the Iranian remedy if I kept it up.

"Jim," a pleasant voice said, "this is John."

I smiled. For a moment I thought it was Jon Sager calling. That would have been most welcome, a boost of support from my favorite Dewsweeper. But then I realized it was John Halpern, Mom's doctor.

"Jim," he repeated simply, "your mother just passed away five minutes ago."

My brother and his new wife arrived at the hospital a few minutes ahead of me. They'd flown in the evening before and stayed somewhere in Portland. My brother's eyes were red and swollen. My children came a few minutes later, to sit and say goodbye to their *Gammy*, as they called her.

At one point, for some mysterious reason, Jack noticed that the paper calendar on the wall of Mother's hospital room was a numerical day behind. He pulled off yesterday's date. My brother and his new wife stayed only a few more minutes. They slipped out to "get some air" before they headed back to the airport. To be honest, I really wasn't sorry to see them go.

When my children left the hospital room with their mother, I sat for almost two hours waiting for Bracketts Funeral Home to come and collect Mom's remains. She looked remarkably at peace, her silky white hair swept back, her lips almost curled in a faint secretive smile. Every now and then, I glanced at the wall calendar myself, wondering what it was about that date that teased my brain. Then the duty nurse came into the room and handed me, of all things, a golf club. It was the seven-iron I'd been holding when John Halpern phoned me on the golf course.

"I believe this is yours," she said. "You were carrying it when you came in. You must have just forgotten it."

"Runs in the family," I explained.

"By the way," she added quietly, pausing by the door, "I was with her when she passed away. I was changing the sheets. Such an adorable lady. I was just chatting away and she was listening and smiling at me and the heart monitor suddenly went flat. If it helps, I've been around this hospital a long time and I've never seen a more peaceful death. I probably shouldn't say this. But it was almost like she was . . . grateful."

I told the nurse I was grateful that she'd told me this and thanked her for returning my golf club, feeling my own tears beginning to push forth at last. She left and I sat there looking at my mother and then it came to me why I knew this date.

It was just hours before my parents' fifty-ninth wedding anniversary.

• • •

CHARLIE Chaplin once observed that life is a tragedy when seen in close-up, but a comedy in long-shot. That sometimes seems like a pretty good working description of my golf game, as well.

The next morning, as my mother had wished me to do, and as family tradition seemed to dictate, I drove over to Martindale Golf Club in Auburn and teed off with a pair of young studs half my age in the State Amateur qualifying event.

Jeffrey, who had a looping country swing, double bogeyed the first hole, while Chad, a young assistant from some club downstate, with a swing and host of mannerisms copied from Greg Norman, opened with a birdie. I somehow thumped a sand shot onto the putting surface and sneaked a long par putt into the cup.

For the next two hours, I walked along the cool, wet fairways deep inside my head, thinking about how my mother always took such pleasure in the stories I brought her back from my travels through the golf world and the people I'd met in the past twenty or so years. Her own golf game was comical, but she loved the game with the pure passion of a club champion—which may say as much about the values of golf as it does her.

On the ninth tee, I was surprised to realize I was just one over par. The hole is a long and steep downhill par three of 230 yards. I pulled out a five-wood and hit the ball as hard as I could, rolling it onto the green. I made my par.

Frankly, I wasn't even thinking about earning one of the twenty-four spots available in a field of sixty-one players. Or maybe I was. Perhaps I was really thinking how wonderful it would be, under the circumstances, to bring tricky Martindale to its knees and make that State Am field with the next generation of Dodson golfer on my bag, rooting me on the way Jake Ives and Eddie Kingman rooted for their fathers.

Probably, I wanted it *too* much. I hooked my first drive of the back nine far into the hemlock woods. The ball struck a large tree and wound up wearing a massive glob of sap. When I tried to

chip safely out to the fairway, the ball stuck to the face of my club
and squirted wildly left. It might have been funny if it hadn't
been so painful, and it never even occurred to me to go find an
official and replace the ball. I just chipped and played, growing
more numb and more indifferent with each swing, squirting
three more woeful shots down the hill to the edge of the green. I
recorded 9 on the par-four tenth hole.

Eleven was a dangerous par-three with a slick Redan-style
green. I flew the green, chipped poorly back, and *four*-putted for
a triple bogey. In just two holes, I'd ballooned to nine over par.

Frankly, I've never been so tempted to quit and walk off a
golf course in my life. In fact, at any moment, I was sure I would
do just that. The day had grown unbearably hot and I was as miserable in body and soul as I've ever been with a golf club in my
hand—maybe as miserable as I've ever been, period. I double-
bogeyed the next two holes, hating everything about the game,
realizing how right Marcel the filmmaker had been—realizing I
had no business playing in tournaments.

I still don't know why I didn't quit. I walked every last ago-
nizing step of that miserable damned qualifying round, wordlessly signed my card for a 90, the second worst score of my
adult life, then got in my car and drove home, where I downed a
quart of cold water and two beers and lay under a slowly turning
ceiling fan on the sun porch until it got dark.

• • •

THE truth is, I might not have picked up a club for a month if my
cousin Bob Tracy and his wife, Claire, hadn't arrived that very
night for a vacation visit with my mother that was scheduled
months before. Bob isn't really my blood cousin. He's my mother's
oldest friend's son, the guy I always wanted to be when I grew
up. My mother, in any case, simply adored Bobby, as she always
called him.

In retrospect, he and Claire and Wendy (who was en route from Syracuse) were the perfect people to have assembled around me at that moment. Nothing felt quite . . . *real* to me; the jolt of losing my mom in the blink of an eye hadn't fully sunk in and even the schizophrenic rounds of golf I'd played that week had the quality of a strange underwater dream, or a nightmare.

The next morning, a beautiful summer morning, the four of us went to breakfast and thence to Mom's pretty apartment to sit and share memories about her. Mrs. Congeniality's favorite perfume still lingered in the room's air and a slim book of verse was open where she'd been reading it and paused.

I went to the bedroom to fetch a sapphire necklace and a set of diamond earrings Mom planned to pass along to her oldest granddaughter, Rebecca, my brother's teenage daughter, and was startled to discover that all my mother's important pieces of jewelry were missing. Boxes were empty, as if looted. It was unthinkable that the Highlands staff had taken them—the room was not only protected by a coded entry door but the Highland's staff had impeccable credentials.

It came to me where the jewelry had gone. My brother had obviously taken it, during his sortie to "get some air" before leaving town. I might have been outraged if I hadn't been, once again, deeply surprised and profoundly saddened by his actions. I walked out to the living room and told Bob and Claire this latest indignity and Bob shook his head. "I'd like to kick his ass," he said quietly. "I bet your father would, too."

Before we left, we stopped by the common room to thank Norman and his staff for being so helpful and found the Gang of Four watching an old Bob Cummings comedy.

"Where *is* your mother?" demanded Helen, the elegant dowager who always wore formal pearls, smiling up at me from her wing chair, at least remembering I was my mother's son. "We've been waiting for her *all* morning. There is a van ride up to Rockland this afternoon."

"She passed away yesterday," I explained gently, realizing how *unreal* the words sounded to my own ears. It simply didn't seem possible Mrs. Congeniality was gone.

Helen's tapered fingers flew to her open mouth and the other Gang of Four all gasped. Norm smiled sadly at me from across the common room. I knew he had already broken the news to them, perhaps several times, but it probably had just slipped their minds.

Outside, Bob seized me firmly by the shoulder. "Wendy, Claire and I have made an executive decision. One that your mom would definitely approve of. Something that'll cheer us all up."

"What?"

"You'll see."

We fetched Jack and the three of us shouldered our bags and walked around Brunswick Golf Club in the fading afternoon light. Bobby plays with ridiculously ancient clubs and employs a simple "feel" swing—he's the kind of guy, in other words, you'd never wish to meet in the semi-finals of any golf tournament. He shot 75 as if it were nothing. I managed 76, proving I should always just play for the heck of it.

I have no idea what Jack shot because in true Dewsweeper fashion, he didn't bother keeping score at all. He just whacked balls and had fun, impressing Bobby and me with his new grip-and-rip swing.

· · ·

ONE week later, I flew to Indianapolis to interview Pete and Alice Dye for a column, bearing my mom's ashes in a two-thousand-year-old Maine slate urn, then flew on to Greensboro, where Pat McDaid picked me up at the airport.

I sat with my Aunt Daphne, Bob Tracy's sisters, my brother's former wife and his grown children, and several of my mother's best chums at the memorial service, trying to remain unperturbed by the fact that my brother arrived in a shiny black Mercedes with his new wife decked out in a showy black funeral hat.

He'd lost his mom, too, I reminded myself, and this wasn't the time and place to try and square things with him. I either had a lot to say to him, or nothing at all.

Instead, after the opening hymns, I got up and spoke briefly about Mom's life in Maine—how she'd dearly missed Greensboro and her house and garden and church circle and so many loyal old friends—but how she'd dived enthusiastically into her new life up in the godless frozen north with an open mind and a cheerful heart and given me and my children an incomparable gift in the process.

I talked about how she'd charmed everyone she met at the Highlands, including some old rogue called Stan, enjoyed a lot of nice dinners with her Yankee grandchildren by the sea, even described how she'd recently predicted she would soon be reunited with her husband.

"Jimmy," whispered one of Mom's closest neighbors as she hugged me after the service, "I feel so awful. I think I may have killed your mother."

I had to smile at this strange remark and told her that was completely ridiculous.

"No. Really. I phoned her the night she had the stroke. I told her that her house had been sold. I think . . . it broke her heart."

This lady was one of my mother's oldest friends, a dear woman who had been a friend of my family's forever. I told her she had nothing whatsoever to do with Mom's death. On the contrary, I said, her twice-weekly phone conversations kept Mom going during homesick stretches in Maine. I thanked her for that loyal friendship and explained that being late for a dinner date with my father was really what broke my mother's heart—and maybe her bickering sons.

The Irish Antichrist drove me to the airport. He asked if I was okay. I said I was fine—but might not come back to town for a while. Something needed to heal first, I said, best done from my hill and mowing crop circles.

"Do you think you can make the Dewsweeper trip to England?" I added that a friend I'd met at the President's Putter was a member of Westward Ho! and had e-mailed me an invitation to play the first round of the Blarney Cup there.

"Absolutely," Pat said. "I've even gone back to my old Callaway blades and plan to kick your ass the way I did at Ballybunion during that hurricane."

"I wouldn't brag about *that*," I reminded him. "After all, you shot ninety-one."

"True. But you and Jon Boy shot ninety-threes."

That had been my actual worst score as an adult, the third round of the first Blarney Cup. But that was another story entirely.

"Well, don't say you weren't warned," Pat said, then gave me a long hug good-bye.

TEN

THE MEMBER-GUEST

FRANKLY, I needed a shot of Wendy and Syracuse and the Dewsweepers and I didn't even mind that a dreary Leatherstocking mist was later falling on the qualifying round of the Onondaga Member-Guest tournament. I sometimes play very well in the rain as it happens, and it was comforting to be hacking around the old course with Lester and his son Terry, who'd just arrived from San Francisco.

Lester was his usual steady self, hitting every fairway with monotonous repetition and talking about his lettuce patch and Sheila being off for the week at "piano camp" in Minnesota, while Terry walloped massive drives and admitted he was only "slightly concerned" about the 50-percent drop in tech stocks in the past six months. I told him about the dot-com millionaires I'd met in the bar at Spanish Bay back in February, the former wind-surfers turned golfnuts who planned to play their way around the world.

"Yeah, well," quipped Terry, "they're probably parking cars somewhere or bagging groceries these days. This is the big shake-out everybody's been predicting. Reality time, I'm afraid."

Jon and I exchanged almost no words during the qualifier. There was a noticeable absence of banter and none of the usual good-natured needling. There was obviously a great deal on his mind, but he did not want to talk about it so I did not press him. Still, he fired a highly respectable 78, good enough to offset my indifferent 82 and place us in the tournament's first flight. However sharp my game had been just ten or so days ago, I now felt mostly out of synch.

My partner dropped me at Wendy's house and I watched him drive back up the block and pull into his own driveway. I walked into Wendy's house and found her sitting at the kitchen counter drinking a cup of lukewarm coffee. As I put down my golf bag, she smiled sadly at me and explained that she had more bad news. She'd just learned that my Aunt Gladys, my mom's older sister, my cool West Coast aunt, had suffered a stroke almost identical to my mom's and passed away the previous night.

· · ·

They say it never rains on a golf course. But in life, obviously, when it rains it pours.

Luckily, the tournament gift was an attractive water-repellant knitted wind shirt with the handsome Onondaga Indian chief head emblazoned on the breast. I immediately put mine on, prior to our opening match of the member-guest, because the rain was coming down at a cold and steady clip.

Our opponents were a couple decent guys in matching designer rainsuits. They beat us easily 3-and-2 in the match, during which, once again, Jon and I said almost nothing to each other. As we came off the eighteenth green, a massive thunderstorm broke over Syracuse and the rains picked up with a vengeance.

Play was suspended. It suddenly grew so cold my fingertips went numb. Our riding cart was one of the few that had no bag protector, thus we had to employ locker room towels to try and cover up our equipment. Jon vanished. I walked into the grill room to try and get warm and stopped to look at a framed photograph of Bill Mitchell, Onondaga's legendary longtime head professional, the Mal Strange of Syracuse, then fetched a cup of coffee and walked into the trophy room to kill time looking at an antique club display donated by a late club member named Larry Sovik, a renowned Onondagan golfer who played many of his rounds with Hagen and Sarazen, and even a few times with a promising young junior member named Jonathan Sager.

Tony Langan, a retired lawyer, saw me and came over. We shook hands. Tony's nickname around town was "the Blade" due to the smoothness of his putting stroke back in the days when he and his twin brother Art were the most famous golfing twins in New York State. Tony won the city golf championship three times between 1946 and 1952 and Art, the city's junior champion for many years running, won medalist honors at the 1947 U.S. Amateur.

The Blade asked me how Jon and I were playing and I hated to tell him it wasn't pretty. Neither of us was in synch yet, and we might not get there, given the circumstances.

"Oh, this weather will clear up," the Blade assured me with his lopsided Irish smile. "You should know how fickle Syracuse weather is by now.

"How's the putting holding up?" he asked.

One sunny afternoon the Blade had consented to share his putting secrets with me, advising: *Plant your feet in cement, weight on the left side, hit on the upstroke and let the putter go at least three inches past impact with the ball. Speed is the game! Don't fall in love with the line! The secret of putting is to never let the right hand roll over. Sometimes you stroke it and sometimes you tap it. The trick is to know which you should do!*

The Blade's putting tips had worked pretty nicely, I admitted, but my putting thus far in the member-guest was pretty awful. Who could figure out this screwy game?

"It'll come around," he assured me with a wink and gentle pat on the shoulder, wandering off to find one of his sons. "Just keep those feet in cement!"

I resumed my study of antique clubs, thinking about my Aunt Gladys, thinking about my mother and my brother, wondering what was chewing at my playing partner, probably thinking way too much. My feet *were* in cement but the last thing on my mind, really, was a reluctant putting stroke that wouldn't come around.

Someone else walked up and spoke to me, a guy who was one of Jon's better friends at the club.

"Hey, you ever see your friend Barney Adams any more? If you do, ask him when he's going to come back and visit his hometown."

Barney Adams, the innovative CEO of Adams Golf and inventor of the Tight Lies fairway wood, was a local boy made good. As a working-class kid living in Marcellus, twenty miles west of Syracuse, he used to hitchhike to Onondaga Country Club and caddie for Bill Mitchell. Later, he snagged an engineering scholarship to Clarkson College in Pottsdam and—small world—worked for a couple summers as a summer intern at Crouse-Hinds with Bill Tuck.

Barney and I had been good friends for several years and nobody had been happier to see his little company grow from a struggling custom-fitting outfit barely scratching out the monthly rent into one of the golf industry's true innovative forces, signified by his well-publicized public stock offering in 1999 that was still the largest IPO in golf history. Since then, though, the golf equipment business at large had slipped into its own private recession and once-mighty stocks like Callaway and Adams had taken it on the chin.

Anyway, I wandered off to try and find a Dewsweeper and found Terry Austin in the locker room, wiping his face with a towel. I asked him how it was going. "Do you mean the new economy or my old golf game?" he asked with a laugh.

"Whichever you like best at the moment," I said.

His smile broadened. "Both are pretty *unlikable* at the moment. Fortunately, at least in golf, I've got my dad to carry the load." He and Lester had won their opening match. That was something good, at least.

• • •

Our second match got delayed two hours. It was nearly two o'clock when we started off the back nine beneath menacing clouds and threatening rumbles. I doubled-bogeyed the opening hole. Jon did, too. There was no ham-and-egg left in us, apparently. Just egg on our long faces.

By the sixteenth hole—the seventh hole of our match—the rain was coming down in violent gusts again. Club grips were soaked and so were our brains. It was growing darker and colder by the minute and we took to sniping at each other for this or that minor infraction—a poorly parked cart or crossing the invisible line between his side of the cart seat and mine, petty annoyances that made us appear to be a couple of cranky old marrieds. Rainwater sloshed in the dash of the cart. "Are we having fun yet? You're supposed to be the damned *mudder* in the group," Jon said angrily to me at one point, then grinned slyly, displaying a welcome bit of his old pluck. "Why don't you *do* something."

I birdied two holes back-to-back. He birdied two holes in the final four we played but it wasn't enough. We lost again 3-and-2.

The third round the next morning was just plain dreary and cold. My Tommy Armour clubs felt like blunt instruments. Armour, the story goes, once hurled a set of uncooperative clubs into the waters of the firth from a passenger train crossing the Forth Rail Bridge on his way home to Carnoustie. That's how I felt. I suddenly wished I could throw away my club because, as the saying goes, when all else fails, blame the arrows instead of the Indian.

Somehow, though, we played a bit more like ourselves, both shooting 79 and hamming and egging a bit to take our final match of the member-guest to the final hole. The sun began to come out, the earth to warm. But it was too late for us. We were dead last, I believe, in the loser's bracket of the first flight.

"Let's get out of here," Jon proposed, "before somebody says something to me that *I* live to regret."

· · ·

INSTEAD of going home, we drove around town and wound up, of all places, at St. Mary's Cemetery in Dewitt. By then it had become a decent summer afternoon. Thinking of Tommy Armour, I was tempted to make a joke about us coming there to bury our golf clubs, since they'd already buried us.

"What a week," Jon said. "First your mom, then the Civitellos."

I asked what he meant. The Civitellos were the Sagers' neighbors, and Mary Civitello, a physician, was Karen Sager's best friend.

"You haven't heard?" Jon seemed incredulous.

I shrugged, pointing out I'd just rolled into town and had my own concerns.

"Holy cow," he said, shaking his head. "I thought you *knew* what happened. It's just awful."

He explained that he'd come home on Sunday morning after dewsweeping with the boys and started his usual weekend lawn chores, just as Karen and Sarah pulled into the driveway from church. They were in a panic because a police cruiser was parked in the Civitello driveway.

"Karen made me walk up the street to find out what was going on. So I did. Suzy, a sweet kid who was a freshman in college, was in the house alone. She was dead."

According to the police, her father had returned home from a trip to Albany and discovered the girl's lifeless body. Mary Civitello had been away, too, at the time, up at the family's house on Lake Ontario. Jon had actually been allowed by the police to clean up a patch of vomit where Suzy had apparently thrown up

after coming home from a party with friends the night before—
he hadn't wanted Mary to have to see that. According to the authorities, it appeared that the girl had strangled on a piece of
cake and died of asphyxiation.

"It's every parent's worst nightmare," he said. "That's why I
can't keep my mind on golf or anything else."

I shook my head and asked how Mary was holding up.

"Devastated, of course. Who wouldn't be? She's a basket
case. Karen's with her around the clock. But Karen's a mess, too.
She and Sarah haven't stopped crying in days," he confided, falling
silent for a moment. "This thing is so horrible it doesn't feel real.
You know what it reminds me of? It reminds of the surreal time
when Bill died. He's buried right over there."

Bill was Karen's older brother, the beloved swimmer she followed on scholarship to Notre Dame, the uncle Billy Sager was
named for. I knew Bill died in the crash of a Northwest passenger
plane in Detroit in August of 1987, but I didn't know much else
about it. So I asked Jon to tell me about it.

"Karen and I were in Laguna Beach visiting my grandmother
at the time. She was six months pregnant with Billy. We heard
about the crash on the news and Karen knew Bill was on a Northwest flight, heading to Korea to teach a training class. He'd come
home to see the whole family before going to Asia—almost like
he had a premonition or something. Bill worked for Motorola.
He had his Ph.D. in chemistry, a fabulous teacher and a great guy.
You'd have loved him. Everybody loved Bill.

"I tried to act unconcerned, telling her there was no way he
was on that plane. But the truth was, I felt really funny all the way
home from California. Something wasn't right. I'll never forget
arriving at the Syracuse airport. Karen's brother Joe was there to
meet us. Joe lived in Philadelphia. The moment Karen saw him,
she knew. She came apart at the seams. We all did. It was like an
out-of-body experience. A hundred and fifty-four people died in
that plane crash. Only a small baby shielded by her mother's body
survived."

The tragedy, I knew from Karen herself, dramatically altered the Sager household. For one thing, a short while later, Karen informed Jon that she needed to return to the Catholic church. She and Jon had been teaching youth Sunday school classes at Dewitt Community Church for a couple years, but Bill's death opened wounds only the faith of her family could heal. Jon consented, giving up his family's church for hers. That was how the Sager children came to be raised Catholic.

Jon, ever the dutiful seeker of facts, became quietly obsessed with the tragedy, going so far as to have his congressman secure the government's video reenactment of the crash when the FAA and NTSB both stonewalled him. He discovered well before the public did that the crash was caused by pilot error. The pilot neglected to extend his flaps for takeoff properly.

"Since that day, every time I fly now, I turn and look out the window to see if the flaps are down," he said, as we sat there in that pretty cemetery, each of us reeling in our own private ways from the summer's cascade of sudden deaths of beloved persons.

I didn't know what else to say so, a bit pointlessly, I admitted to him that ironically I did this same thing whenever I flew in an airplane—possibly because of that very same crash. I routinely glanced out the window to make sure the pilot had his flaps down before takeoff, prepared to do I don't know what if they weren't properly extended. There were those tiny degrees of separation at work again.

"Hey," Jon said, clearing away his throat. "Want to go get a beer? I know where Al Devendorf might be hanging out."

I told him a beer would be good, with or without Al Devendorf. Frankly, nothing would go down better.

• • •

WE drove to the Retreat in Liverpool, not far from where Karen and her brother Bill grew up. The bar was crowded but Al Devendorf had once again eluded us. A jolly dark-haired guy named

Mike, an acquaintance of Jon's, was there, however, straight from a golf outing north of town, and immediately began regaling Jon with details of his latest sexual escapades in his company's secretarial pool. Jon listened to Mike with a tolerant smile, glancing at me every now and then. When Mike wandered off to get another brew, Jon explained that his nickname for Mike was "Dash Riprock"—Jethro Bodine's buffoonish skirt-chasing mentor in *The Beverly Hillbillies.*

"Boy," Jon said. "Did we stink out there or what?"

"I'm hoping it's just a mini-slump. Mid-season blahs. But I don't know."

I added that this year, curiously enough, some of the worst scores of my life had been born of testosterone-driven tournaments of one kind or another, while some of the best scores of my life were achieved in simple, grab-a-round loops where nothing was really on the line. The trick to being *stupid happy* in golf, it was beginning to dawn on me, was not to notice what the hell I was doing—or particularly care. Just hit the ball, walk after it, and hit it again.

"Damn right. It's called *dewsweeping,*" he agreed, sounding a bit more like his old welcome self. "I have an admission to make. I hate member-guest golf tournaments."

"I hate them, too. Even if they give you attractive free wind shirts."

Jon smiled.

"In that case, here's what we'll do. Next year we'll have our own Dewsweeper Invitational. Everybody will bring a guest and we'll do a three-day tournament that includes the best and worst of everything—best shot, worst joke, lousiest score, that sort of thing. We could do it on the Robert Trent Jones Trail—Green Lakes, Seven Oaks, Cornell, and maybe even Tully. You'll be fined for slow play or for taking the whole thing too seriously. Sound good?"

"Great. But what's Tully?"

"A town south of here. That's the short little course Jones allegedly designed for a buddy on a cocktail napkin, widely acknowledged as being his worst course design in the world. Remember? That was reason number five to come to Dewsweeperland in the first place. Bill Tuck honed that dry heave of a swing he owns there as a young man, when his body weight was double what it is now."

I smiled at this classic Sagerism. It was good to have Jon back, however briefly, regardless of what the world was flinging at him. I noticed that Dash Riprock had found a new lust interest and completely forgotten us.

"Let's go pick up the girls before we're late for the tournament dinner," Jon said, placing his half-empty glass on the bar. He sounded reenergized. "Lester's saving us all seats on the porch and he gets out of sorts if we're late. With Sheila away he'll think we no longer love him."

• • •

THE next afternoon, in tribute to the late Trent Jones and a dry run for the Dewsweeper Invitational, Tuck, Cahill, Sager, and I drove down to Tully to play the Hill-N-Dale Golf Course. As advertised, it was little more than a cow pasture equipped with nine small push-up greens, the kind of endearing "starter" course McDaid liked to call a "goat farm classic," with a friendly staff and cheap green fees, cold beer, and paying customers who roamed the premises in sneakers and tank tops.

"You've gotta love a place like this," Jon enthused, taking a warm-up cut on the first tee, "I mean, this is the kind of place you find all over Scotland."

"I didn't know you'd been to Scotland," Tuck reminded him.

"I haven't," Jon confirmed, jerking a thumb at me. "But *he* has. Right, Lump?"

"Right, Patch."

I confirmed that there were courses like this little goat farm all over Scotland; every village had at least one. Scots had this crazy egalitarian notion that everybody from the castle laird to the village butcher's assistant should be allowed access to the links, and places like Tully's Hill-N-Dale kept that spirit alive and well, or so it seemed to me.

"Speaking of Scotland," said Tom, "how's the Dewsweeper trip to Britain shaping up? I haven't heard any more about it. Are we going or what? Russ was asking me the other day."

"The Lord of Layering needs to start planning now," Jon said with a laugh. "Russ will need weeks to pack all of his layers of clothing."

I explained that the trip was shaping up quite nicely, as a matter of fact. I'd just heard from Donald Steel and his associate Martin Ebert and they were putting together an intriguing itinerary of old established British clubs we might be able to visit in late September, places most American golfers never set foot. The working list included Woking in suburban London, Woodhall Spa in Lincolnshire, Seacroft and Ganton farther up the coast. Maybe even Royal Worlington could be arranged; that was the home of the Cambridge University golf team, the nine-hole course Bernard Darwin called the "Sacred Nine."

Just to tantalize them a bit, I pointed out that Woodhall has been described as England's greatest inland course and mighty Ganton was where the women's Curtis Cup had just been decided in favor of the USA. A Walker Cup and a Ryder Cup had also been decided there and I, personally, was dying to see the place. Donald Steel, I added, maintained that Seacroft was one of the finest hidden gems of true links golf—and Donald should know since he was the dean of British golf architects and literally wrote the book on the subject.

"Will we get to meet him?" Tom wondered.

I said I hoped so; Donald and Martin were Dewsweeper kind of guys.

"No Scotland?" wondered Tuck.

"We can go to Scotland, too," I said. "But getting on the Old

Course will basically be impossible. September is the most popular time of year and everything is booked solid." I pointed out that there were some pretty famous alternatives around St. Andrews that might fill the void nicely, though—including Gullane, North Berwick, and maybe even the highly regarded new Kingsbarns course.

Finally, I explained that I was even working on a private luxury coach to haul us from London to Scotland in style.

"Count me in," declared Tuck. "You just take us there and we'll play 'em. Can we please play *here* now? This place means something to me."

"We know," Jon deadpanned. "It's where you broke one-fifty for the first time and learned to smoke cigars."

"That's right," Tuck replied. "I was only ten years old at the time."

"That means you weighed more then than you do now."

Because Trent Jones's Tully course was located near Preble, New York, Jon had named it "Preble Beach." It was no Sacred Nine, but it wasn't without eccentric interest. The second hole, for instance, was a novel downhill four-par that asked you to smack your tee shot *over* a row of fully mature hardwood trees to an unseen fairway. I'd never seen anything in the world quite like it.

"Looks like a hole he designed on a cocktail napkin after one too many cocktails," Tom Cahill mused as Tuck and Jon marched ahead of us to try and find the tee shots they'd launched into the tree branches.

"By the way," Tom said, "so sorry about your mom. It must be tough."

I thanked him for saying so. Thanked him, as well, for the nice sympathy card he and Nancy had sent days after she died. That meant more than he knew, I admitted.

"Well," he said, "that's what golf buddies are for."

As we approached our shots, I asked Tom how his son Patrick had fared in his big golf tournament in Rochester. Patrick, a member of Country Club of Rochester, was a fine young player with his mother's good looks and his father's sweet disposition. While Jon and I were flailing in the dreary Onondaga rain, Tom had been up in the hometown of Trent Jones caddying for Patrick in a four-day regional golf association event that attracted five hundred of the district's finest golfers.

"Oh, it was great, really great. He made the thirty-six-hole cut," Tom related with obvious pleasure, stopping by a mud-freckled ball that turned out to be my wayward hook. "And then he went on to actually finish tied for first on Friday. He played beautifully on Saturday and I thought, by golly, for a while that he might even win the thing, but he tied for third in the finals—just two shots out of first. I was very proud of him. He's such a good kid."

"Chip off the old block," I said, remembering the fun we'd had up at CCR with Patrick.

"Nice of you to say so. Nancy would thank you."

"Nancy who?" I asked innocently and Tom laughed.

• • •

ON my way out of town the next evening, I stopped by Russ and Jiggy King's house to tell Russ he could start packing his layers of clothing for September, that the Dewsweepers were going to do England and maybe parts of Scotland as well.

"We're ready for England," Russ said, after he showed me his new English threshing barn and we took Cokes out on the sunlit deck of his magnificent post-and-beam house. "But do you suppose England is ready for the Dewsweepers?"

"Wow," I said, halted in my tracks by the view.

The house sat on the crown of sweeping hill, surrounded by a hundred acres of golden waving wheat, with fifty-mile views in three directions that included Onondaga and Oneida lakes, the city of Syracuse, the foothills of the Adirondacks, even the smoke-stacks of the Nine Mile Nuclear Plant way up on Lake Ontario.

"See?" the dean of Dewsweeper protocol said, pointing to a

small ribbon of green over several small hilltops to the left. "There's the seventeenth fairway at Onondaga. Remember when I told you that you could see it from my porch, whenever that was?"

"Three years ago," I reminded him.

"Seems like we've known you for much longer than that," he said.

I appreciated him saying so. I'd come to think of the Dewsweepers as my home away from home.

"Say, how did you and Jon do in the member-guest?" he wondered.

"We finished it," I replied with a shrug, "or it finished us. I'm not exactly sure which, really."

"I never liked playing in tournaments much. They're just so serious. It's far more satisfying to take Bill Tuck's dollar."

I agreed, explaining how the idea of playing in tournaments always pumped me up, but actually playing in them always seemed to let me down. I pointed out my recent horrifying free falls in the Brunswick Club Championship qualifier and the Maine State Amateur as state exhibits number one and two.

"Well, you can't count those," Russ said gently. "Under the circumstances."

"Yeah, well. If I've learned anything the hard way this year, it's that I should just play for fun," I replied, admiring his extraordinary view again. "What a view. You're a regular Ozymandias up here. Lord of all you survey."

"That really does make you a Dewsweeper," he said. "That's why the Dewsweepers started, you know."

I glanced at the Dean and admitted I didn't even know the history of the Dewsweepers—or, for that matter, how Russ hooked up with them. I knew Russ hailed from a famous family of Syracuse architects and Tom Cahill had told me he'd taken up the game of golf late in life, but I didn't know a whole lot more than that. If we were going to steam to England in each other's company, I said, I had a right to know these vital facts.

Like Bunny Dugan, there was an old-world air of formality about Russ I greatly admired——a warmth and a reserve that complemented each other. He smiled as if he thought I might just be trying to be polite and then gave me a brief sketch of the life that brought him to his glorious hilltop.

If Jon Sager was a true son of Syracuse, Russ King was a genuine patriarch, head of the state's oldest architectural firm, dating to 1868. His grandfather, Melvin King, went to work at age thirteen as a raw apprentice and chauffeur for the great Archimedes Russell, the famed Syracuse architect who designed so many of the city's grand churches and neogothic and Victorian mansions along James Street, as well as several buildings at Cornell University, following the Civil War.

Russell eventually made King a full partner in 1903, living only another ten years, and it was Melvin King who drew up the architectural plans for the classically ornate Onondaga County Courthouse and operated the architectural firm until his son Harry graduated from Syracuse University and joined the firm to make it King and King.

Russ, an only child, grew up in the city's Bradford Hills neighborhood during the Great Depression only a half block from the house where a younger Tom Cahill lived, and he knew "in his bones" by age thirteen that he wanted to be an architect like his father and grandfather. "There really wasn't much of a decision to make," he recalled. "I knew it was something I wanted to do even if there was little or no money to be made in architecture at that time." During the depths of the Depression, he explained, his father and grandfather drew $5 a week in salary from the company bank account and his mother Gladys had to work as a secretary for L.C. Smith at the typewriter factory to help make ends meet.

"My dad used to take me out to prospective job sites and let me hold the dumb end of the measuring tape"——little sorties that more or less ordained his eventual place in the family firm. Harry King survived those challenging years, in part, by designing Coca-Cola plants and factories for the defense department, moved into medical institutions and churches after World War II, and designed several of the city's most prominent architectural landmarks.

"My father was probably the hardest working man I ever saw in my life," Russ said, "and whatever he committed himself to, he gave it everything he had. That had a tremendous impact on me. He seldom took time off and didn't even seriously take up golf until he was nearly forty years old. He used to ride a bicycle, if you can believe it, out to Drumlins to play golf with friends early on weekend mornings during World War II when gas was rationed. He was a Dewsweeper too. And he eventually became so taken with the game he used to say there were only two men in town who could get him to give up the golf course—Mr. Fairchild and Mr. Meech. They ran the city's funeral home."

Not surprisingly, Russ's life and working career—and even his sporting passion—mirrored his father's. After completing his degree in architecture at S.U. and marrying his sweetheart, Jiggy Silcock, in 1952, Russ served in the amphibious forces in Korea and returned to his father's firm in 1956, assembling a distinguished forty-five-year vita that included several S.U. science buildings, S.U.'s Bird Library and the award-winning S.I. Newhouse Communications building, which he did in conjunction with I.M. Pei, as well as major hospital projects in upstate New York.

In the early eighties, Russ's twin sons, Jim and Pete, joined the firm, making King and King the oldest architectural firm in continuous service in New York State, possibly in the United States.

"Like my dad before me," he said as we soaked up the afternoon sun on his hilltop deck, "having my own sons join the firm left me time for other things I'd always wanted to do. I'd been a devoted skier since I was a kid, but I also tried playing golf just to see what all the excitement was about. Brother, did I ever get *hooked*. Like father like son, I guess."

Just then, Jiggy joined us on the deck, bearing a tray of nuts and soft drinks.

"I started playing early with a group of guys who are either retired or moved away now," he remembered. "I guess that was fifteen or twenty years ago maybe—Herb Hooley and Maury Finnegan and the infamous Miles Murphy you've heard Jon talk about. Great bunch of guys. None of us were very good at the game, you see, and we had busy families, so playing early, before anyone else came out, seemed like the reasonable thing to do. Since some of us were just learning the game we didn't even bother keeping scorecards. We just played for the heck of it. It was fun. It became our weekly thing. That was the start of the Dewsweepers, though we didn't call ourselves that. I forget who gave us that name."

"I love the fact that Russ took up golf," Jiggy interjected, pulling up a chair and joining us. "The game suited him in so many ways. Like his father, he's got all of this creative energy and really can't stay in one place too long. So golf and skiing were perfect for him. They kept him going down a hill or walking along a fairway—out of trouble." She laughed robustly.

"There was something else about golf I loved," Russ admitted. "It was the most civil game I'd ever seen. I'm old-fashioned, I suppose. But I like the fact that even with all the jokes and carrying on and so forth—especially from Jon—underneath it all lies a great respect for the traditions and a respect for each other. What other game has that quality?"

Sipping my Coke, I admitted I couldn't think of one. As the declining sun warmed my face, I realized that this conversation on top of the world was pleasing me far more than the Onondaga member-guest had. The hike around the Tully goat farm had made the trip worthwhile, too. If you looked out from Russ's deck, you didn't just see a trace of Onondaga's distant green fairways. You could also see the end of summer coming.

Russ smiled almost slyly. "Did I ever tell you about the first time Jon played with us?"

"No," I said. "But please do—in case it involves something

personally embarrassing. I can maybe use it to get him to stop calling me Lumpy."

"He calls you Lumpy?" Jiggy seemed gently appalled but couldn't avoid smiling. "That *Jon*. He's a rascal."

"That's why we love him," I said. "He calls Russ the Wandering Golfer," I pointed out. Due to the fact Russ carried so many articles of clothing and other gear in his golf bag, layer upon layer, he sometimes appeared to be a homeless hacker ambling along the sod.

"An old ski trick—lots of layers," Russ proclaimed and picked up his tale about Jon joining the Dewsweepers.

"Somebody invited him to join us. I forget who—maybe Herb Hooley. This was ten or fifteen years ago. Anyway, Jon was a young hotshot lawyer just starting out, solemn-eyed and a bit on guard. Of course, I knew both his parents very well. Ruth was known at the club and around town for all her charity work and Rod Sager and I served together on a couple boards.

"Anyway, we're teeing it up there on the first tee—it's wet and early and Jon seems a bit a bit gun shy, almost nervous, maybe just aware that he's the young guy playing with all these old farts. Also, he was so much better than we were you wondered why he was playing with us. So I offer him my hand and look him straight in the eye and say rather sternly, 'We're glad to have you join us, son. But we have three cardinal rules that must be observed at all times. Do you want to hear them?'

" 'Yes sir,' he said.

" 'Good. First, we only play to have fun. Nobody takes this game all that seriously. Understand? Sometimes we don't even bother to write down our scores.'

" 'Right.'

" 'And we never play for more than a buck—no big money to be made here.'

" 'I understand.'

" 'Oh, and one more thing. We play a Floating Flannigan.'

" 'Never heard of that, sir.'

" 'Of course you haven't. We invented it. A Floating Flanni-gan is a mulligan that carries over from the first tee and can be used on any tee.'

" 'Fine by me.'

"I thought that would be it—he would think we were just a bunch of old farts who couldn't even compete with him. He didn't say much that first round, as I recall, but he showed up again the next week, so there must have been something about us he liked after all." Russ smiled. "Maybe it was the Floating Flannigan that hooked him."

"Maybe he was an aspiring old fart."

The Dean's smile widened. "Maybe."

I asked how his game was progressing. "My game right now is like a bad inner tube. I get one thing fixed and then another part springs a leak. But at least I'm only one buck down to Tuck right now. That's all I really care about." He told me about how he and Jiggy had recently been dining in the Seneca Room at the club and glanced over to discover Bill Tuck mere feet away trying to hit a recovery shot out of the bushes just outside the dining room window.

"I thought I'd be clever so I pulled out a dollar bill, tapped on the glass, and waved it teasingly at him. I suppose he might have been thirty yards from the eighteenth green. Damned if he didn't chip in from those bushes. He's amazing."

"That's okay," I consoled him. "You'll have all of England to earn it back."

"Hey," Russ said, "do you suppose we'll need to wear neckties and jackets in the bar and all that sort of thing? I've heard that's the tradition over there."

Absolutely, I said. The Dewsweepers couldn't do England without proper neckties and jackets.

"I like that tradition," Russ said.

I told him that didn't surprise me a bit.

ELEVEN

GOOD GOOD

LOOKING back on times when his life or his game was off, according to the late great Bernard Darwin, Harry Vardon—golf's first supreme stylist who won six British and one U.S. Open, popularized a novel overlap grip, and struck the ball with such regal ease he rarely even took a divot—used to lift his glass and say, "Whatever the situation I found myself in, there was only one thing to do, namely, go on hitting the ball."

That's more or less how the month of August passed for me back home in Maine. I stayed close to the hutch, as Old Harry might have said, built a new flower garden in memory of Mrs. Congeniality, mowed lots of crop circles, drove my kids to and from church camp, and ventured forth every few days to hit the ball with Terry, Tom, and Sid. I couldn't avoid the feeling that something irreplaceable had been lost—two things if you cared to count the schism with my brother—but the unexpected graces of the game gave me much needed perspective, a decent Vardon grip on what was really important.

My new Ping clubs arrived, for example, the same afternoon Wendy came for a week's visit, bearing her own new custom-fitted clubs but also the unhappy tidings that not only would her

former husband not agree to renegotiate the terms of their original visitation agreement, which would permit her and her children to relocate to Maine and a marriage to take place, but, in
fact, he planned to challenge her in court for physical custody of
their children. Her lawyer, an affable Columbo sort, assured her
that, given their parental histories, it was highly unlikely that any
court would reverse custody, but pointed out that courts were
unpredictable and the protracted legal wrangling might go on for
weeks, if not months, possibly years.

So instead of our new extended family being nicely united in
one place by Labor Day, as hoped and planned, Wendy might be
"legally stuck" in Syracuse for the unforeseeable future. Ironically, the relocation hearing that would ultimately determine
whether there was to be a backyard wedding with an Irish fiddle
band and Dewsweepers dancing with their wives beneath the
harvest moon had been set for the very afternoon we were
scheduled to embark for England.

I was discouraged by this development but not, I suppose,
particularly surprised. It had been *that* kind of year, the kind of
year that made you wish you were a kid again and only concerned
about beating your best friend at his own game, or so I grumbled
something to this effect as we sat together on the porch having,
in tribute to France and our friends from Chantilly, a glass of
chilled Sancerre rouge, watching a beautiful summer afternoon
expire, and periodically slipping indoors to catch the closing action of the PGA Championship on TV, where Tiger Woods was
poised to capture his third major in less than a year, having, with
or without the assistance of Hughes Norton, *that* kind of year,
too. In Tiger's case, however, it was the kind childhood dreams
are made of.

"Forgive me for whining," I said, "but it doesn't seem one
damn bit fair." I was thinking about not having Mrs. Congeniality
around and the rift with my brother and the distinct possibility
that the wedding would have to be postponed indefinitely, know-

ing full well life isn't meant to be fair but wishing, by jeepers, it somehow could be.

"I'll bet the other players feel that same way about Tiger Woods," Wendy observed dryly.

"Forgive me for whining a second time, but has *anything* this year really worked out?"

She smiled patiently, as if she were trying to potty train a toddler who kept wetting his Keds due to an awful aim. She tasted her wine as if it brought back excellent memories.

"Just the small stuff. Thank God for that."

I looked at her and realized she was right, of course. The "small" stuff of life, which was much bigger than perhaps anyone realized, *was* working out pretty nicely, all things considered. She and I had never been closer or happier, our children were all healthy and safe, and the resolution I'd made in the pink light of the New Millennium to *work less and play more* seemed to be paying unexpected dividends—having reinvigorated my golf work life and brought me closer to the game than I'd been in years. If it was impossible to say if I'd fully "rediscovered" the joy of playing as I'd hoped I might, I'd undoubtedly grown closer to the things that mattered most.

So what if roughly half of our ordinary days were divided by 492 miles of interstate, three states, eight turnpike toll booths, and eighty-two highway exits (I know because I counted them)? We had each other, four great kids, and a whole lifetime to chase the ball together down the fairway. Tough weather makes good timber, as they say in Maine. Whatever doesn't kill you just makes you stronger—which, by the way, is also the official travel motto of the Massachusetts Turnpike Authority.

That was just one more thing I loved about Wendy Anne Buynak—her remarkable ability to peer through the fog of life and find the ball in any kind of rough, grip down, and keep on hitting the ball down the fairway. She was Harry Vardon's kind of gal.

I thanked her for reminding me of this small truth, apologized for being such a moping boob, and realized she was staring at the lengthening shadows on the lawn and clearly pondering some deep and meaningful thought. I asked what it was and she slowly smiled and said, "Do you think we might have time to get in a quick nine before dark? I sure would love to give those new clubs a swing."

There, I realized later, lay all the proof I required that the golf gods give and the golf gods take away. While Tiger was busy claiming title to his fourth major to cap off the greatest year in professional golf since Ben Hogan in 1953, my golfing soul mate and I wandered around a nearly empty golf course, hitting balls and taking stock of our "small" blessings in the fading Sabbath light.

Moments after finishing, totaling up our scores on the members' porch, Wendy suddenly glowed like a firefly in the twilight. "Holy crow," she said with an excitement you could feel to your fingertips. "I *almost* broke fifty and you shot *even* par!" I laughed at the sweet irony of Old Man Par's timing. He'd finally showed up, but I'd almost failed to notice. At the end of the day, I suppose, as Vardon himself might say, these small graces are better left unexplained.

• • •

THREE days later, I met Sid, Tom, and Terry at the club for our usual Wednesday four-ball. Sid was feeling better thanks to his new medication, displaying encouraging bits of the gruff and gently profane charm that made him such a thorough pleasure to be around. He was clearly buoyed by the fact that his three sons were coming to town that weekend for the annual Watson family golf tournament that marked the end of another summer, but he didn't like it one bit when I airily proposed that Tom and I be permitted to play Terry and himself for two bits a hole. In ten years of playing together, I can't even count on one hand the times Tom and I have played together against Terry and Sid. Or yes I can—it was *once*. We tried it purely as an "experiment" to see if Terry and Sid could actually function as partners instead of opponents. The tension that ensued from their union wasn't pretty.

"That will never happen again, no *way*," Coach Sidney snapped, as if I'd just made the most absurd suggestion he'd heard since some administrative sissy suggested putting face masks on NFL football helmets.

"It's either you and me against Terry and Tom or the old guys against the young guys," he declared, settling the matter once and for all. He frowned at Terry's droopy socks and scuffed golf shoes. "By the looks of those socks, Terence, you must be doing your own laundry these days."

"What's wrong with my socks?" Terry sounded deeply wounded, slipping me a tiny smile. The gauntlet had been thrown down and he loved it.

"Nothing except they're ugly, dirty, and mismatched. I just wondered if maybe Nancy had left you. She usually dresses you a little better than that."

Bunny Dugan, regal as Densmore Shute in his button-up white polo and faded green Augusta National cap, winked at me as if to say, *Here we go again.*

Terry and Sid pleasantly sniped at each other like old times for several holes, a true indication that God was in his firmament and all was well with creation. On the fourth tee, speaking of Divine intervention, at the difficult and lengthy par three over the lake, Terry and I both placed three-iron shots on the edge of the dangerously tilting putting surface and Sidney hooked his long-iron into the pine woods left, swearing in a manner that made me remember Longhurst's helpful injunction that a perfectly timed, well-chosen blue word can help restore the balance of nature.

Tom teed up his ball and made his usual abbreviated caddy-swipe with his trusty five-wood.

"Oh, shoot, *that's* no good," he groaned tragically, watching his low fader zip across the lake and just clear the lip of the guarding cross bunker. "That's just *terrible*."

"Want to bet?" I managed to get out nanoseconds before his ball struck the front of the green, rolled up the slope like it had eyes, and trickled delicately ten feet across the green from left to right—dropping sweetly into the cup for an ace. I smiled and dutifully clapped my hands—this was, oddly enough, for all my years and miles along the golf trail, the first ace I'd ever actually witnessed—and Sid and Terry both glanced over at me from the gravel path where they'd shouldered their bags and were happily arguing, for the zillionth time, about which of them always seemed to have more luck with errant balls flying back out of the woods into play. Sid claimed his poor shots almost always stayed put in trouble because pull hooks had natural over-spin and always traveled farther away while, conversely, Terry enjoyed outrageous good fortune because he typically pushed his misses far to the right and, as Lee Trevino was supposed to have said, everyone knew you could talk to a fade but a hook simply wouldn't listen. I think that was the gist of this particular moment's debate.

"What the hell happened?" Coach Sidney demanded.

"Tom made a hole-in-one," I replied simply. "And you both missed it."

"Oh, great," Sid snarled with mock annoyance. "My partner makes an ace to put us one up and I miss it completely. Thank you *very* much, Terry."

"Well," admitted Tom, almost sheepishly, visibly blushing. "It was really kind of an . . . accident."

"Yeah, right," Terry said. "How many does that make for you now?"

"Just three."

"Just three more than me," Terry said.

"Or me," I chipped in, noting that I was *still* founder, CEO, sergeant-at-arms, head doorman, and general dogsbody of the International Hole-in-None Society, which I founded several years back on the rough theory that those of us who haven't had this

unique experience need a place to go for a little fraternal comfort when some 30-handicapper with a swing that could slice
watermelons launches a ball off the bunker rake and the side of a
nearby golf cart into the cup to register his *seventh* ace. The good
news was, I'd still never made a hole-in-one. The bad news was, if
I ever did I would have to throw myself out into the street.

Terry said with a sniff, "Well, Sidney, if you had just hit the
ball to the green where it's *supposed* to be, we wouldn't have missed
Tom's great shot, would we? Let that be a lesson to you . . ."

On the very next hole, a back-to-back par three of just 120
yards over the opposite edge of the same lake, it was Coach Sidney who dropped a brilliant wedge shot inches from the cup and
nearly scored the ace. The tap-in birdie put the Old Guys up,
two-zip.

After halves at six, Terry and I both attempted to drive the
sharp dogleg right on seven and wound up miles in the woods—
proving the gods play no particular favorites with slicers, either.
"Isn't this great," Terry remarked as we set off to hunt for our lost
balls—his filthy X-out rock and my bright white Titleist Professional. "I wish we could go on like this forever."

I knew exactly what he meant. He didn't mean losing balls
and being about to go three down in a golf match. He meant the
fine summer day and the even finer summer companions, the
lively give of a friendship that spanned almost two decades and
whose mortality had dramatically revealed itself in the previous
year. He meant how wonderful it was to see gunnery sergeant
Bunny Dugan score an unexpected ace and how glad he was to
have Sidney back in fighting trim, gently needling him about his
floppy socks or his outrageous good luck or whatever else he
could think of because Terry, in fact, was like a fourth son to Sid.

When Sid gave up ice hockey after a hall-of-fame coaching
career and hired Terry away from Barney Adams's alma mater,
Clarkson College, in 1983, one of the most productive friendships in college athletics was begun. Terry had gone on to build
his own college hockey dynasty at Bowdoin, amassing one of the

finest coaching records in the nation. But more important, he found both mentor and friend in Sid Watson, a guy who would be there when he was needed most.

One similar "ordinary" summer morning four years before, the summer before I met Wendy, Terry phoned me out of the blue and asked if he could "just come visit." This was most unusual. We always met at the golf club just after eleven, moseying out just ahead of the daily "Gangbusters" group. But something in his voice told me he needed to come to my house for some other reason. I didn't ask what. He arrived and we sat in wooden chairs beneath the big shady beech tree on the lawn, and Terry kept looking at his massive hockey-player hands, opening and closing them as if they were in great arthritic pain.

His ruggedly handsome face looked awful, untouched by a razor in days, ravaged by days of lack of sleep. We talked, as I recall, for a couple hours, a jabberwocky of mid-life male topics crazily skimming from the origins of one's faith to the raging civil war in Bosnia to his daughter Kelly's new job and boyfriend, Sid's fast-approaching retirement, and yet another serious feeler he'd received from a major Division One hockey power looking for a savior.

I listened as Terry rambled on almost incoherently at times, wondering what I could possibly say or do to help him through whatever deep and unexpected funk he'd slipped into, realizing that even though I'd pretty well worked through the baggage of my own recent divorce, my grip on reality probably wasn't all that keen at that moment, either.

Before this moment, I would have told you Terry Meagher was the most mentally stable bloke I knew. If *he* could find life silently unraveling in the quiet rooms behind his eyes then nobody was safe. He talked, I listened, and what it took me some weeks and several in-depth conversations with Tom and Sidney to fully comprehend was that "listening" was all Terry really required from me that day. He needed a friend, nothing more, nothing less.

With steady support from wife Nancy, Sid Watson, a gifted

psychologist, and his old coach and mentor from his playing days at Boston University, the fog lifted and Terry emerged from his ordeal a wiser and stronger man—undoubtedly an even better coach. The mysterious illness probably cost him that big Division One job, but as he often pointed out to me, it also gave him a much deeper understanding of the meaning of his own life and his role as a teacher. Little by little, his own players began turning to him for insights in dealing with the pressures of their lives, and people he never would have pegged as potential victims of depression began to seek him out for counsel. His teams continued having sparkling records and Terry now displayed the ease and confidence of a man who had been through the darkest night of the soul and learned that whatever didn't kill you probably did in fact make you stronger. He seemed at peace with his life, wiser than ever, though still essentially clueless about the quality of golf balls.

"Hey," he said now, four golf seasons and a couple light-years from that epiphanal summer, as we stumped along looking for our lost balls, about to go three down to the Old Guys. "I'm so sorry about your mom's death."

I thanked him and reminded Terence that he'd already told me this a few dozen times since her funeral in June. That was another thing I liked about Terry. He could almost be *too* thoughtful at times. But, on the other hand, if anybody understood the psychological difficulty of losing a mother, it was Terry Meagher. His mother, Doreen, died the winter before his depression struck, and her loss may have been the trigger to his illness. Terry was the oldest of nine children raised on the modest income of a Canadian railroad worker in a small town in rural Ontario. His mother not only taught him to ice skate and work hard, but also never to complain and always tell the truth. As a result, he was the first in his family to go off to college on a scholarship, followed by several of his brothers and sisters. One brother made it all the way to the National Hockey League. Another brother died of AIDS. Terry's mom was a rock through the good times and the bad.

Then, while Christmas shopping at a mall a few days before her family assembled for the holidays, she suffered a massive heart attack and died. It devastated Terry that he never got to say good-bye to Doreen. If anybody knew what losing Mrs. Congeniality meant to me, it was Terry Meagher.

I was about to thank him for caring so much when a different voice rebuked us sharply from the fairway.

"You know the problem with old men playing with younger guys? The younger ones can rarely keep up."

It was good old Mike Linkovitch, grinning at us from the recesses of his cluttered golf cart. Link was Sid's oldest pal in town, Bowdoin's legendary head athletic trainer who'd also wound up in several national athletic halls of fame. Link, now retired, was the group's usual fourth player on Sunday mornings, filling in when I went to church instead of played golf for fear that some USGA official in the sky might be keeping a scorecard of another kind. When he wasn't roaming the course in his golf cart or down in the bullpen swatting practice shots, Link was doggedly searching for lost balls, needling Terry or Sid, or trying to wheedle free test equipment off me. He quickly spotted my new Ping irons and wondered if they were "any good," which was his code phrase for "gee, I'd really like to give those babies a spin sometime."

I pointed out that these particular irons weren't clubs I was testing for one of my magazine columns. These were custom-made irons I fully expected to play with until I became an annoying old fart who roamed the course in a golf cart looking for balls on the cheap and bothering people trying to play a decent game of golf.

Link gave me an apish grin. He liked it when I gave him *crap*. I liked it when he gave me *crap*. Nobody could give Terry crap, of course, because he was far too earnest and sweet. Only Sid could really give Terry crap, which is what he did now—hollering at Terry (and, by extension, me) to either play ball or concede the hole to the Old Guys. There might be something wrong with

Sid's heart, I thought with a surge of relief, but there sure is nothing's wrong with his bark.

Terry said, "My mother used to say, 'If you've lost something, quit looking for it and it will eventually come back to you.' "

"Really? Does it work?"

"More often than not it seems to."

I suggested we give it a try. We declared that we'd lost our balls and conceded the hole to the Old Guys. Moments later, ten or so yards farther along, I swear on the grave of Old Tom Morris, both balls presented themselves, sitting up pretty nicely on a patch of grass in the woods.

. . .

AFTERWARD, I drove to the Highlands to meet the folks who were building the new golf course and sit in on their first planning session. I hadn't set foot on the property for almost a month and, to be perfectly honest, hadn't even permitted myself to drive past the entrance of the Highlands because of the powerful feeling of loss that came over me when I realized my mother's apartment was still there but she wasn't in it. Sorrow is so easy to express, as singer Joni Mitchell once observed, but so hard to tell.

The course was going to be a fine nine-hole affair, possibly with a teaching center that specialized in teaching golf to seniors and kids. My primary suggestion to the project manager and the architect, thinking of crafty old Tom Simpson and the late Trent Jones, was to create greens that featured lots of slope and strategic possibilities and old-style bunkers that would frame the holes in a classic manner but not penalize older or younger golfers too much to spoil their day. Forget trying to build a "signature" course and aim, instead, for a golf course that was fun to play, a wee bit eccentric, and would keep newcomers or old hackers like me coming back for more. The project manager seemed to appreciate this modest viewpoint and wondered if I would come

back when the shaping commenced that next spring. I replied
that nothing would please me more.

After the meeting, I strolled over to return an extra set of my
mother's apartment keys to Norm in the assisted living wing and
we chatted pleasantly for a few minutes in the empty common
room. The door swung open and the Gang of Four bustled in
from an afternoon van ride along the coast. Helen, fingering her
pearls, saw me and demanded: "Where on *earth* is your mother?
We've been looking for her all morning long."

Norm and I both laughed at this. Mom would have laughed,
too, and it prompted me to vaguely wonder if there was an
outside chance that Doreen Meagher's rule might apply in this
situation—*quit looking for it and it will eventually come back to you.*

· · ·

With that in mind, I kept on hitting the ball.

Bunny Dugan phoned and wondered if I wanted to meet him
for nine. It was late afternoon and he'd played that morning with
Sid, Terry, and Link. I said sure and drove to the club, only to discover Tom had phoned Chris Doyle, the pro, and asked him to
give me his apologies for having to postpone our round. Tommy
had taken a sharp turn for the worse and was back in the hospital
for another treatment and Tom needed to be with him.

I was putting on the practice green when Mike Doran
sashayed up. Mike, I believe, was fifteen, a vision of myself at that
age and maybe Jack in a few years—somewhat small for his age, a
short and blond high school freshman in a sun-bleached Penn
State cap who'd recently made his varsity golf team, artfully dressed
in a deeply faded polo, shapeless khakis, and battered unlaced golf
cleats he appeared to have picked up from a thrift shop. He played
with a set of Wilson Fat Shaft clubs I'd tested and given to him after Mike Linkovitch declared they "weren't all that hot," which
was his code phrase for *I'd rather try the new Taylor Made clubs if
you've got them.*

Mike asked me how my summer was going. I said fair to mid-dling and asked him how his budding golf game was doing. He shrugged cooly and explained that he'd just lost the junior club championship to Chris Doyle's son Joe, the club cart boy, who proved practice does pay off and maybe puts you on the road to Carnegie Hall after all.

"But I shot thirty-three on the back yesterday. Wanna play nine?"

I had nothing better to do—or maybe too much. In any case, it seemed like a good way to get ready for the Darwinist rigors of the Blarney and Dewsweeping England, an impromptu match against a flat-belly who was clearly on the way up.

"Sure. What'll we play for?"

Another Cool Hand Luke shrug. "I don't know. How about you buy me a ham and cheese sandwich every day until school starts."

"Okay. Assuming you win. Let's say you mow my lawn while I'm away in England."

"You're going to England?"

"Yeah," I lied with a perfectly straight face. "It's work."

He had me two down with three to play. Then I rolled home a long eagle putt on sixteen, and managed to halve with a birdie on eighteen. We both shot 35, even par.

Mike, I learned, was reading the Harry Potter books. We talked about them on the way to the practice green to settle the issue with a nine-hole putt-off. He was about to go camping with his family and said he hated to miss the state juniors. Apologizing for sounding like an old fart, I remarked that there would proba-bly be lots of golf tournaments ahead for him but probably not too many camping trips with his family.

"What's it like to lose your mother?" he wondered suddenly out of the blue, the way a kid does.

I told him it was like losing your best friend, the person who is always there to pick you up when you're down.

"My mom always picks me up at the golf course," he said, putting a new spin on the old theme. "It must be like that."

"Yeah. Just like that."

I had him two down with two to play and then he canned a couple long putts to halve the match. We shook hands on our draw and agreed to settle our differences somewhere down the fairway. A few minutes later, a car pulled up and Mike's mom got out and waved. She was a pretty mom. He blushed, shouldering his faded bag.

"Well, I gotta go. See ya," he said.

"See ya," I said.

• • •

Keep on hitting the ball . . .

My kids came home from camp. Jack resumed his golf tutorials with Mal Strange and I couldn't resist sneaking down to the bullpen to watch. He made several beautiful swings with a three-wood and launched some surprising drives. Mal spotted me and came over in his golf cart, leaving Jack alone to finish off a few shag balls.

"He's excited about going to Scotland," Mal said.

"I'm excited about him going," I admitted.

"Great little swing, eh? I told you it might surprise you."

I admitted I was pleasantly surprised. Jack's swing was *far* superior to mine at his age. He looked like a young Mike Doran. It was rapidly becoming a summer of small wonders.

"At this point," Mal said, "you just want him to have fun out there."

"At this point," I replied, "that's all I want to have out there."

I suddenly remembered to ask him about Pops Erswell—this cockamamie idea about him *inventing* the pull cart.

Mal smiled. "I think it's actually true. Pops was quite a character. He'd been a Maine guide and an Indian fighter somewhere out west before he became a golf pro. He was still here when I

was a kid and caddied here. Pops was your classic old Yankee tin-
kerer. He welded a small rack onto some bicycle wheels, and several of the wealthy summer members urged him to patent the
idea before someone else did. Well, he never would do it—Pops
was stubborn as a mule—though he made and refined several
models of the contraption and sold them. That was in the 1920s,
I think. He could have been a rich man."

As Jack trudged up the hill toward us, swinging his tour
spoon like a Shropshire boy scything grain, Mal continued: "Pops
also invented a device to hold your wrists in place during the
swing and conducted a one-man campaign to have the hole
widened by a quarter of an inch. He wrote the USGA and the
Royal and Ancient several passionate letters citing his own statis-
tics to prove how widening the hole would be much fairer to the
average player. I think they actually corresponded and even officially considered it for a while."

"Amazing," I said, thinking once again about the game's unexpected connections.

"What's amazing?" Jack wondered.

"You," said Mal with a large smile, taking the words straight
out of my mouth.

•　•　•

RAYMOND Floyd, on the other hand, was frowning.

He glanced up from his lunch and saw Rees Jones. This was in
the magnificent grill room of Atlantic Golf Club on Long Island a
few days later, where I'd gone to visit Susan and Rees Jones the
day before I attended Wendy's custody hearing and left for England with the Dewsweepers. The two men shook hands and Rees
introduced me. I'd met Raymond Floyd on a couple of occasions—
back when I interviewed him for an article on the Ryder Cup
matches in 1989 and then, a second time, a decade later, at Winnie Palmer's funeral. He didn't seem to remember me from either of those encounters, which was no big deal to me.

The two men chatted for a moment and then Rees and I strolled outside to see if the starter could work us onto the golf course. As the young starter checked his sheet, Rees looked back at the dining room, shook his head a little, and wondered if I thought Raymond Floyd seemed unhappy.

"I thought he might at least make some comment about the golf course," he reflected with the faintest smile. "I mean, we architects are pretty sensitive guys, you know? These things are our babies and I'm pretty proud of how Atlantic turned out."

He was joshing, of course—though not entirely. Golf architects are like anybody else. They have healthy egos. I replied that I wasn't the fairest person to ask this because Raymond Floyd always seemed unhappy to me, though it was difficult to figure out why. The guy had won twenty-two regular Tour events and a couple majors, including his sensational U.S. Open just down the lane at neighboring Shinnecock in 1986, and had one of the great shotmaking games of all time.

I explained how he'd been my late father's favorite player— mostly due, I think, to his vaunted short game skills and Carolina connections. But I didn't care for him much because he had once nearly chewed off my head when I asked him a fairly innocent question.

Rees grinned. "What on earth did you ask him?"

"Nothing too awful. I just wondered if Ryder Cup players would ever stop acting like spoiled brats and get back to competing like gentlemen. This was just about the time the 'War by the Shore' garbage was starting up."

"You said that? What did he say?"

"He said I didn't know what the hell I was talking about. If I'd been a player I might know something. But I was just a reporter. He was right, of course—except for one thing. I was a fan long before I was a reporter. I never cared much for Raymond Floyd after that, to be honest."

I added that if the poor quality of the behavior on both sides of the ropes at Brookline was any indication of how things had evolved since then, I probably wouldn't soon care about the Ryder Cup, either. Give me the high drama of a junior club championship semi-final any day over a bunch of spoiled and colorless millionares who are so oblivious to the traditions of the game they threaten to go snowboarding in Peru unless their demands for compensation are met. Cliff Roberts and Henry Longhurst both warned forty years ago that too much money would ruin professional golf, and the spirit of the competition certainly seemed imperiled by mammon of late. I hoped Curtis Strange, the American captain for the 2001, could restore some sanity—and fun—to the proceedings. At the very least, he would probably dress the American contingent better. He'd personally told me he was considering plain white shirts and ordinary khaki pants—my very own basic golf mufti, as it happened.

"You're beginning to sound like a curmudgeon," Rees said with a laugh. "But I basically agree with you."

"Beats those crazy team shirts Julie Crenshaw picked out—although I'm half convinced the wife of a buddy of mine in Syracuse really selected them. She buys her husband's golf duds by the shipping crate from a discount warehouse that specializes in recycled hotel draperies."

"No. I mean about the effect of money in golf these days. We've all benefited from it but it does have a downside. We start to take things for granted and there's so much of it around you wonder why nobody seems all that happy. Floyd's not alone by a long shot. Think about it. Look at all the fallout from Brookline. You've got equipment companies battling the governing bodies over new technology and players threatening to form unions, Casey Martin taking his case to the Supreme Court. I don't believe there's ever been a more contentious time in golf—lawsuits, arguing, deals going sour. I see young kids at amateur tournaments these days, or for that matter guys our age—most of them really aren't having fun. Some of them don't know why they are even *there*. You can see it on their faces. They're there for something else—fame, money, parental pressure, I don't know what. I just think they might be missing the point of the game. I think all of us might be, at times."

"Funny you'd say that," I said, and told him I was trying to work less and play more, desperately attempting to put the fun back in my golf game.

"Any luck? Having fun, I mean."

I said I'd had my moments that summer. Falling in love with Wendy Anne Buynak as she fell head over heels for the game at Pebble Beach, Bunny Dugan's ace, and the joy of beholding Jack's rapidly evolving golf swing. The Dewsweeper trip to Cape Cod had picked up my sagging spirit when I needed it most and a couple *stupid happy* rounds at Chantilly and Fontainebleau may have conclusively proved God is a Frenchman after all.

"So God's really French, eh? Why didn't *He* allow Jean Van de Veldt win the Open, then? By the way, what's a Dewsweeper?"

"A guy who takes the game but not himself very seriously."

The starter was finally coming back, a touch red-faced and deeply apologetic.

"I'm sorry, Mr. Jones," he said. "But we don't have any two-ball slots for another hour or so."

Rees patted the young man gently on his shoulder. "Don't worry about it. Popular game. We'll find someplace to go."

We collected our bags and started for the parking lot, and I explained to Rees that a round of golf wasn't really all that necessary. I'd mostly come to visit and chew the rag, as they say up in Maine. Golf architects interest me *far* more than Tour players, as a rule, and that morning Rees and his daughter Amy had shown me something quite extraordinary—a "secret" new Rees Jones layout being built through the stubby oaks and remains of the Bridgehampton Raceway, featuring wonderful elevation shifts and a glorious view of Peconic Sound, a fantasic new course called the Bridge. When it opened for play sometime in late 2001, the Bridge was certain to be hailed as one of the great new courses of the year, and to burnish Jones's reputation as America's top classic designer.

"I have an idea where we can go," Rees said suddenly. "Given your contrarian views of the modern game, you may like it better anyway."

I followed him down the road a few miles to the Maidstone Links, in East Hampton. Designed and laid out in the early 1920s by the great Willie Park, Jr., the two-time British Open champ who made the memorable assertion that "any man who can putt is a fair match for anyone," Maidstone is built miraculously on just 140 acres of sand dunes and salt marsh, famous for its charming "road holes," cross-bunkers, and natural waste areas, an antique gem I'd long hoped to someday have a chance to play.

There was no one about and so we shouldered our bags and went straight to the first tee, placing our next dinner evening out on the outcome of the match. During his high school and college days at Yale, Rees was an accomplished amateur player but never quite the match of his older brother Bobby, who played on the U.S. Juniors and helped Yale win the Eastern Intercollegiate championship. But as he proved by recently winning all of his matches in the National Team Fourball Championships with partner Vinny Giles, Rees was no slouch with the sticks, either, as custodian of a solid three or four handicap.

If you believe what has written about Robert Trent Jones's two sons, they grew up competing intensely against each other both on and off the golf course for the affections of their famous but emotionally remote papa. If golf in the past half century has become a large and not entirely happy big business, Trent Jones is one of the major reasons why. He not only revolutionized golf course design and made the position of "course designer" a respectable and formally recognized profession—prior to Jones the great course architects were often simply regarded as "builders" by the people who hired them—he also invented the concept of a "signature" golf course, popularized the game as no architect before him had, and established the gold standard for self-promotion and dogged pursuit of paying customers, setting out a blueprint for aspiring young architects everywhere, including his own sons.

No one was quite sure what the total output of the Jones family was, though *Sports Illustrated* recently put the number at over seven hundred golf courses during a fifty-year span, a prodigious accomplishment that prompted some wag to refer to the Jones boys as the "IBM of golf."

The afternoon Chris Doyle informed me that Trent Jones had passed away, I attempted to phone Rees and offer my condolences but he was already en route to Florida to give his father's eulogy. A few days after my mother passed away, Rees had phoned me just as I was heading out the door for a flight to North Carolina to do the same thing for my mother.

Our friendship had grown in recent years through a shared passion for old golf courses and traditional designs. In my opinion, as a fan of the work of both men, the Jones brothers couldn't have been more philosophically different, and yet each bore traces of their father's influence.

Bobby was what I thought of as a "big-canvas" designer who created lush "signature" courses that dazzled you with their visual splendor and technical challenge, much in the way his father startled the golf world with his eye-popping designs at the height of his career; he also had his father's knack for showmanship and gift for self-promotion, which perhaps explained why he worked as much as any architect on earth, creating lavish layouts from California to Southeast Asia.

Rees was the quieter soul, influenced by his mother Ione's taciturn personality, a more introspective sort who cut his teeth in the trade by working on several of Trent Jones's famous Open course renovations before striking out on his own in 1974 to apply what he'd learned from his father. In his heart, I knew from our conversations, Rees had always felt a little slighted by the great man and handicapped by the fact that he didn't have his father's famous name. That belonged to his brother, Bobby.

"It was tough in the beginning, leaping out on my own. I literally rented a small office and waited for the phone to ring," he once told me with a solemn laugh. "I waited and waited and waited." He designed several fine courses but really didn't begin making his own mark until he remodeled Brookline for the U.S. Open of 1988. "That really opened the door for me in ways nothing else could have because it showed that I understood what the classic architecture meant and I had some creative new ideas of my own."

After Brookline, the offers came his way in a steady stream and he went on to create some of the most acclaimed golf courses of the past twenty years, including Atlantic, Nantucket Golf Club, Hunstville, Ocean Forest, and highly regarded Red Stick in Vero Beach. He also remodeled eight or nine classic Open courses along the way, including the original Bobby Jones's beloved East Lake in Atlanta, and inherited his father's "Open Doctor" title— so, in effect, he'd acquired his father's true legacy, if not his name, after all.

Sports Illustrated writer John Garrity summed up the natural rivalry between Rees and Bobby this way: "Bobby, who tires of reading that Rees is the best of the Joneses, counters by describing his brother as a 'gentleman architect, part of the East Coast establishment.' His own mission, Bobby says, is to democratize the game and make it more accessible to the masses, which is why he builds more daily-fee and housing-tract courses and why he follows his father's example by taking golf to foreign countries."

In my book, the brothers didn't even compete and there was plenty of room in the golf world for both designers.

In any case, as we moseyed down Maidstone's charming first fairway, which was framed by a small uneven lane, scraggly rough, and whole exposed sandy patches that gave the old course a welcome *under*-manicured look, I asked Rees how he and Bobby were getting along since his father's death. Thinking of my own situation, I wondered if Trent Jones's death had made it easier or more difficult for the brothers to see eye to eye.

"Bobby and I are just different sorts of men," he reflected. "And even though we don't understand why the other does what he does sometimes, particularly in family matters, we've managed to keep it civil and respect each other's work. He does his thing and I do mine. I think the rivalry stuff has been blown way out of proportion. We do such different kinds of work, I don't think we really even compete with each other for jobs. We pretty much reconciled our personal differences years ago, but Dad's death, I think, brought a lot of things into focus. Death reveals a lot in families—the good and the bad."

I told him I couldn't agree with him more and then filled him in on the unexpected rift that had separated my brother and me over the past seven or eight months. If anybody could understand the disappointment and loss of faith I felt, it would probably be Rees Jones. We were both younger brothers who preferred the old ways.

"Boy that's a *tough* one to swallow," he agreed. "You wonder how two brothers who come from the same family can wind up looking at the world so differently."

"Look at you and Bobby."

He smiled. "Touché."

"I clearly don't understand my brother. But I think I'm getting over the anger of what he did. He obviously felt he needed to do it. It would sadden me to think we might never speak again."

"You'll hear from him again," Rees assured me, sounding like the older brother I wish I'd had. "When he needs something, he'll call you."

"You think so?"

"Guaranteed. That's the way it works in families. Question is, will you be there to help him out again."

Unsure of this answer myself, I proposed that we forget the unsolvable conundrum of older brothers and simply concentrate on the mystery of golf design. I asked him if Maidstone was his kind of golf course because it certainly was mine.

"Oh, yes. This is just about as fun as golf courses get, in my opinion," he answered quickly. "Everything you must do is visible, no tricks, no gimmicks. It's honest architecture that reveals the shot you must make and asks you to make it. The only trick—and it's not really a trick at all, it's more of a visual hazard—is the eighth hole. Wait till you see it."

The eighth hole was a partially blind par three that no designer in his right mind would dare try building today, requiring a nimble pitch of 130 yards over the shoulder of a dune to a postage-stamp green tucked in the lea of another sand dune.

Rees lofted a brilliant shot over the dune, leaving his ball two feet from the half-hidden pin. I pushed my shot over the green and went one down in our match.

"I should have given you a couple strokes," he apologized as we hoofed to the ninth tee. "After all, I know this course pretty well."

"That's okay," I said, and told how I was recently two down with three to play to a fifteen-year-old phenom in unlaced Footjoys who seldom went home from the golf club except to sleep and read Harry Potter books. A great deal had been riding on the match—well, a ham and cheese sandwich—but I'd somehow sucked it up and pulled out a magnificent halve.

"That's *exactly* what I'm talking about," Rees crowed happily. "Golf needs more matches for ham and cheese!"

He asked how the big wedding preparations were coming along and wanted to know a date so maybe he and Susan could make the festivities. We were passing through the same dunes where Impressionist Childe Hassam painted some of his finest oil landscapes in the late 1920s. I explained that there was an unexpected hitch and the wedding might have to be postponed, but that was sort of the way the year's big plans were going for us.

"Sorry to hear that," Rees said. "On top of everything else."

"It'll happen when it's supposed to." I heard myself saying something I think I was beginning to finally realize. "You can't force a wedding, I suppose, any more than a golf shot."

"Good way to look at it."

So we finished our tour of Maidstone speaking only of happier subjects—the impending Dewsweeper invasion of Great Britain and his daughter Amy's recent homecoming from graduate school in Boston; happier memories of his larger-than-life father and my most congenial mother.

I was still one hole down at seventeen, the dangerous two-shotter where you must first calculate how much of Hook Pond to bite off and then deal with the road and an out of bounds that come quickly into play. I chipped close and, proving the truth of Willie Park's maxim, sneaked a wandering downhill putt into the cup to tie our match.

We played eighteen in near darkness, leaning into a sharpening ocean wind that smelled of the approaching rain as we walked up the hill. Rees hit another brilliant approach shot, this one coming to rest inches from the cup. I hit my seven-iron to a respectable two feet. I was about to mark my ball when Rees, holding the stick, looked at me with those famous spaniel eyes of his father, and smiled.

"What do you say . . . good good?"

I picked up my ball and we shook hands—shades of what the Ryder Cup used to be.

Good good was fine by me, another great thing about golf, another small reason to keep on hitting the ball.

TWELVE

FUG

"Tшат area to the right of the fairway is a place you will wish to avoid at all costs." Charles Churchill spoke like a gentle prophet of doom. "If you go in there you may not lose your ball but may well wish you had, for it is a place of uncompromising difficulty, a locally feared vegetative hazard we simply call *fug*."

"Sounds like the kind of year some of us are having," snorted Jon Sager, waggling his Terminator driver as if he intended to take out his life's frustrations on an innocent little ball.

"Speak for yourself and the Lumpster," advised the Irish Anti-christ, doing one of his technically correct LPGA-approved body stretches. "My year's been great and it's about to get a whole lot better. Come to me, sweet *Blar-nay* Cup."

"Then I must count myself fortunate to have you as a part-ner," Charles Churchill said pleasantly to Patrick, liberating one of his two Labs from her lead while giving the other a gentle tug. One beast was a yellow called Mashie, the other a blackie named Niblick. Or maybe I've got them backward. Anyway, Charles, a former Senior Master and longtime cricket coach at Summer-fields, Bernard Darwin's old prep school near Oxford, and a member of the Oxford and Cambridge Golf Society (Oxford '61) who'd led fourteen expeditions of British prep school golfers to the United States and probably carved his way 'round more famous courses in America than the three Blarney competitiors combined, was graciously putting us up for the opening rounds of the Cup. Due to the fact that McDaid and Sager had arrived almost five hours behind schedule and our opening round at Saunton had to be scratched, that left only Westward Ho! and Rye to decide the issue of winter bragging rights before our planned rendezvous with the Dewsweepers in London for a Saturday night dinner at the Savoy.

If Saunton was a scratch, Royal North Devon, as the club is properly called, appeared in grave danger of becoming a wash. The flat expanse of common grazing land between Westward Ho!'s handsomely unadorned white clubhouse and the sea is called the Burrows, but it was wreathed at that moment in a chill September mist interspersed with small fits of Atlantic rain that obscured most of England's oldest royal links land, dashing any hope of seeing the picturesque harbor village of Appledore.

"Peculiar name for a challenge cup," Charles said. "How on earth did you arrive at it?"

"The inaugural cup was played in Ireland," I explained, "in honor of Patrick's ancestors who were deported from the country in 1910 at the height of the troubles."

"Which reminds me. How *does* an Irishman go on vacation?" Jon asked. "He changes bars."

"It's true," the Irish Antichrist confirmed, ignoring the Sage of Syracuse. "My grandfather was sent from County Clare to America as an indentured servant along with two hundred other men. Curiously he was carrying a passport issued by the British War Office. So he may have been an informant for the Crown. Anyway, he went to Tennessee and went on to have five sons, four of whom became millionares. So I guess it worked out pretty well."

"Fascinating," said Charles. "And what courses did you play and who won that first Blarney Cup?"

Pat explained that we started at Lahinch and went on to Old Head, Ballybunion, and finally Tralee. We also did a couple turns around the Killarney Golf and Fish Club. I considered interjecting edge-wise that Killarney had special significance to me because it was built on Lord Brabazon's old estate, designed in part by good old Henry Longhurst. But it didn't seem particularly relevant to the discussion so I kept mum. Besides, Longhurst was a Cambridge man.

"Jim won," Pat revealed, "which was fairly rude considering they are *my* people. But at least I carried the day at Ballybunion."

"An old Tom Simpson course," I put in even more *un*-relevantly, in case anyone was interested, which they obviously weren't.

Jon laughed. "Right, Charles. He beat us with a ninety! I wouldn't boast about *that*."

McDaid felt moved to defend his honor. "To put it in perspective, Charles, the winds at Ballybunion were seventy miles an hour, the rain was sideways . . ."

"Bill Clinton had been there the day before us," I interjected, feeling increasingly irrelevant to the tale, which in fact I turned out to be that rainy day in Ireland.

" . . . and we were hitting three-hundred-yard three-woods downwind and drivers on par threes upwind. It wasn't pretty."

"It *was* fugly," agreed Jon.

"Which made the hot lunch afterwards most welcome," I remembered. "We found a great little pub where a young waitress wanted to have relations with Bill Clinton, as they say, and the older one wanted to chase him out of town with a pitchfork."

"No," Jon corrected. "The best part was trying to liberate the Clinton poster from the pole afterwards. They had put up hundreds of these posters with Clinton's mug saying 'Ballybunion Welcomes President Clinton' on them. Jim desperately wanted one. We almost got arrested trying to get it."

"I wanted one for Arnold Palmer," I corrected him. "It was Arnold's seventieth birthday and I needed a gift. What do you get a man who owns his own jet and several golf clubs?"

"Anyway, the Lumpster boosted Pat up the pole and a constable—"

"The Guardia," Pat corrected him.

"—*whatever*. An Irish cop pulled over and asked just what we thought we were doing? He told us to go down the block to the presidential gift shop and *buy* one of the posters from the village council. Turns out they changed the name of the shop out of respect for Clinton. It was formerly called Monica's Gifts."

"The next day at Tralee," I finished the protracted Canterbury golf tale, "I beat them both like a couple old rugs on a fence and took home the first Blarney Cup."

"Yeah, well," sniffed Jon beneath his Onondaga cap, "let's talk about the next year at Kiawah and the greatest shot ever made . . ."

"Oh, brother," sighed the Irish Antichrist. "I knew *that* was coming."

A throat was discreetly cleared.

"Perhaps we should actually *play* and chat before the weather turns really ghastly," Charles said, mercifully putting an end to this discussion—proposing that he and Patrick play Jon and me in a best-ball four-ball.

"You mean it *gets* worse than this?" Jon wondered.

"Oh, much worse," Charles seemed pleased to inform him. "I'm afraid this is rather mild for Westward Ho!"

. . .

Our charming host pegged up his ball and gave it a very smart crack, sending it away in the mist with the no-nonsense efficiency that did his 8 handicap no dishonor whatsoever. McDaid teed up and made one of his patented LPGA-tutored perfect swings, drilling his opening shot dead into the rushes of the small burn fifty yards ahead of us.

"That would be one," Jon intoned like James Earl Jones, causing both Charles and me to laugh.

"What do you say we give him a mulligan," I suggested charitably, being officially undefeated in Blarney Cup competition.

"So he doesn't ask for some cheese with his whine," Jon added, winking at our host.

"How very gracious," Charles observed. "Not normally done in the average challenge cup."

"Who said anything about being average? We're well *below* that, Charles."

This time the Irish Antichrist sped up his swing and pulled his ball sharply to the left into a lank area of tall wet grasses.

"That's not the fug," Charles advised. "But it won't be an easy second shot from out there, I'm afraid."

Jon led off for our team. He positioned his feet for a long low draw, stared at the wall of mist, and drew back his battle-scarred Terminator so far past parallel it reminded me of a famous photograph I'd been looking at just the night before, of the great Bernard Darwin in action. Jon often audibly grunts at the top of his backswing but this time, mysteriously, he didn't, perhaps indicating that due to the uncertain conditions he was attempting to "steer" his tee shot rather than simply slug it with his usual bravado. In any case, his ball vanished far to the right, last heard wailing as it flew toward the perilous fug.

I selected a five-wood and poked a safe shot two hundred straight ahead, prompting Charles to say "Not bold but smartly played," prompting my fellow Blarney competitors to hoot and hiss and make generally unbecoming noises about the quality of my manhood.

"Nice shot, Alice," the I.A. chided.

"Safe but not exactly the way it was done back when men were men and sheep were afraid at Westward Ho!" smirked the Sagacious One.

"See what I must put up with all in the name of friendship?" I said quietly to Charles, as we all shouldered bags and fell in step along the first fairway.

"You appear to relish it just the same," he observed dryly and I realized he was right. I did relish this banter. It was when my Blarney mates weren't needling each other or me that you had to start to worry.

Half a dozen sheep did indeed palely loiter just up ahead, but herds of roaming sheep are central to the elemental charm of Royal North Devon. The course occupies ancient common lands where sheep and horses are permitted to wander free, which makes where you step or place your ball something of an adventure. Supreme naturalness is the course's principal virtue. "Go to Westward Ho!" wrote Darwin in his 1910 classic *Golf Courses of the British Isles,* "and it is a reverent pilgrimage."

That's what it was shaping up to be for me, at any rate. Historically speaking, though the raw and windy links land shaped the attacking flat-footed playing styles of two-time British Amateur champ Horace Hutchinson and his former boot boy John Henry Taylor, who went on to win five British Opens and become part of the Great Triumvirate with James Braid and Harry Vardon that dominated golf at the turn of the century, the course was also the spiritual home of my funny gold-toothed mentor, David Earl, the Duke of Earl, who always found something to laugh about and claimed that he never had a bad day on the golf course, even when the card indicated otherwise.

Regardless of the fitful weather—which, to be honest, I rather fancy on a links land because it means you're playing the course at its most challenging—I was determined to have a good time no matter how I played, à la Ballybunion, where the three of us got soaked to the bone and blown to smithereens but had one of the most entertaining afternoons of our lives, trading barbs and taking home a pile of funny memories, if not Bill Clinton's smirking mug on a poster. Though I couldn't have known it from the outset at North Devon, the whimsical golf gods would thoughtfully grant me a most unexpected dispensation—a very fine score indeed. One of my best ever, as it happened. But that was yet to come.

At the most dauntingly famous hole of the outward nine, the legendary fourth with the formidable "Cape bunker" staring down players from the tee, said to be the largest cross-bunker in the civilized world and a sight meant to strike terror in the stoutest of hearts, I once again chose discretion over valor and pelted my three-wood safely over the trouble, as did our team's opponents McDaid and Churchill.

My partner, the Sage of Syracuse, however, ripped his low-flying tee shot straight into the bunker's massive wooden "sleepers," from which it caromed back into the sand. "You'd be well advised simply to wedge yourself out and hope for little more than that," Charles warned him fairly enough.

But standing thirty yards back and to the left side of the fairway, near an out-of-bounds stake where forensic evidence suggested a herd of sheep had recently passed, I realized that Jon was aiming to accomplish far more than that.

He swung savagely and I saw his ball strike the wooden sleeper and ricochet violently upward. For a baffling moment we all gazed heavenward wondering where the orb might have gone. Then I heard a soft but telltale thud mere feet to my left and discovered that my partner's ball had come safely to earth again, cushioned by a large moist pile of sheep doo.

Wishing to be helpful to my partner, I enthusiastically called out to Jon that I'd found his ball.

"The good news is, you're still in bounds. The bad news is, you're in something else."

"Crap!" he bellowed, climbing out of the pit.

"Excellent guess! Recent vintage, by the look of it."

"Well, I'm taking relief from the sheep's relief!"

As Jon stalked toward me to examine the damage, I couldn't help imagining Bernard Darwin and the Duke of Earl sitting together on the members' porch of Heaven having a good laugh at this little scene—the kind of moment of rude hilarity only the game of golf can really present in its unadorned glory. Bernardo, as the greatest of England's golf writers was affectionately called by his peers, was renowned for the ferocity of his temper and the Duke loved nothing better than to savor another man's comic misfortunes on the links. He must have been enjoying my year immensely.

Jon must have been on the same wavelength because, surveying the challenge, he laughed, shook his head, and observed, "I wonder what our friend Bernardo would say about this? Too bad Pinkie didn't have a club for *sheep dip*."

The reference was to the delightful hour or so we'd passed the previous evening in the cozy home of Charles's friend Pinkie Aarons, just doors down Isha Street, who turned out not only to possess maybe the greatest collection of antique kitchen utensils anywhere on earth—whisks and eggbeaters and the like going back three *hundred* years—but also one of the great private golf libraries and a collection of rare antique clubs begun by her late husband Herbie.

While Jon admired various peculiar "speciality" clubs that came from an age when there was no restriction upon the number of clubs one could carry in competition, Patrick and I vanished into Pinkie's vast and entertaining library that featured antique primers on the game and beautiful first editions of Darwin, Vardon, and several other deities but also a curious little blue tome that turned out to be a privately printed "memoir" of Bernardo's toddler years, penned by his father, Francis Darwin, a physician who worked as a botanist and the brother of Charles Darwin of *Origin of the Species* fame. It was called "The Story of a Childhood."

October 16, 1879:

B is developing a greater power at being naughty. Miss Drummond from Holwood was lunching and he totally refused to say, "How do you do?" This was not taken any notice of but when he was going out of the room she asked to look at his soldiers and, after refusing, he took them and showed them. When he'd nearly got it right I asked him if he would show them another time and he said, steadfastly, that he would not. So I took them away and burnt them, which caused a fresh outburst of rage and grief.

It was only after I finished reading excerpts of the memoir aloud to the others and the laughter subsided that I was moved to discover another coincidence of timing—or as I was coming to think of them this year of small discoveries, another unexpected "connection" to the game.

That very day was Bernard Darwin's birthday.

Darwin's respect for Westward Ho!'s so-called "Rush Holes" was immense and, as we discovered, well justified. The tall and spiky sea rushes come into play along the left border of the tenth hole but seem to close dangerously all around you on the eleventh tee, making this one of the narrowest and most harrowing driving holes in all Britain. My partner drilled his tee ball straight into a wall of rushes and the ball dropped straight down as if it had run into a velvet curtain, and I thought of Darwin's stern admonition the previous evening:

Once you get in the rushes, you may stay there a long time, and your niblick must be a trusty one to mow them down. They are like wire and it is quite queer to feel your niblick rebound off a clump! I know nothing like them anywhere, and they certainly come under "Things to be avoided" as they have a distinctly sharp way of reminding you that you are off the course.

I watched my partner violently attempt three times to advance his ball, hacking at the stubborn grasses where only the fittest survive. He finally gave up and picked up and issued another burst of strong but necessary words, not having the kind of easy walk he'd had around pretty Eastward Ho! on that past and faraway spring afternoon.

The sun suddenly bobbed out at fifteen, the long and dog-legging four par where, peeling off my soaked wind shirt, I faced an approach shot unlike any I'd ever had. A group of mares and their foals were peacefully munching grass between my ball and the just-visible top of the flag stick, a scene as bucolic as any Thomas Constable painting. I hated the thought of disturbing them so I took one more club than normal, a nine-iron, and struck the ball as firmly as I could, hoping to cover the 150 or so yards to the putting surface without their notice. One of the mares lifted her head and I could swear she watched my ball fly over her head.

Sometimes it really does pay to be more lucky than good and I was surprised to discover my ball sitting a foot uphill from the hole. Jon and I were two holes up with four to play. As I walked around the other side to examine the putt from a second angle, though, the Irish Antichrist smiled evilly and said, "Uh oh. One-stroke penalty."

Charles appeared gently baffled. "What on earth did he do?"

"We have a little rule in the Blarney," Pat blithely explained, "where you're docked a stroke for reading a putt twice. Keeps play moving nicely."

"Or hinders your opponent's attempt to make a timely birdie that could cinch the match," Jon more accurately summed up.

"I seem to recall a mulligan on the first hole . . ."

"Okay. We'll let it slide this time."

Our host smiled. "My, but you chaps do get on. It's a wonder you don't play stymies. I rather like that rule, though. Seems quite sensible to me."

I made the putt and could have sworn Niblick winked and smiled at me. My Buddhist friend Bill Kimpton would have said I was *one* with Westward Ho! and its critters. I realized that I'd unexpectedly slipped into the blessed state of *stupid happy*.

"Do you see that building on the hill?" Charles said pleasantly as we approached the seventeenth green, indicating a line of ornate rooftops on the eastern hill. "That's a school Rudyard Kipling attended for a while. I don't know if he played golf here or not, but he well could have, I suppose."

I remarked that Rudy would have been crazy not to play here.

But then, even without consulting the card I knew I was having one of the best rounds of my life. Perhaps that was *because* I hadn't been consulting the card and was thoroughly enjoying the rough splendors of Westward Ho! I imagined the Duke of Earl's gold tooth flashing when I signed the card for a one-over 73. Both Charles and Pat, it emerged, had soldiered around with respectable 81s, while Jon had labored mightily just to scratch out 85. On the official Blarney tote board, I had six points to Pat's three to Jon's zilch.

"What exactly does one *get* in terms of an award for winning the Blarney Cup? Is there an actual cup?" Charles wondered, as we started up the soggy footpath to the clubhouse, following Niblick and Mashie to lunch.

"There is an actual silver engraved cup from Auchterlonie's of Saint Andrews," I explained. "Jon even commissioned a local craftsman to make a wooden carrying case for it with a shamrock seal. It looks like an IRA bomb carrier. But mostly, you get to shamelessly lord it over the other two for a solid year."

"Well in that case, it would appear you chaps have some jolly work left to do in order to catch the leader," our host pleasantly commented to McDaid and Sager.

"Jim is a mudder," Jon dismissed me as if that were only one evolutionary rung above philandering president or lying insurance agent—pointing out something I perhaps truly hadn't fully considered until now. "He plays his best when the courses and conditions are the worst. It's disgraceful."

"Except at Ballybunion, of course," Pat said.

"Do we need to hear any more about *that*?" I asked, pausing to give Nibbie a good scratch behind the ear for her excellent moral support.

"Are there any sheep at Rye?" Jon wondered. "I've seen enough sheep for one trip."

"No sheep at Rye," Charles attempted to console them. "But Rye is magical in other ways. *Anything* is possible there."

• • •

SENIOR Master Churchill had thoughtfully arranged luncheon and a surprise guest for our enlightenment. David Stirk was a longtime member of Westward Ho! and a distinguished historian of the game, author of several comprehensive books on everything from the history of caddies to the origins of the game's rules and hardware. If anyone would know whether old Pops Erswell invented the pull-cart, it was likely to be David Stirk.

Stirk was waiting for us on the club's now-sunny porch, a dapper English physician with a rosy complexion who was eighty-four years old but looked ten years younger than that and, according to Charles, regularly bested his age 'round Westward Ho! After we took seats and ordered the day's special plate of fresh salmon and peas and had pints of bitter safely in hand, I mentioned Pops Erswell to David and wondered if there was any chance Pops could have invented the American pull-cart or the British "trolley." I also filled him in on Pops's running correspondences with the USGA and the Royal and Ancient, his passionate petitions to have the hole widened by a quarter inch for the sake of the average golfing Joe.

"Most interesting, " David replied, sounding a lot like Dr. Watson puzzling over a delicious mystery. "But I don't believe it's recorded who exactly devised the trolley. It could well have been some clever person from your side of the water, of course. But I can tell you something fascinating I discovered from my own inquiries regarding the circumference of the hole. I've studied this phenomenon on golf courses from Saint Andrews to Malaysia, and it has remained consistently true in every situation. What amazes me is that no one ever comments upon it—or particularly takes notice."

He explained that ten or twelve hours after a greenkeeper cuts a four-inch hole for the cup early in the morning, that same hole has become, on average, anywhere from an eighth to one-sixteenth smaller. In effect, it shrinks during the day.

McDaid, the Blarney's second-biggest mouth but most inquiring mind, wondered why that might be true.

"Natural contraction perhaps plays some role in it," Stirk said. "As the green dries out, the hole contracts. But my own theory is that the steady pressure of feet compacting the area 'round the hole as the day progresses may be the real culprit. In any case, it constitutes a real advantage to players who play in the morning, the earlier the better."

"In other words," said Jon with immaculate timing, "it pays to be a Dewsweeper."

"Oh, I would definitely say so," Stirk agreed. "The evidence is conclusive."

We had a toast to this fact and then the peas and salmon arrived and Stirk entertained us with tales of a village surgeon's life and left us smiling with an account of a club secretary who'd recently caught a pair of lovers copulating in a bunker while he was attempting to make an important pitch shot.

"You can't do that here!" the secretary thundered at the tresspassing lovers.

"Why ever *not?*" the young man demanded, scarcely pausing in his exertions.

The club secretary thought for only a moment and indignantly replied, "Because you're not *members!*"

. . .

On the long drive to the southeast coast and the enchanted village of Rye, we saw several closed petrol stations.

"Hope *that's* not a sign of things to come," Jon reflected. "Hate to think of the Dewsweepers hiking from one golf course to the next."

"Big strike looming," Pat said. "Read about it in the *Times* yesterday. Prices have gone through the roof and farmers and lorry drivers, I guess, are ticked off. They want Tony Blair's head."

"I know where they could get Bill Clinton's head, on a poster. Probably pretty cheap by now."

"Hey, maybe the farmers could use a good employment lawyer," Jon joked. "I mean, Sarah's headed to Oxford anyway. I'm sure Karen wouldn't mind a year in England."

"We sure could have used a good lawyer," I said, and went on to explain about the comic opera I'd sat through in Onondaga Court House just hours before my flight to England.

The custody hearing went nothing like we'd hoped and expected it would. Wendy's affable lawyer couldn't seem to remember her former husband's name, forgot to mention most of the relevant points of her case for relocation, and seemed completely stymied when his opposing counsel brilliantly used technical points to shoot holes through Wendy's relocation petition. After a series of maddening delays, the judge extended the hearing to late November but suggested Wendy go ahead and "get married and move on with your life," implying that he planned to ultimately rule in her favor somewhere down the line. In the interim, the court-appointed guardian suggested that since the new school term had already commenced, Wendy's sons "temporarily" reside with their father, pending the late November hearing.

There was no way on earth, I pointed out to Jon and Pat, that Wendy would agree to give up her kids just for a new life in Maine with me, even temporarily. We'd both agreed that sort of arrangement was no way to begin a married life.

"So what will you do?" McDaid wondered.

"The wedding is off for now, I'm afraid. I was just waiting for the right moment to break the news to you guys."

"That's really crummy," Jon agreed. "But, on the plus side, you're leading the Blarney Cup by an Irish country mile."

That made me smile a bit.

"A small compensation from the gods."

• • •

Rye, Darwin's spiritual home, where he ended his days living in a stone tower, was indeed magical. But the golfing magic was mostly in Jon Sager's hands in a two-ball Scotch foursomes match we conducted with Peter Gardiner-Hill, a delightful former captain of the R&A I'd met during the President's Putter, who shepherded us around the fabulous old links land and was gracious enough to treat us to a fine buffet lunch afterward in Rye's cozy dining room. The overwarm room was crowded with old stags and young bucks wearing school neckties and talking about their weeks in The City or the impending fuel crisis, which of course explained the sign by the road as we left Devon. The buzz seemed to be that the government was digging in its heels and the situation would only worsen before it eased up—vast shortages and more closures were predicted by week's end.

I decided I simply wouldn't think about that, either. The civilized world was perhaps fraying at its edges around us but at least we had a week of golf with each other and the Dewsweepers ahead of us, not to mention a slap-up buffet to balm the gentle beating Jon and I had taken at the hands of McDaid and Gardiner-Hill.

To briefly recap, under the alternate-shot format that few Americans ever play, every time I placed us into the gorse or deep grass, Jon's heroic copper wedge seemed to bail us out of trouble. We managed to hang close until the penultimate hole, at which point Gardiner-Hill's royal and ancient charm was exceeded only by his putting brilliance. He smoothly rolled home a twenty-footer to seal the match in their favor and we went in to lunch.

"One thing you can say about Rye," boomed the old fellow in line directly behind me, watching me slice off large portions of roast beef, "they do a very fine tongue, indeed!"

Tongue? I heard myself wondering. What kind of *tongue* would that be? Perhaps I paled a wee bit around the gills at this prospect, glancing past the jolly old fellow and the horns of my dining dilemma to see my friends chortling like teenagers caught writing blue words in the chapel hymnal.

In life as in golf, as Gardiner-Hill or some other tongue fancier of the Empire may have said, the key to success in the game is really all about the follow-through, playing on whatever life or the golf gods hurl at us.

Any lingering disappointment I felt over the fact that Rye's quaint two-ball rule meant there was no way to further contest the Blarney Cup on this particular trip—one more best-laid plan turned to sheep dip, as it were—was quickly muted by the fact that in this place and among this race of jovial golfing scions it truly was impossible to remain unhappy for long. No wonder, I thought, Darwin had chosen to come here and spend his final days. No wonder he had his own *armchair* at Rye.

In short, with a stiff upper lip, I took my tongue and ate it.

Everything about Rye *is* magical, from the warm and clubby fellowship of its membership and glorious views of the old town that sits like a fairy-tale village on the distant hill across the links land, to the golf course itself—a subtle but deviously brilliant par-sixty-eight test of one's golfing nerve that seems to grow, in the manner of the Old Course at Saint Andrews, more addictive every time you play it. I'd been around Rye now three times and, though I hadn't even managed to break 80 yet, couldn't wait to have a crack at it again.

Jon and Pat must have thought so, too, because after lunch I found them both lingering in the clubhouse library as if they were reluctant to leave, having a last sip of something and perusing old golf books. John looked quite comfortable in Bernardo's personal chair.

"I hate to be the bearer of bad news," I said to them, "but we've got a three-hour drive to London and a Dewsweeper dinner at six."

"*Five* hours to London, if you're driving," Jon said and laughed—a reference to the fact that I'd taken a couple short cuts I knew like the back of my hand and gotten us thoroughly lost in the countryside of southern England on the way to Rye.

"By the way," I pointed out, "that chair belonged to Bernard Darwin."

"No kidding? So I guess I shouldn't test its sound-dampening characteristics."

"Not unless you want your golf partner to beat you to death with an antique spoon."

"Bite your tongue, Lumpy."

"I tried that already. To be honest, it wasn't as bad as I thought it would be."

· · ·

FIVE hours later, give or take an hour for the unscheduled but deeply interesting side tour of South London's mazelike streets, I was thrilled to see the big silver Mercedes Perry Golf bus parked directly in front of the Basil Street Hotel in London, a modest pitching iron from Harrods, with none other than Bill Tuck and Jim Hathaway standing out front as an official reception committee.

"You guys are late," Jim said pleasantly. "What took you so long?"

"He knew a shortcut," Pat explained, jerking a thumb at me.

"Well?" demanded Bill. "Who won the Blarney?"

"The Lumpster," Jon said, unpeeling himself from the cramped backseat of our Renault. "But it's a win with an asterisk. Like the Opens during the war, it doesn't really count." He theatrically massaged his back and explained that we had all agreed that I would get to keep the cup another year, but it wouldn't count in the official total: the golf equivalent of kissing your sister.

"I think picking the most cramped and uncomfortable rental car in the British Isles was part of his game strategy," Jon complained and then snorted when I wondered if he wanted to go with me to drop off the rental near Marble Arch.

We were running two hours behind schedule and dinner at the Savoy was in exactly one hour's time. My good friend John Hopkins, golf correspondent for the *Times*, had agreed to meet us for dinner and convey tales of Ryder Cups past (John had covered them all since 1981), and my old friend Andy McKillop would also be there, with or without his lovely wife, Beth. It was, for me at least, a big social occasion and I didn't want anything to screw it up.

"I'll ride with you," good old Bill Tuck cheerfully volunteered from somewhere beneath his snowy eyebrows. He was already cleaned up and strapped into necktie and jacket.

He climbed in and moments later we were zipping along Hyde Park Row.

"Hey," he said, "Jon seemed kind of grumpy. Everything okay with him?"

I said he probably was just a bit groggy after his heavy lunch at Rye and from sleeping through most of the unscheduled tour of South London.

"Been a tough summer for him. I still don't think he's over Suzy Civetello's death. Also, he mentioned that his big promotion has been 'postponed' indefinitely, which translates unofficially to 'canceled' due to a shake-up higher up the corporate chain."

"Corporate culture is totally baffling," Bill agreed, shaking his head, looking out at the big luxury hotels we were passing. "I learned that the hard way."

Tuck, I knew, had taken over as president of Crouse-Hinds and within a few years halved the company's production costs and tripled its sales. But as he'd once explained to me, even that wasn't enough to please the company's Texas-based owners and he'd been ordered to do more. "Cut more costs, fire more people, make more money. More, more, *more*," he'd summed it up, explaining how it finally got to be too much for him. He drew the line at firing more people and "forced" management's hands. They offered to send him out to pasture with an enhanced retirement package. He took the latter deal and now devoted his days to working out at the gym and advising budding Bill Tuck at the S.U. Business School. The business world needed more guys exactly like Bill Tuck, it seemed to me. And more straight-talking Jon Sagers, too, while it was at it.

"He'll be all right," I said, scanning the street behind Oxford Circus for the National drop-off agency. "It's me I'm really worried about."

"In case I forgot to tell you," Bill said, "I'm sorry about your mother."

"Thanks," I said. "But this week's crisis is about Wendy. We're having to postpone the wedding. I guess I'll have to keep coming to Syracuse for a while longer."

He smiled. "That's too bad. We can probably find something useful for you to do, though. Maybe we could play golf or something."

A car ahead of us veered down a steep entrance ramp to a corrugated metal door that suddenly opened. I almost followed him until I realized it was the Hertz rental agency. Half a block later, though, the National agency appeared and I did exactly what the other driver did but *this* corrugated metal door remained shut. I tooted the horn and we waited for it to open, the nose of our Renault steeply canted downhill, inches from the door. I tooted again. No response within.

"I guess they're closed," Bill said. "Look . . ."

A small faded notice on the wall advised us to fill out a form (there were none) and leave the car in the garage back up the ramp. I placed the Renault in reverse but the car wouldn't back up. In fact, on the contrary, it lurched wildly forward—pressing against the door hard enough to bend the metal slightly.

"*Whoa!*" declared Friar Tuck, suddenly anxious enough to unplug his stogie. "Better back this pony up!"

"I'm trying, for Pete's sake!"

"Put it in reverse and gun it," Bill advised in his best Syracuse Business School voice, assuming executive command.

"I did that already," I replied somewhat testily, angrily disengaging the shift and slamming it into reverse position for a second time.

"We seem to have lost our reverse gear."

"Nah, you just missed it," he assured me. "Really give it some juice this time."

I released the brake and gunned the engine. The Renault plowed violently forward, pushing up the shrieking metal door like the lid of a giant inverted sardine can, setting off a bank of bright yellow strobe lights and a genuinely annoying alarm bell.

"Fug," I believe I may have said when we came to safe stop, halfway *under* the door.

We got out and walked up the ramp to see if we could find an attendant to shut off the alarm and phone the constabulary or a representative of National Car Rental. Instead, we found a hysterical Pakistani garage man in a glass booth frantically waving his arms and telling us to go away.

"I'll go tell the others that you'll be late for dinner—assuming you're not dining in jail tonight," Bill proposed beneath his jaunty cigar, starting off on foot for the Savoy.

"Don't feel like a rat abandoning a sinking ship or anything." I couldn't resist calling after him and could swear he was laughing.

A small crowd gathered and began offering thoughtful advice. A very proper Englishman wearing a bow tie wondered if I shouldn't dial up the American consulate and demand immediate assistance and a sweet-looking tourist couple from Iowa suggested tossing the keys in the nearest waste bin and phoning in a stolen car report. A young man with pinkish hair and gecko eyes even helpfully offered to steal the car for me.

Instead, I sat down on the curb to wait. Chin in palm. The Job of modern golf travel. I picked up someone's discarded copy of the *Sun*, hoping the sight of a topless Page Three girl might lift my spirits. It was just my luck that someone had torn out that particular page so I read instead a sad story about how London's vaunted Millennium Dome was a major bust and even the Japanese consortium of businessmen who'd hoped to purchase the thing and turn it into an all-you-can-eat sushi bar or indoor driving range were backing out of the deal.

After a small eternity passed, during which London's streets began to grow noticeably darker, a young policeman strolled up. He pulled out a pad and took down my statement, nodding as if he'd heard my sob story many times before.

"If I may ask, sir, are you here for business or on holiday?"

"Golf trip with friends," I replied, proving I could get my favorite subject into just about any conversation, including a travel calamity.

"Tough way to begin a trip," he commiserated.

"We're taking a bus from this point," I explained.

"I see." He nodded and jotted that down. "I trust," he added gently, "that you *won't* be driving the bus."

I assured him that I wouldn't.

"Very good. An honest mishap." He snapped shut his little book and suggested I give the car rental agency a friendly call to let them know how I'd creatively parked their car. "By any chance," he wondered, "did you take out the additional insurance protection?"

Before I could reply, the alarm bell suddenly stopped and the bank of bright flashing lights died. It vaguely occurred to me that I might have shorted out the entire building's electrical system.

The constable smiled and so did I—but not just because the silence was golden. In fact, come to think of it, I *had* purchased the deluxe insurance package which basically protected me against anything life or England could throw at me—or, more likely, vice versa.

"In that case," he said, "you needn't have stayed here all that time. You're free to go on your way. Cheerio. Have a pleasant *and* safe journey, sir."

I thanked him, turned, and sprinted toward Marble Arch with as much dignity as a lumpy man of forty-six years could muster, praying there was an empty taxicab somewhere in the vicinity. By now the Dewsweepers would be tucking into their Beef Wellington, I calculated, lapping up the cream of the Savoy and enjoying John Hopkins's tales of Ryder Cup triumphs and disasters.

My own social disaster was looming, too—one more Great Expectation turned to dust, the story of my life in the New Millennium. After a frantic ten-minute search, though, I spied a taxi disgorging customers across Oxford Street and bolted toward it, dodging honking cars, arriving just as the cabbie was preparing to pull back out into traffic.

"Sorry, mate, I'm going off duty," he said politely, flicking off his light. Clutching his door handle, I spotted a copy of *Golf Monthly* lying on the seat beside him.

"You a golfer?" I gasped.

He issued a surprised smile. "As a matter of fact I *am*."

"I'm terribly late for a special dinner at the Savoy," I pleaded my case. "Ten friends, all golfers, on the golf trip of their lives."

"In that case, get *in*!"

His name was Steve Driscoll. He was a 5.6 handicap and had just played in the annual London Taximan's golf tournament. His son Jack was just twelve but already a 15 handicap. Except for the fact that he was English and drove a cab and I was American and didn't, we seemed at that moment in time to have the whole world in common.

"My boy already hits the bloody ball further and straighter than Monty," Steve said with paternal pride only golf dads like us could appreciate, as we careened through Knightsbridge's back streets to the Basil Street so I could sprint inside and fetch a necktie and jacket and be off again in a bolt.

A little while later, my new cab-driving golf pal and fraternal brother-at-arms deposited me at the steps of the Savoy, steadfastly refusing to accept my ten-pound tip for a job brilliantly well executed.

"Next time you're in town maybe we'll have a game," Steve said, waving me off merrily. "Just remember, always mention golf and you'll be away!"

This was useful knowledge to have, I thought, as I bounded through the hotel's revolving door, only to find seven Dewsweepers and my two London friends sitting 'round a large and elegantly freighted table in the Savoy's main dining room. The boys from Syracuse were all beautifully dressed in navy blazers and being lavishly entertained by Hopkins of the *Times*, having cocktails and prawns whilst waiting patiently for me to appear for supper.

"It's about *time* you showed up," Jon said loudly enough to turn half the heads in the room toward us.

"Gentlemen, recharge your glasses, please! I give you the Jean Van de Veldt of rental car drivers!"

THIRTEEN

NECKTIES THAT BIND

I couldn't believe my ears. Someone was grumbling about neckties.

"Maybe those of us who don't want to eat could just skip lunch and go on and play," Jim Hathaway proposed, glancing at the bucolic grounds of Woking Golf Club as a perfect Sunday afternoon settled over it.

I smiled at Jim, conveying I don't know what. He seemed like a really nice fellow, though I couldn't say I really knew him. He'd played with the Dewsweepers for over a decade but never much when I seemed to be around, perhaps because he was apparently working all of the time. He did something in computers and the others were always needling him about spending half his life in the Cincinnati airport. He'd been invited to come along when John Zawadzki had to scratch because he'd accepted a new job as president of the Savings Bank of Utica. Disappointingly, Peter Marshall had also been unable to make the trip, but on the plus side that opened up a spot for the Irish Antichrist to join us after the Blarney Cup.

"Jim," I said, remembering this was his first trip to England, "here's the thing." I explained to him how British golf clubs are final outposts of civility where one is expected to wear a necktie for most indoor activities. Donald Steel and Martin Ebert, our hosts at Woking, had not only gone to tremendous lengths rustling up several prominent members to play with the Dewsweepers, but they'd also invited us to Sunday luncheon and, for that matter, arranged most of a tour ahead that week—a golf connoisseur's itinerary if there ever was one, as he would soon appreciate.

Woking, I pointed out, was probably London's first great suburban club, one of the classic so-called "heather" courses with a pedigree that even exceeded those of Walton Heath and Sunningdale, not to mention the home club of some of England's greatest champions including amateur champs Freddie Tait, Roger Wethered, and Gerald Micklem, plus a prime minister or two, and the first club Bernard Darwin joined after vacating Cambridge. That made Woking, I gently inveighed, a legitimate *shrine* of golf—at least to me.

"So here's my suggestion, Jim," I said, realizing what an overstuffed bore I must sound like to him. "Either you put on a necktie or I strangle you with it. Besides," I added, "Bernard Darwin always said wearing a necktie keeps the wearer young."

"He's just suffering from Post Rental Car Return Syndrome," McDaid said with a grin, patting me gently on the back. "Let's humor him, Jimbo, and put on neckties."

"We're *delighted* to put on neckties, right, fellas?" declared Russ King, Dean of Protocol, uncapping his dreaded red Sharpie marker. He had already used it to brand scarlet Xs on the hands of Dewsweepers who made what he considered to be off-color or unbecoming comments in the presence of the Queen or her loyal subjects, even though the Queen was off visiting cousins in the Netherlands. Thus far Jon had already "earned" a couple Xs for classic Sagerisms, while Friar Tuck and I had each accumulated one X apiece—the Friar's for describing his new hard-body workout routine as the "Noassatall Program" and me for telling the chaps a moderately blue joke at the Savoy that caused a wine steward to giggle and spill a few precious droplets of the outrageously priced wine he was dispensing. The wine had been ordered by the Irish Antichrist, the international wine buff and bon vivant—who got an X, as I recall, for simple wine snobbery.

The dreaded Sharpie hovering, Hathaway wisely beat a retreat to fetch his coat and tie with no further comment. To his credit, he was the first to pull me aside an hour or so later, as we shed luncheon mufti and put on golf duds to prepare for afternoon Scotch foursomes, to say how delightful the lunch and fellowship had been, capped off by Donald Steel's droll observation that his young collegue Martin Ebert had once again "overclubbed" by ordering eight bottles of wine for sixteen diners. Hathaway had already fallen under the spell of the British club golf and as he wandered out to join the others in the teeing area I assured him the best part was yet to come.

"Golf heals all wounds and wounds all heels," McDaid chipped in pleasantly from the bench a few yards away where he was lacing up his golf shoes.

I knew he was addressing me but I was suddenly pretending to study a framed copy of the club by-laws dating from the late 1800s, worrying about how uncharacteristically down in the dumps Wendy sounded on the phone the night before when I slipped away from the rowdy Savoy dinner to phone her back in Syracuse to see how she was bearing up after the unexpected collapse of her relocation hearing. I'd casually asked her what she planned to do that week while we were gone and she sighed and answered: *I don't know. Clean up the garden. Chase the wild men around the house. Load the dishwasher and drive the school shuttle. The usual stuff. Don't feel like doing any of it, to be honest. This is so unfair.*

"The wedding is definitely on hold," I explained to my oldest friend.

"That's too bad. Anything I can do?"

Pat was a rainmaker, a guy who got things done, a happy and

well-adjusted Hughes Norton without all the baggage. I started to laugh and say, *Here's the list: bring back my mom, patch things up with my brother, and find me a killer lawyer to win that relocation case.* Instead I smiled and said, "Yeah. Don't complain if I whip your scrawny butt out there. I feel like playing some golf this week. This was Darwin's club, you know. And tomorrow was Long-hurst's favorite place."

He grinned as if we were both thirteen again.

"Bring it *on*."

I double-bogeyed two of Woking's first three holes, leaving a very nice Woking member named Gerald Bristowe in the lurch in our alternate shot match against Donald Steel and the Irish Antichrist. Thanks to my dismal start, and McDaid's fine one, Gerald, a retired broker from The City, found ourselves two after three and would have been down three if he hadn't potted a handsome cross-green putt to salvage par with Donald.

It wasn't until the famous fourth hole that my wee funk began to lift, thanks to the entertaining misfortunes of Bernard Darwin himself. The hole is a short four-par that plays just a dog's whisker over three-hundred yards, framed by eruptions of heather and forest on one side and by the busy suburban railroad line Darwin took great delight in riding out from central London.

"This is the place," Donald said as if beginning an Arthurian tale, "where Darwin is alleged to have had one of his most memorable blow-ups. The story goes that he came to this spot in a medal competition having just missed a succession of close putts that would have given him a brilliant score. Once again, he drove safely into the fairway and required only a short pitch to the green, which he left only a few feet from the hole. Unfortunately he missed *that* putt as well, sank to his knees, and dropped his anguished face to the green. One account holds that when he lifted his head again he had actually taken a bite of the turf. But in any case, he reportedly stretched out his arms, looked to the heavens, and cried, 'O God, are you satisfied *now*?' "

McDaid laughed. "Sounds like Jon Sager on a good hair day."

"Don't tempt me," I said. "I can feel his pain from here."

"I think we *all* can," Gordon chipped in pleasantly, winking at me as if to say, *Right, laddie.You've had your neat little brood. Let's see if you can play the game now.*

After we all hit shots safely into the short grass and started down the fairway, I relayed a fascinating tidbit I'd picked up just after lunch while I was nosing around the clubhouse and came across a copy of James Connelly's history of Woking Golf Club aptly called *A Temple of Golf.* In it, Connelly—who was playing, I believe, in another group with Lester and Jon—relates how this very hole even had a life-altering influence on none other than Tom Simpson, the crusty beret-wearing aristocrat so near and dear to my cross-bunker-loving heart.

It seems that early in his life Simpson was playing as a guest of a competition at Woking and wandered out to have a look 'round the premises during a weather delay. He wound up at the fourth tee, utterly enchanted by what he saw—a very short hole that was long on strategic brilliance due to a set of clever "double" cross-bunkers that gave the hitter the option of choosing to play right or left of the sand hazards or prudently choosing to lay up short of them. The most direct line to the hole was also the most treacherous, whereas the "safe" play to the left resulted in a difficult pitch to the green.

Simpson, at that point in time, was a very fine player who had never designed a golf hole. He was so inspired by what he saw at Woking that day, though, he soon afterward abandoned law at London's Temple Bar in favor of golf course architecture, forever crediting Woking and Saint Andrews as the primary sources of his inspiration.

The hole seemed to inspire me, as well. I wedged my ball to within ten feet and made the putt for my first birdie and felt my troubles begin to drift away a bit.

A couple of pleasant hours later, with deep shadows stretching across the emerald green turf, Gerald and I were thoroughly subdued by Steel and McDaid and I found myself walking up the final hole toward Woking admiring its simple but magestic white clubhouse on the slope above the final green. It did indeed resemble a temple spun of sugar in that late and valedictory light. The other groups had already finished, and a lively buzz of conversation could be heard drifting down from up on the columned terrace where the Dewsweepers and their new mates were sharing a Pimms cup or two.

"Could you do this every day of your life?" Pat reflected happily, falling in step by my side, our clubs gently clicking with each step, admiring the same scene up the hill.

"No," I said. "You might start taking it for granted. I'd hate to take this for granted."

"I don't think I would. This place is like Augusta National with a British accent."

"I'd say more like Pine Valley with a regimental stripe necktie on."

"The necktie that binds."

We walked on a bit, approaching a couple balls lying on the perfect turf of the fairway. I noticed, as I said this, that Jim Hathaway and Jon Sager had moseyed down the slope with drinks in hand to watch us finish.

There was a mirrorlike pond guarding the final hole. I deposited my approach shot into the heart of it, sending out a widening circle of ripples. Gerald Bristowe put his approach into the bunker and we hailed the victors, shaking hands all around.

Jon presented me a chilled pint glass of Pimms. I normally didn't care for Pimms—too sweet and fruity. But like everything else at England's Temple of Golf, this tasted wonderful and refreshing.

"I've been sent to tell you to go shower and put on a proper necktie or Russ will put a big red X on your forehead for offending our hosts."

"Very funny. How'd you do?"

"Not bad. Not good. But what a golf course! I could play here every day for the rest of my life."

"McDaid said the same thing. I'll bet Karen wouldn't even notice you were gone. "

"Are you kidding? She'd throw a block party."

I went into the dressing room to fetch my stuff and paused on my way back to the terrace to admire a large and famous oil painting of Bernard Darwin, the man some Woking members affectionately call "The Great Thunderer." It was probably the most famous picture of him anywhere.

Bernardo sits on a bench among the heather, slightly stooped of shoulder with black hair sleekly oiled and a long iron lightly cradled in his arms, a man about my own age wearing a weary but contented little smile

Someone stepped up behind me.

" 'The bravest, stupidest race in the world,' " Donald Steel mused quietly over my shoulder. "That's what he called us, you know. 'The unconvincible, inextinguishable race of golfers.' "

I turned and my debonair host smiled at me, his own face flushed from the afternoon's exertions and his graying hair combed back and looking eerily like Henry Longhurst had looked in my memory on that long-ago late afternoon at the bar at Sedgefield. Donald reminded me of some famous English actor whose name was just beyond reach.

"Will you come and have a drink?" he asked, the soul of English hospitality.

"It would be my pleasure," I replied, and meant it.

· · ·

REFRESHMENT was happily taken, as Father Longhurst might have said, and further plans made.

That line comes from my favorite essay in *Spice of Life*, a collection of Longhurstian musing on golf and sport, and has either nothing or everything to do with golf and friendship. The piece is called "Death in the Forest" and relates how one bright September afternoon at Killarney, in Southwest Ireland, after a difficult morning of deer stalking with his dear friend Count Castlerosse, Longhurst peered down the scope of a Mannlicher 303 at his overtaken quarry, a lone and magnificent stag. *Then, instead of pressing the trigger, I laid down the rifle and gazed at this magnificent creature I was about to kill. Death seemed a monstrous penalty to exact for his negligence. We had won the game, according to the rules, and had crept successfully upon him without revealing our presence. Who was I to say the beast should die?*

Was it just happy coincidence or simply another of golf's exquisite gossamer threads of connection that thirty-some years later, just at dusk, McDaid and Sager and I had come to that identical spot on the old Castlerosse estate, the spectacular seventeenth hole of the golf course Castlerosse later built there with the able input of Henry Longhurst, during the final round of the first Blarney Cup. Just as Jon teed up, a lone stag appeared within a few yards of the tee where we stood and stared at us as if taking our full measure before wheeling and thundering into the forest and rendering, perhaps the first time ever, the three of us completely speechless.

Here was no venemous rabbit or sparrow or pigeon, no enemy of man, but a noble specimen of God's handiwork—the Monarch, indeed, of the glen! My mind was a turmoil of opposing emotions.

Had he been alone, Longhurst confessed to his readers, he would have let the stag go his merry way. Instead, faced with the prospect of explaining away such complicated feelings to his host, one of Britain's greatest sportsmen, not to mention his bloodthirsty hunting guide "Old Dan" . . . *my courage deserted me. I raised my rifle again and a second later the stag was dead . . . and I knew how the Ancient Mariner felt when he shot the albatross.*

I have shot my stag, he finished the tale. *I shall never shoot another.*

· · ·

THE day after Woking, I described this coincidence to Donald
Steel as we sat together on the "Longhurst" memorial bench ("To
Henry Longhurst from his friends at Clare College, Cambridge")
after we'd completed our rounds at Royal Worlington and New-
market Golf Club, on the outskirts of the tiny village of Mildenhall, not far from Cambridge University, the golf course Bernardo
called "The Sacred Nine," the finest nine-hole course on earth.

A student of modern American architecture might wonder
what Bernardo was smoking or drinking when he made this dec-
laration, because Royal Worlington appears flat and almost fea-
tureless at first glance, little more than a glorified hayfield in
places.

The irony was, though, that hayfield had beaten us all pretty
soundly, and the Dewsweepers were once again replaying the
dramas of their two-ball matches with Martin Ebert and several
of the club's members, including a local aristocrat called Peter
Mason, who wondered if our traveling band of hackers might be
interested in coming by his house for a final round of golf on his
"garden" golf course.

We were all sampling Pink Jug, the infamous traditional Cambridge libation that involves, if I heard correctly, equal parts
Pimms Number One, brandy, Benedictine, Princess Margaret's
preferred brand of gin, some *vin ordinaire*, various tropical fruits,
a bitter dash of this and a bolstering thimble of that, all shaken
and strained through a filthy Cambridge University athletic sock.
For all of that, it's remarkably refreshing and I'm reliably informed that just two of them can make you forget your own
name, rank, and serial number.

"You know," Donald said, "I was lucky enough to have known
Henry pretty well. When I began writing for the *Sunday Telegraph*,
of course, he was still doing his column for the *Sunday Times*. We
were, as they liked to say then, 'bitter rivals' but saw each other

quite regularly and had, I think, a great deal of affection one for the other."

This didn't surprise me to hear. In his earlier days, Donald had been a crack player himself and once made it into the field of the British Open. His first reporter's job straight out of Cambridge had been to cover the British Open at Birkdale in 1961, the one Arnold Palmer won in a gale, capturing the hearts of Britain's golf fans in the process, proving golf really was a small world after all. After a distinguished career in journalism, Steel had followed the lead of Tom Simpson and moseyed into course design and made himself into Britain's leading course architect, with something like a hundred courses worldwide to his credit now.

Thanks to my own keen interest in the subject and growing friendships with Donald Steel and Rees Jones, I sometimes fancied that I might try and do the same thing someday before I grew too short of memory and long of tooth. On the other hand, maybe the one-hole golf course I'd already built in my backyard and the nine-hole course I was helping to design at the Highlands would be as far as my own design ambitions got. You never know what's going to happen in life or golf, I suppose.

In any case, I was happy to be seated on my silent mentor's memorial bench sipping Pink Jug with a true blue-blooded son of the game. I mentioned my close encounter with Longhurst at the bar at the Greensboro Open in 1971, the year I failed to find a job as a PGA caddy and the year he wrote about giving up the game.

"Did you speak with him?"

"Nope. Too star-struck, I suppose. Just stood there on my hind legs drinking a Coke and shamelessly eavesdropping."

"Pity you didn't converse. You'd have liked Henry. I certainly did. He gave me a couple very useful pieces of advice when I first joined the profession and I've never forgotten them," Donald obliged me. "The first was, never write about the rules of golf because someone will always write and say you're dead wrong. Rules, he believed, were a deadly subject. That attitude fits his character. Henry was a bit of a loner, a champion of lost causes, far more interested in the spirit rather than the letter of things.

"He was also, as you know, very well traveled and worldly. He'd written about oil wells in the Middle East and politics in Africa. That relates to the other bit of advice he gave me—try everything at least once in your life. So he went up in planes and down in diving costumes in true sportsman fashion—or shot the stag you mention for the experience of knowing that he couldn't do it again.

"Golf meant the most to him, of course. That was what carried him through life in grand style, especially when he got into broadcasting, perfecting the silence that's worth a thousand words—which we can only dearly wish was practiced on air these days. His own game, early on at least, was very good, and no one is quite clear why he gave up playing it at such an early age—I believe he was only in his late fifties."

Donald paused and glanced across the little gravel courtyard where McDaid was thoughtfully aiming his digital camera at us as we sat on the Longhurst bench. We both smiled, the way you do when someone threatens you with a camera. This was a photo, I thought without saying so, that I really hoped came out.

The Irish Antichrist knew, even if the other Dewsweepers didn't, how much this particular stop in the journey meant to me. Most golf writers get into the business because their heroes are the game's greatest players, the people they most wish they could be like. As a kid, I'd certainly worshipped Arnold Palmer and others, but the reason I'd gotten into golf writing probably had far more to do with the literary dash of Henry Longhurst than the playing bravura of Arnold Palmer.

Corny as it may sound, I sat there thinking how incredibly lucky I was to be sitting right *here*, still eavesdropping shamelessly on my mentor thanks to Donald Steel.

"Two final stories say a lot about Henry, I think, and maybe golf itself," Donald resumed. "After years away in the war, he returned here to Mildenhall, as this place was often called in those days, rather full of fear and trepidation that things had perhaps changed in his absence. Before the war, you went into the clubhouse and rang a little bell and the little hutch door opened and a man whose name, I believe, was Haywood or something like that cheerfully said, 'Good afternoon, Mr. Longhurst. What can I get you, sir?' Well, Henry came back after this great lapse of time full of dread that the war had changed everything. He loved this place and didn't wish it to be altered in any way. So he rang the bell and the little door slid open and there stood Haywood or whoever he was, as if only minutes had passed since they last saw each other. 'Good afternoon, Mr. Longhurst. What can I get you, sir?' This gave Henry a tremendous sense of relief and joy. He cared more about the ordinary pleasures of this game, the small moments like that.

"The other story concerns when he was finally made an honorary member of the Royal and Ancient Golf Club. Henry was a little slow to buy the drinks, perhaps feeling that was the price of having him to entertain you. Anyway, never at a loss for the right words for any occasion, he finally stood up and said something to the effect that he was so deeply touched by the honor of being made a member of the great governing body of golf, he wasn't really sure if he should burst into tears or buy the house a round of drinks. But he added, he felt just sufficiently in control of his emotions to avoid doing either.

"When he died, my own tribute to him was written in the car park of the Dutch Open," Donald concluded. "I said there are many reasons the game of golf has grown so immensely popular but people searching for an explanation shouldn't overlook one important factor—Henry Longhurst. He made ordinary people see bits of themselves in the game. He gave golf such a human face. He called it the Esperanto of sport, a universal language."

I thanked Donald for these insights and wondered, not for the first time, when *he* planned to make time to set down his own memories of the game. Engaging private glimpses of Longhurst and Darwin, one suspected, were just the aperitifs of a rich club dinner speech simmering inside his head. That's when the name of the famous British actor he resembled popped into my head—James Mason.

Steel actually blushed a bit. "Perhaps I shall. But first I've just agreed to write a modern history of the Royal and Ancient."

I told him how pleased I was to hear this and then we both fell silent and eavesdropped on an amusing tale Martin Ebert was telling the other Dewsweepers that sounded like something straight from Henry Longhurst.

It concerned a physician whose woeful playing record at Oxford was matched only by his abysmal performances at January's President's Putter, the annual mid-winter competition of the Oxford and Cambridge Golf Society at Rye.

"Faithfully he came back, year after year, always to be eliminated in the first round of play," Martin related. "And you could see the heavy burden on him. So one year I asked him if he'd ever considered alcohol as a possible solution, thinking perhaps a wee nip or two before the round might steady him a bit and ease his nervousness. It could certainly do no worse, I reasoned.

"He admitted to me that he had indeed tried this approach, but the results turned out rather badly. Seems he showed up early in the car park one year before the start of the Putter and got out a fresh bottle of gin. Down she went, as he waited and waited—the entire bottle, apparently. After a while he made his way to the clubhouse, only to discover that he was an entire day *early* for the competition. The poor fellow couldn't legally drive anywhere for hours! He was trapped in the car park!"

"With a story that depressing," Jon reflected as our laughter subsided, "we could declare that guy an honorary Dewsweeper."

· · ·

PETER Mason led us to his fifteenth-century manor house called Wormil Hall, hard by the River Lark, where Lords Darby and

Banbury supposedly once tossed a coin to determine whose name would grace England's most famous horse race and where Mason, who made his fortune in the wholesale flower business, sometimes invited guests to play a charming makeshift course laid out through the estate's sprawling gardens.

Mason's wife, Nikki, joined us, a stately and regal blonde proffering champagne and smelling faintly of Chanel. And as Brittania's sun set and Wormil's lurchers "Cable" and "Fathom" roamed about us, we chose up teams and played a final team match, five-on-five best-ball—divots hacked from the perfect billiard-table lawn, shots fired gamely over unsuspecting orchard trees, at small clay pots bearing red flags, balls lobbed bravely over the greenhouse ("Automatic disqualification for breaking any panes!") and the immaculate groomed hedges of a classical Greek swimming pool. Despite a "hole-in-one" by the Irish Antichrist—warranting immediate expulsion from the HIN Society, he was summarily informed—the match came down to the final hole, a long pitch to the final flag just off the main terrace.

Bill Tuck executed it brilliantly in nearly complete darkness to take the match for Lady Mason's team, then topped off this brilliant feat of artful shotmaking under the influence by summarizing our collective gratitude to the golf-mad couple in a way Father Longhurst probably would have found touchingly appropriate.

"Thanks for having us," Tuck declared, executing a solemn formal bow from the waist and managing to fire up another Don Dominco as we all receded across the gravel to the waiting bus, bidding adieu and waving good-night. "This has been the most fun we could have had with all our clothes on!"

• • •

LATE the next afternoon at Woodhall Spa, well up the road in rural Lincolnshire, deep in the greenest heart of England itself, the other Dewsweepers and I stood beside the eighteenth green of a magnificent course originally laid out by Harry Vardon in 1905 and sometimes hailed as England's "greatest heathland course," watching that same wily Tuckster prepare to hit a critical sand shot out of the final bunker.

Once again, the Angry Yoots were playing the Hostile Elders, only this time Hathaway and I had combined to carve out a slim win over Tom Cahill and Russ King and now McDaid and Sager were one up over Austin and Tuck with one hole to play. But Tuck had the luxury of an extra shot.

He wiggled his diminutive feet into the sand of the reasonably deep bunker and glanced playfully over at me from beneath his big Santa Claus eyebrows.

"You know," he teased, "if this goes in you'll have only yourself to blame."

"Why is that?"

"You gave me the best tip I ever heard about the sand."

"Whatever it was," I said, "forget it and do what you *used* to do."

"No way," he said, gripping his stogie with his bare teeth. "You said always keep your lower body quiet on sand shots. I've done that ever since and it works. Watch this . . ."

For a moment, there was complete silence. Tuck concentrated and slowly drew back his sand wedge. At the top of his backswing, someone in the crowd loudly passed gas, laughter exploded, and so did Tuck's golf ball, flying ten feet past the hole.

"You know," Jon said with perfect timing, glancing around for the offending party. "It's tough to keep your lower body quiet on important sand shots."

• • •

AFTER that came Seacroft, a marvelous windswept seaside links in the slightly down-at-the-heel holiday resort of Skegness. We posed for a group photo on the first tee, thoughtfully taken by the club's secretary, and then marched out in two four-ball groups to wage battle beneath a lowering North Sea sky and play a course Donald Steel maintained was one of Britain's "best kept secrets."

It was all of that and more, and somehow the Angry Yoots won again, to square the year's running total of match wins apiece, carried by Jon's fine chipping and Hathaway's sensational putting touch, prompting a lively dinner discussion afterward over what the spoils of the Dewsweeper matches should be. Ganton, tomorrow, would be our last chance to play Yoots versus Elders because club matches had already been arranged for us at Gullane and Kingsbarns in Scotland. So it was all or nothing at mighty Ganton.

"I think a nice wool sweater would suffice," Tom Cahill suggested, perhaps remembering how cold we all got in the Seacroft wind that afternoon.

"That way," agreed Lester, glancing at Jon, "you young punks will be reminded of this humiliation every time we wear it to the course at Onondaga."

"No good, I'm afraid. They don't sell child-sized sweaters at proshops, Lester," Jon told him.

"How about if we play for a dollar," proposed Tuck, who was almost as famous for his thriftiness as for his stogies.

"It would have to be a pound sterling," weighed in Russ King, Dean of Protocol. "This is, after all, Great Britain."

"What about a good bottle of wine?" said McDaid—and everyone immediately hooted him down.

"I've got it," said Jon. "This is *perfect*. At our final dinner of the trip, on the last night in Scotland, the guys who lose will have to say two things they *admire* about the guys who win." He chuckled evilly. "That'll be like eating crow—or uncooked haggis."

"That could be really tough to do," said Lester.

"Precisely. It's going to be a long winter in Syracuse. That'll wear much better than any wool sweater."

· · ·

THE North Sea rain that threatened at Seacroft arrived with a vengence up the road at Ganton the next morning.

This was disappointing because Ganton was not only the spiritual home of Harry Vardon, the place he served as head green-keeper and professional when he won three of his six British opens and returned from America with the U.S. Open trophy in 1900, but also the place that had hosted several British Amateur Championships, the Ryder Cup of 1949, and most recently the Curtis Cup matches won by America that very summer. The Walker Cup was scheduled to come there in 2003.

Col. Bob Woolsley, the club secretary, couldn't have been more sympathetic about the turn of weather, inviting us to take a sandwich in the clubhouse's bar before the round. As the others pulled on their rain gear and headed to the putting green instead, I took Woolsely up on his suggestion and nosed around the clubhouse looking at old photographs and memorabilia of past champions, a Who's Who of the game. After a few minutes, McDaid and Sager joined me, but most of the others stayed outside—peculiar, I thought.

There wasn't much Dewsweeper joshing and joking around—no smart-alec cracks, no summarily issued red Xs for endearingly unbecoming behavior. When the gale finally slacked off a bit, the guys simply hastened to the first tee with drawn umbrellas as if they had a duty to do and they meant to do it.

We played the famed course at a hurried pace, a little over three hours, seldom pausing to admire the great flowering banks of hundred-year-old gorse and fierce bunkering and minuscule greens that define one of Britain's greatest tests of golf.

That was a shame, we all later agreed, sinking into our bus seats like remnants of a vanquished army, bidding a solemn adieu to mighty Ganton through rain-freckled windows. For the record, Hathaway and McDaid had tied Cahill and Tuck. Jon and I had also evenly matched Lester and the Dean of Protocol.

Neither Yoots nor Elders had won the day at mighty Ganton, which seemed oddly fitting.

Lester nicely summed up impressions for both teams. "I believe that might have been the hardest golf course I ever played." Fortunately for all hands involved, Ian the bus driver had proved as skilled at locating fresh cans of Guinness Stout as he had been at finding petrol on the sly—since every roadside station we'd passed in almost four days had been shut down, some actually blockaded by angry protesters.

"Well, here's to ties and today at Ganton," someone said. "Not much fun in either case."

We raised our beers but I looked back—making a mental note to return someday when the sun was shining and I could take my time going 'round.

"Look on the bright side," Cahill said after a few minutes up the road toward golf's Holy Land, as always attempting to find the bright spot in an otherwise gloomy afternoon. "At least nobody has to buy a sweater."

"Or say nice things about each other." Jon's voice resonated from the back of the bus.

We all laughed and raised our Guinness cans to that unexpected bonus.

• • •

It was about that moment when I had a startling realization: I was ready to go home to Maine.

This awareness had nothing to do with the Dewsweepers. Instead, it may have simply had to do with the fact that it had been a long and difficult year and the end of another golf season that was already in sight; back home I had a wood pile that required attention, a new barn's foundation that had just been laid, and various loose ends of life that needed tying up before the winter weather came. Blink an eyelash and it would be the start of what a good friend calls the "Official Indoor Golf Season in Maine."

Or maybe, crazy as it sounds, I was a little tired of golf. The truth is, after five straight days of golf—further proof I could never be a serious tournament player—I abruptly lose perspective and my swing thoughts go weirdly blank, my shots become out-of-body missiles headed God knows where. The only real cure for this condition is self-imposed rest and a little useful distance from the physical exertions of the game. Besides, in less than a month's time I was committed to return to Scotland with Jack in tow to lead that father-son tour of several well-known golf courses. With that in mind, I felt an almost overwhelming desire to bolt for home and immerse myself in mundane chores so I'd be chomping at the bit to play golf one last time when Jack and all of those fathers and sons hit the links.

That next morning at Gullane, I walked out to the club's "new" practice area where McDaid and Sager were already warming up for our scheduled Ryder Cup–style match against several members of Gullane Golf Club, in the cozy East Lothian village of the same name that is also home to mighty Muirfield and, in a word, *crackers* for golf.

I saw an unexpected sight that stopped me in my tracks and made me smile.

A kid about Jack's age was using a long whippy pole with a rubber tip to "scrape" the heavy dew from a nearby putting surface. I walked over and asked him if the instrument he was using had a name.

"Aye. The Big Dewy."

Jon walked over, too.

"Ever heard it called a dewsweeper?" I asked the kid.

The boy looked at me. "*Dewsweeper?* Can't say as I have. But that's not a bad name." He nodded and smiled. "I may call it that from now on."

"Personally," Jon said, "I like the Big Dewy. I believe that's what McDaid calls his morning ablutions."

· · ·

THE match at Gullane was arranged by my friend David Kirk-wood, a certified golfnut who hails from a distinguished family of Edinburgh jewelers. David rustled up six other Gullane members to hustle six Dewsweepers whilst he and George Barnes, a former Gullane club champion, challenged the Irish Antichrist and me to a team bestball.

"You should know," David warned, fixing me with a stern eye as only cagey Scotsman can do, "Old George and I have never lost a match with or even been tied by foreigners—neither English *nor* Colonial." He smiled and I smiled and we shook hands, placing a wager on the match of dinner with all the trimmings at the Old Clubhouse Pub.

Knowing myself as I do, given sore feet and slumping golf psyche, I was worried about playing indifferent golf even though Gullane Number One might rank as my favorite course in all of Scotland. Given the suddenly fine tempo of his swings, on the other hand, I was pretty sure my old saddle pal McDaid would play his best golf of the trip and find a way to save the day.

As it happened, through, for approximately fourteen and one third holes I played some of the smoothest golf of my life and was only one stroke over par while, conversely and inexplicably, the Irish Antichrist was maddeningly in and out of the gloriously photogenic hayfields that girdle Gullane links, struggling to find his game, the strain visibly showing on his annoyed leprechaun face. Our opponents played steady golf, seldom missing fairways and almost always getting up and down from trouble. Perhaps because I was so weary I didn't attempt to hit the ball hard, I managed to keep drives in the fairway and somehow keep even with our proud opponents.

They finally went two holes up at fourteen, however, and marching up the murderously long par-five fifteenth into the wind, I lagged back to help Pat look for yet another wayward tee shot in the tall grass.

"I'm done," he admitted glumly. "I can't feel a thing with my swing."

"Baloney," I said. "One good swing and you're back in it. Better yet, we are."

We found his ball a moment later, perched nicely on a clump of East Lothian hay. I watched him pull out his three-wood and halfheartedly take aim.

"Forget those guys and pretend it's just you and me out here, you scrawny little Irish twerp. Whoever wins this hole is the undisputed Champion of the World and gets all the Cherry Coke he can drink."

"You sound about fourteen."

"There were worse times."

Pat, concentrating on his ball, laid a gorgeous swing on the ball and it landed and stopped on the left side of the green, reminiscent, as I later told him, of Jon Sager's miraculous "Blarney Blast" at Kiawah Island from deep in the sea oats of the Ocean Course's final hole, in near darkness no less, leaving him a mere tap-in for birdie and a sweet *halve* of the second annual Blarney Cup, a spectacular finish that we still had not heard the end of yet.

Taking dead aim from much closer range, I hit what I thought was my best shot of the day, a high-flying nine-iron than came up six inches shy of the crowned putting surface and trickled back down into a steep-walled bunker. The Irish Antichrist rose to the occasion, however, by draining a brave sidehill putt for birdie that surgically halved Scotland's lead by half. The Colonials were one down with three to play, and our undefeated opponents, who had never even been halved by foreigners, grew visibly silent, maybe even a bit worried.

For the record, on the final hole, I had a chance to tie our proud Scottish hosts. All I needed was ten feet straight up the grain to place the ball in the heart of the cup for a birdie and an all-square match. I got nine feet, eleven and three-quarter inches and we lost the match by one hole. I was suprised to learn I'd finished with a 74, my bonniest Gullane score ever, something nice when you least expect it, another small grace of the game. We shook hands with David and George and thanked them for a good match.

As we stood off to the side of the green to watch Sager and Hathaway finish their match with Gullane's famous golf historian Archie Baird and another gentleman whose name I couldn't remember, Kirkwood told me a joke about a young London dot-com millionare who burns out and moves to a lonely stone hut in the Scottish highlands that was so fall-down funny I wish I could repeat it here—or at least find a way to use it in a club speech somewhere down the fairway.

"What's so *funny*? It's not polite to laugh at someone's misfortunes," Jon, somehow under the impression I was laughing at him, remarked pointedly as he approached Gullane's final green, needing to make par to halve with Archie and his partner, which he did.

I told him the joke as we stood aside and watched Austin and Cahill complete their circuit of Gullane links with a narrow loss. He was still laughing over the dot-commer's misfortune when King and Tuck finished behind them, having gotten soundly clocked by their Scottish hosts.

"What's so funny?" the Dean of Protocol politely demanded to know, perhaps fearing we were laughing at him.

"I can't tell you," I said. " 'Lest I earn another X."

"You better give him an X just on general purposes," Jon said, shaking his head. "He's outta control."

And so, the Dewsweepers, to no one's particular surprise, wound up buying dinner that night at the Old Clubhouse Pub. The toasts were as bawdy as David Kirkwood's joke, and barbs flew like Bill Tuck's wildest sand shots. The actual Ryder Cup teams,

I think, could have learned a thing or two from the Dewsweepers and their boisterous Gullane comrades on that chill September evening. It reminded me of that great spring night after getting drubbed at Kittansett by the Sons of Massachusetts.

Maybe losing was what we did best.

• • •

THAT next afternoon, a cold but clear Saturday, we played one more team match with several of the local members of Kingbarns—and lost that one going away, too, I'm afraid.

Our collective feet ached, sixteen hands had more or less gone numb, but no one even thought of complaining because Kingsbarns is one of the great new links lands of the world and it showed us every bit of its glory in the late afternoon sun.

"I don't know what I would do if I didn't have this," Jon remarked quietly as we finished together at the eighteenth hole, walking side by side at the spectacular four-par that ends by a three-hundred-year-old stone farmer's bridge accidentally unearthed by American architect Kyle Phillips when he was building the place.

My ball had vanished in the waving fescue and my nose was leaking miserably. Jon's approach shot had missed the final green by a country mile. Both of us were grinding just to break ninety in that stiff and unforgiving sea wind—no longer even bothering to mark down scores, in true Dewsweeper fashion.

I was fairly sure he didn't mean that awful approach shot. Perhaps he simply meant the trip, our friendship, this game. Who really knew. At least I *hoped* so. For what it was worth, I really needed it, too. If nothing else, this long and testing year had taught me that even horrible golf with buddies was a tie that binds.

"We're skimming the cream, my boy," I came back instead, explaining that's what Henry Longhurst once said to Ben Wright shortly before he abandoned playing the game.

"Why do you think he did a stupid thing like that?" Jon wondered.

"He said he couldn't bear playing poorly anymore."

"Too bad he didn't know any Dewsweepers. Then it wouldn't have mattered. They would have found a way to keep him going."

FOURTEEN

THE HOLE IN THE SKY

O<small>N</small> the same late October weekend Wendy and I had planned to get married, I drove instead to Syracuse and played a final round of the season at Onondaga with the Dewsweepers.

There were six of them swaddled up and waiting for me to join them on the first tee—Jon, Tuck, Lester, Russ, Jim Hathaway, and Peter Marshall. Tom Cahill had taken Nancy Who to the Cape, or he would have been there, too.

The club was days if not hours away from closing for the long winter hibernation, and since no other golfers were dumb enough to be out in the cold, we all teed off together, a small army going down the first fairway, my first *sevensome*.

I asked Lester how Sheila and Woody Austin were doing and how his lettuce patch was holding up with winter on the doorstep.

"She's fine, hitting the ball a mile with her new driver. He's crazy as ever, I'm afraid."

"In other words, don't go visit them without a cup on," Jon said.

"My lettuce is doing great. I hope to have it all the way to Thanksgiving this year—if it doesn't snow tonight."

"I heard there are flurries in the forecast," Bill Tuck broke not-so-gently to him, grinning and cigarless for a change.

Tuck's wife, Toni, I learned, was off at some important field trial for bearded collies and Tuck had somehow shaved another five pounds and probably a stroke or two off his weight and handicap respectively.

"Pretty soon he'll be scratch," Jon said, "but all that will be left will be two big eyebrows and an orifice adorned with a cigar."

"True," Tuck allowed, "but at least I'm two bucks up on Russ King."

Lester wondered how things were going with Wendy.

"She's fine. Nothing gets her down long." I explained that the wedding hadn't been canceled, merely *postponed*. Time was on our side. Somewhere down the fairway, I said, choosing a somewhat Vardonish metaphor, we would find a way to get her to Maine.

"Well, until then," Russ King injected, "you'll just have to keep coming back to Syracuse. You're one of us now, you know."

I thanked him for saying this and wondered what the Dewsweeper Dean of Protocol had planned for the long approaching months of ice and darkness in America's Snowiest City.

"To pray for a lot of snow so I can go skiing on a mountaintop somewhere Jon Sager won't be able to harass me," he replied with an avuncular smile.

"Yeah, well, *real* men bowl in the winter in Syracuse," Jon said.

On the back nine, the skies turned dark and let loose a volley of cold, heavy raindrops.

"Look at these guys," Jon said at one point, pausing as we reached the brow of the short and ingenious sixteenth hole, a wee gem with a postage-stamp green that looked as if Tom Simpson had had a hand in designing it. There was an unmistakable affection in his voice as he watched his best friends hump along the fairway ridge, pulling on rain slickers, wool caps, and gloves.

"They don't want to give this up. Even in this mess. Nobody wants to be the first to say the season's over."

"I know the feeling—though I can't really say why."

I chose not to elaborate further than this, but I really didn't want it to end, either. The Dewsweepers were great guys and I really did feel like a golfing oddfellow who once again was playing for the friendship rather than scores. I was curiously more at peace with the game than I'd been in a very long time. There were really only one or two loose ends I could think of that needed tying up before I took my son to Scotland and golf would be over for another year.

"Well *I* can tell you why," Jon said with his penetrating Chuck Grodin laugh. "I told you this at Westward Ho! You're a *mudder*. Get used to it."

. . .

THE next morning, I fulfilled my promise to the kid in Jon Sager. I took him to meet Arnold Palmer. We drove to Latrobe through an early-season blizzard off Lake Ontario and discovered a nice patch of Indian Summer waiting for us in Western Pennsylvania.

I couldn't help thinking about Winnie Palmer—knowing how she loved the lingering warmth of autumn, her new red Dutch barn, and the earthy hues and spicy scents of fall in Latrobe.

The hardest year of Arnold Palmer's life—his first without Winnie in almost half a century—was ending and it wasn't made any easier by the fact that Prince, his beloved golden retriever, dropped dead of a heart attack two days before we got there, while sprinting along the seventeenth hole at Latrobe Country Club.

One of the first things Arnold asked me was if I'd played any more golf during the year, and I was pleased to report to the King of Golf that I had indeed played more, worked a bit less, and *dewswept* my way through the ups and downs of maybe the most memorable year of my life. He wanted to know what was up with Wendy and I replied that we were still hitting it down the fairway together, hoping to make ours a permanent official pairing someday very soon.

This news seemed to please him—and maybe remind him a bit of what he'd lost.

That night at dinner, though, it didn't take the Sage of Syracuse long to get the King of Golf laughing, and on the long drive home Jon thanked me for finally introducing him to his lifelong hero, adding, "That guy was so down to earth and genuine that he should be the Honorary King of the Dewsweepers."

"Glad you like him," I said. "I think he liked you, too."

·   ·   ·

BACK in Maine, Indian Summer held on a few more days. Terry Meagher phoned one morning to say Billy Savage, the club superintendent, was about to pull the flags out for the winter. Terry and I have a little season-closing tradition of playing a final round just ahead of Billy as he plucks out the flags sticks, and in years past we've halved the final match more often than not. This match was no exception. Thanks to a fine seven-iron approach on eighteen, I was able to convert a final birdie putt and win the hole and halve our final match of the year. I still owed him a million bucks, but at least it was Canadian dollars.

Afterward, I drove home to mow crop circles one last time and discovered a sad message waiting on my office answering machine. It was from Jane Dugan. Tommy Dugan had passed away the night before. Tom was fine, she said, deeply relieved his son's long ordeal was finally over, and the two of them would be starting out early in the morning for Florida.

I couldn't help thinking how ironic the timing of these conclusions was when the phone rang and an even more ironic conclusion occurred. Or maybe it was a new beginning in disguise.

It was my brother calling. He sounded different.

He explained that he and his new wife had separated, and it did not look like they were going to get back together. She wanted nothing to do with him, he told me. He began to break down and wondered if I could help him out, financially speaking. Am I my brother's keeper? Maybe not. But maybe so. I promised I would help him out and I promptly did, too.

A short time later, I was sitting in a crowded pub in Greensboro where McDaid and I had resumed our friendship many years ago when my brother came through the door. I'd stopped off in town to see his children and the Irish Antichrist and Terry, on my way back home from an interview before Jack and I embarked for Scotland.

My brother looked well, like a million bucks in fact, as if he might be headed to a GGO party. He sat down and we ordered iced teas and made easy small talk for a few minutes. I noted how Hams never seemed to change much, which was oddly reassuring. It was loud and rowdy with college kids drinking beer and eating burgers. I ordered my usual Hams cuisine—the Old South burger loaded with onions and chili.

I told my brother I was sorry to hear about his marriage problems. Death cancels all debts, someone said, and I was anxious to pick up the pieces and move on.

"I never should have signed that damned prenuptial agreement," he said, shaking his head. "I feel bad how all of this happened."

In effect, he said he'd been a fool for love, a tale as old as the hills of Galilee and as near as Harvey Ward and Lester Austin. He hoped I could get over it and we could find a way to patch things up and start anew.

Of course, I wanted nothing more, myself. We'd been very good friends for a very long time and I wanted to trust and admire my brother again—I also wanted him to use this expensive lesson to finally take charge of his life.

"Here's the deal," I said, not wanting to rub his nose in it any longer. "We'll wipe the slate clean and start again. All I ask is that you give mother's jewelry to the rightful owner—your daughter."

He assured me he would do that, and later he did.

I asked him what he was going to do now. He was once again between jobs and staying at some friend's "corporate" apartment.

"I've got a buddy in Baltimore who wants me to work for him. Job pays well. It would mean leaving Greensboro, though."

I knew this would be very difficult for him. My brother fiercely clung to the safe harbor posts of the past, whereas I constantly scanned the open waters of the future. Perhaps that explained our essential differences. He stayed, I went. For what it was worth, I said, I thought leaving Greensboro might be the best thing he could do to put his days back in order. Shake the dust off the old hometown, find a new improved life, and get on with it.

"Well, whatever you decide," I said, meaning it, "best of British luck."

This made him smile a bit and we began talking about happier things, almost like old times—the coming Carolina basketball season, the memory of a recent business trip I'd once taken him on to London where we did tourist sights like a couple giddy schoolboys instead of forty-year-old men. My brother seemed pleased that in four more days I was taking Jack on his first pilgrimage to golf's Holy Land. He said he thought our father would approve.

"You and Wendy still planning to get married?" he wondered, too.

"Eventually," I replied, and explained how I hoped things would evolve in that respect somewhere down the fairway. I didn't say it but the thought occurred to me that if the relationship between us continued to evolve in a positive way, I would probably ask him to be my best man, too.

A little while later, we walked outside to the parking lot to say good-bye. It was one of those eerily cool and clammy late autumn nights of the Piedmont South that smell of decaying oak leaves and lonely yards and make me realize how fortunate I am to live in a place where the season ends with the sharpness of a descending axe blade.

He asked where I was headed.

"Home," I said, wearily. It was been a while since I'd been there.

We shook hands and then, awkwardly, we embraced. My brother, unlike McDaid, was not much of a fraternal hugger.

He waved genially and turned and walked hurriedly toward our mother's old Cadillac as if he were late for an appointment. I waited until he was gone, sitting in my darkened rental car, thinking how he would probably never leave our hometown, watching more college students come and go from Hams with their whole lives ahead of them, thinking how I did indeed have much to consider—not to mention be thankful for. Not least of all, perhaps somewhere on a sun-washed deck by the sea, Opti the Mystic and Mrs. Congeniality were having a nice glass of chilled wine together, pleased at the way things were working out down below.

. . .

JACK caddied brilliantly for me at Nairn, in a match with a nice man named Ken and his son Jeff. On the second hole, my son gave me a perfect read on a fifty-foot putt and punched the air like his hero Tiger Woods when the ball fell in the cup for birdie. Together, "we" beat Ken and Jeff by the margin of a single hole in a close but thrilling match.

Then, up at Dornoch, birthplace of a fairly well-known golf son named Donald Ross, I pulled my second shot left into a stiff wind on the long par-five ninth. The ball vanished over the waving beach grass toward the sands of the beach and I couldn't spot it anywhere. Unfortunately, Jack and I were two down in a match to a terrific guy named Chuck Froelicher and his son-in-law Chris. I was about to give up and drop a penalty ball and effectively toss in the competition towel when my eagle-eyed caddie suddenly pointed to the beach, nearly out to the tide line itself.

"There's our ball," he declared. "Let's go hit it."

He turned out to be right. It was our ball, reposing in the sticky wet sand inches from the tide line of the North Sea. The green was maybe 130 yards away, somewhere up over the billowing dune tops. I asked Jack if he wouldn't mind standing on the dune's top between me and the flag stick—a human direction post. He grinned and loped toward the dune like a medieval page on a mission.

I selected an eight-iron and swung hard and watched the ball soar over the dunes and my son's head, causing Jack to neatly piroutte. Seconds later, his skinny arms flew up exuberantly and he was dancing a jig and double Tiger-pumping the sea air. The ball, I discovered, landed a foot from the hole and stayed there, probably the best recovery shot I've ever hit, something nice to remember during the long dark days of the Official Indoor Golf Season in Maine.

I made the putt that turned the tide and "we" won that match, too.

Finally, Jack got to play at Kingsbarns, where the fathers and sons of the tour all clustered ceremonially around the first tee to watch him tee off first. Jack's caddie, a big strapping lad named Ian, glanced at me and smiled as if to say, *Are you sure about this, Dad?* And for what it's worth, my heart was crowding the corridors of my throat.

Jack, though, had no doubt why he was there.

He calmly teed up his ball and took his position and checked his grip, as Mal Strange had taught him to do. Then he stared down the fairway for a moment and slowly drew back his driver. His ball flew far down the middle of the fairway and the men on the tee all whooped and whistled and Ian the caddie glanced over at me and gave me a suprised grin and thumbs-up and I smiled back at him, blinking the tears from my eyes.

Jack shot 130 that day, 65 on the front, 65 on the back, the model of consistency on the first championship course he ever played.

The next day, playing the famed Jubilee Course at St. Andrews with a delightful Florida minister named Scott Whittaker and his lawyer son, Nathan, Jack got tired and I offered to carry his bag for the closing holes directly into the wind. Jack had a grand time talking to Nathan, legal counsel for the Tampa Bay

Buccaneers, and Scott turned to me at one point and observed: "Do you realize it may someday come to this—you caddying for Jack?"

It was a fascinating question, a future I hadn't realized was quite so near. "I hope so," I admitted. "I have a feeling Jack has a tournament game, his bag is the *perfect* place for his old man."

On our last day in the Old Grey Toon, a scheduling mix-up prevented us from playing the Old Course together. As the other fathers and sons teed off on a beautiful and surprisingly clement morning, Jack's disappointment was visible—his grandfather's ashes, after all, lay in a bunker on the Road Hole. Placing my arm around his slim shoulders, I assured him his shot at the Old Course would eventually come and proposed, as an alternative, that the two of us go hack around the wee Strathtyrum Course and then maybe snoop around the town and see a few sights even I hadn't seen in my many trips to golf's sacred home.

The smile came straight back, the Bay Hill cap bobbed.

After golf, we went back to our room at Russacks Hotel and packed our bags for home. The room was named—small world— for Densmore Shute, the quiet man from Boston, Bunny Dugan's old boss, just one more link to a Royal and Ancient game.

After that, we hoofed all over bloody Saint Andrews—through the teeming market streets and into the medieval university, where I informed Jack he was under no obligation whatsoever to someday consider applying to college, though it might make Parents Weekend a *little* bit more interesting for us both, if he did. We ate a big lunch of fish and chips and did the Golf Museum and castle in the afternoon.

We toured the remains of the gothic cathedral, learning about the city's violent ecclesiastical wars, and finally found ourselves paying respects at the graves of Young and Old Tom Morris. In lieu of memorial flowers, Jack left Young Tom one of his most prized possessions—a shiny new "Tiger Woods" Nike golf ball.

As we were leaving the quiet green grounds that surround the ruins of the cathedral, Jack suddenly stopped and peered up at a lone arched window that hovered against the sky, somehow having survived all those centuries of terrible conflict and war caused by God and country and brother against brother.

"Dad," he said quietly, "can I ask you something? It's really important . . ."

"Of course," I said, placing my hand on his shoulders again, hoping I could remember the complicated history of the place.

"Do you think," he began, "if I used a nine-iron, I could hit a ball through that window?"

I looked up at the ancient arch and realized that life really is all about how you choose to look at things. I was seeing an old stone arch. But my son was seeing a golf hole against the sky. This realization made me laugh out loud. It was either laugh—or maybe cry.

"I have no doubt about it whatsoever," I told my son, fiercely kissing Jack's tousled head the way Old Tom must have kissed his son, realizing, as I did, that *there* was the joy that Father Longhurst never knew, the very thing that would, with luck, bring me back to golf for many years to come.

So joy hadn't been lost after all; merely waited quietly for me to catch up, true blue as a boy's upturned eyes or a clearing Scottish sky, the real reason I would go on playing golf, and loving it, for as long as the game would have me.

James Dodson is the author of *Final Rounds*, the 1996 bestseller that was named the "Golf Book of the Year" by the International Network of Golf. He is also the author of *Faithful Travelers* and *A Golfer's Life*, a collaboration with Arnold Palmer that was a *New York Times* bestseller; a four-time winner of the prestigious Golf Writers of America Award for his column in *Golf Magazine*; and the recent recipient of the 1998 "Golf Reporter of the Year" award by the International Network of Golf. He lives on the coast of Maine with his two children.